Mathematics
UNLIMITED

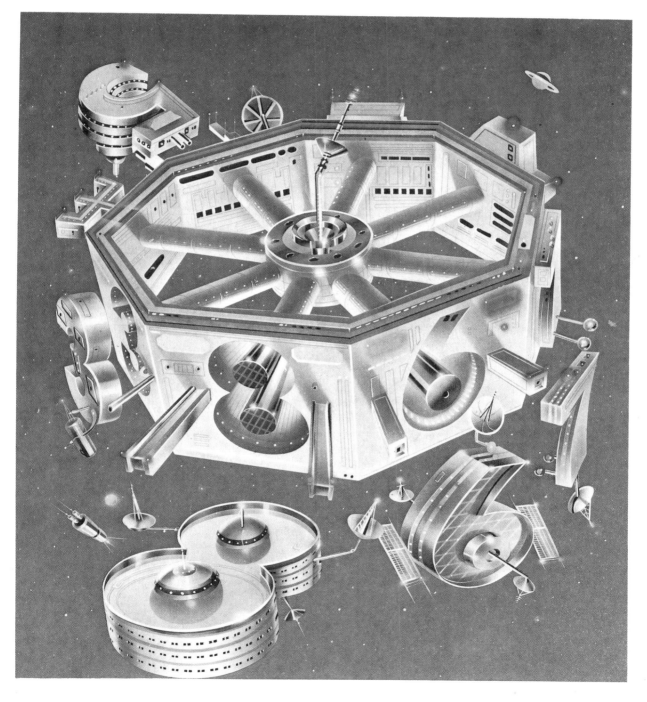

HOLT, RINEHART and WINSTON, INC.

Austin   New York   San Diego   Chicago   Toronto   Montreal

AUTHORS

Francis "Skip" Fennell
Chairman, Education Department
Associate Professor of Education
Western Maryland College
Westminster, Maryland

Robert E. Reys
Professor of Mathematics Education
University of Missouri
Columbia, Missouri

Barbara J. Reys
Assistant Professor of Curriculum
and Instruction
University of Missouri, Columbia, Missouri
Formerly Junior High Mathematics Teacher
Oakland Junior High, Columbia, Missouri

Arnold W. Webb
Senior Research Assoiciate
Research for Better Schools
Philadelphia, Pennsylvania
Formerly Asst. Commissioner of Education
New Jersey State Education Department

CONTENTS

Copyright © 1988 by **HOLT, RINEHART and WINSTON, INC.**

Printed in United States of America

ISBN 0-03-021909-4

901 063 987654

STUDENT RESOURCE BOOK

TO THE TEACHER:

The Student Resource Book contains Practice and Reteach sections that provide additional instruction, extra practice, and review of material covered in the pupil's edition. This book provides a hardbound, non-consumable resource to meet the individual needs of each student.

PRACTICE

This section provides additional practice for lessons found in the pupil's edition. Each page is keyed to the appropriate lesson, but could be used as extra practice or review at any time after the lesson.

RETEACH

This section provides additional instruction on material covered in the pupil's edition. Each page is keyed to the appropriate lesson, but could be used as instruction, extra practice, or review at any time after the lesson.

Write the value of the underlined digit.

1. 7̲19 _____

2. 6,90̲4 _____

3. 8̲1,319 _____

4. 5̲9,002 _____

5. 13̲7,646 _____

6. 17,̲401 _____

Write in standard form.

7. 80,000 + 300 + 2 _____

8. 900,000 + 20,000 + 7,000 + 800 + 40 + 3 _____

9. 10,000 + 8,000 + 700 + 30 + 4 _____

10. 30,000 + 1,000 + 600 + 70 + 6 _____

11. 600,000 + 50,000 + 4,000 + 300 + 20 + 2 _____

12. 20,000 + 3,000 + 900 + 90 + 9 _____

Write in expanded form.

13. 8,954 _____

14. 71,683 _____

15. 444,296 _____

16. 9,851 _____

17. 123,478 _____

18. 54,911 _____

19. 19,672 _____

20. 263,548 _____

Solve.

21. Pablo Picasso created 13,500 paintings and designs in his lifetime. What is the value of the digit 3 in 13,500?

_____

Write the value of the underlined digit.

1. 2,314,<u>6</u>09

_____

2. 1<u>3</u>,491,732

_____

3. 4,5<u>8</u>6,916,300

_____

4. <u>1</u>6,000,932,134

_____

5. 14,09<u>6</u>,475

_____

6. 412,000,000,6<u>1</u>9

_____

Write in standard form.

7. 732 million, 37 thousand _____

8. 154 billion, 82 million, 15 thousand, 6 hundred 11

_____

9. 99 million, 2 thousand, 7 hundred _____

10. 225 billion, 137 million, 985 thousand, 8 hundred 44

_____

Write the word name for each.

11. 679,020,111 _____

_____

12. 802,313,602,033 _____

_____

Copy and complete the chart or write the number.

	Billions	Millions	Thousands	Ones		
13.					=	5,010,225
14.	3	26	309	76	=	_____
15.					=	78,910,562
16.	1	112	680	269	=	_____

Holt, Rinehart and Winston, Publishers • 5

Use with pages 4–5.

Compare. Use >, <, or = for ◯.

1. 3,743 ◯ 3,842

2. 930 ◯ 903

3. 345,011 ◯ 345,101

4. 98,701 ◯ 98,701

5. 8,808 ◯ 18,808

6. 71,814 ◯ 17,757

7. 65,000 ◯ 56,000

8. 2,112 ◯ 11,121

9. 123,456 ◯ 231,456

10. 77,777 ◯ 757,770

11. 898,989 ◯ 898,989

12. 24,422 ◯ 24,420

13. 716,671 ◯ 716,671

14. 6,001 ◯ 6,010

15. 678,876 ◯ 778,876

Order from the least to the greatest.

16. 158, 157, 149, 152

_____

17. 241, 313, 165, 156

_____

18. 756, 509, 821, 312

_____

19. 2,496; 1,231; 996; 2,946

_____

Order from the greatest to the least.

20. 7,560; 8,903; 7,712; 8,900

_____

21. 5,022; 5,018; 5,015; 5,005

_____

22. 11,342; 10,342; 9,612; 612

_____

Read the problem. Help each student below by deciding where in the Help File ideas can be found to help solve the problem.

Mr. Player wants to place this ad in one of the local newspapers. *The Town Gazette* sells an average of 23,782 papers daily, while *The Examiner* sells 25,302. If he wants to reach as many people as possible, in which paper should Mr. Player place his ad?

1. After reading the problem several times, Kim did not understand the question. "What is it that I am looking for?" she asked.
   Where should Kim look in the Help File?
   a. Questions   **b.** Tools
   c. Solutions   **d.** Checks

2. Jesse understood the question. "One newspaper sells 23,782 copies, and the other sells 25,302 copies a day," he said. "But how do I figure out in which one Mr. Player should advertise?"
   Where should Jesse look in the Help File?
   a. Questions   **b.** Tools
   c. Solutions   **d.** Checks

3. Rosa knew she had to compare to solve the problem. But she made mistakes comparing.
   Where should Rosa look in the Help File?
   a. Questions   **b.** Tools
   c. Solutions   **d.** Checks

4. Raul answered the question. "Mr. Player should advertise in *The Examiner*," he said. Then he wanted to check his answer.
   Where in the Help File should Raul look?
   a. Questions   **b.** Tools
   c. Solutions   **d.** Checks

Use with pages 8–9.

Add.

1. 7
$+ 7$

2. 8
$+ 4$

3. 6
$+ 1$

4. 3
$+ 3$

5. 2
$+ 9$

6. 7
$+ 5$

7. 4
$+ 9$

8. 3
$+ 7$

9. 9
$+ 8$

10. 1
$+ 0$

11. 5
$+ 7$

12. 3
$+ 6$

13. 6 + 3 = _____

14. 5 + 2 = _____

15. 2 + 0 = _____

16. 1 + 2 = _____

17. 8 + 9 = _____

18. 3 + 6 = _____

19. (4 + 7) + 5 = _____

20. (1 + 3) + 9 = _____

21. 6 + (4 + 8) = _____

22. 1 + (3 + 9) = _____

23. (6 + 4) + 8 = _____

24. 4 + (7 + 5) = _____

Solve. Write the missing number.

25. 6 + _____ = 12

26. 9 + _____ = 10

27. _____ + 5 = 9

28. _____ + 3 = 7

29. 3 + _____ = 11

30. 2 + _____ = 5

Complete. Identify the property used.

31. 7 + 6 = _____ + 7

32. 3 + 5 = 5 + _____

33. _____ + 8 = 8 + 9

34. (3 + 5) + 4 = 3 + (5 + _____)

35. 6 + (7 + 5) = (6 + _____) + 5

Solve.

36. Harry counted 8 herons. Mary counted 6 herons. How many herons did Harry and Mary see altogether?

_____

37. Jean and Dean counted the same number of ducks. Jean counted 5 ducks swimming in the pond and 4 ducks walking in the weeds. Dean counted 4 ducks swimming in the pond. How many ducks did he count walking in the weeds?

_____

Subtract.

1.	15 $- 7$	**2.**	11 $- 6$

1. $\quad$ 15 $\quad$ **2.** $\quad$ 11 $\quad$ **3.** $\quad$ 10 $\quad$ **4.** $\quad$ 9 $\quad$ **5.** $\quad$ 18 $\quad$ **6.** $\quad$ 12
$\quad\quad - 7 \quad\quad\quad\quad - 6 \quad\quad\quad\quad - 8 \quad\quad\quad\quad - 5 \quad\quad\quad\quad - 9 \quad\quad\quad\quad - 7$

7. $\quad$ 14 $\quad$ **8.** $\quad$ 16 $\quad$ **9.** $\quad$ 12 $\quad$ **10.** $\quad$ 15 $\quad$ **11.** $\quad$ 17 $\quad$ **12.** $\quad$ 8
$\quad\quad - 5 \quad\quad\quad\quad - 7 \quad\quad\quad\quad - 6 \quad\quad\quad\quad - 6 \quad\quad\quad\quad - 9 \quad\quad\quad\quad - 3$

13. $\quad$ 16 $\quad$ **14.** $\quad$ 7 $\quad$ **15.** $\quad$ 12 $\quad$ **16.** $\quad$ 10 $\quad$ **17.** $\quad$ 12 $\quad$ **18.** $\quad$ 15
$\quad\quad - 8 \quad\quad\quad\quad - 1 \quad\quad\quad\quad - 9 \quad\quad\quad\quad - 2 \quad\quad\quad\quad - 4 \quad\quad\quad\quad - 8$

19. $\quad$ 15 $\quad$ **20.** $\quad$ 11 $\quad$ **21.** $\quad$ 14 $\quad$ **22.** $\quad$ 6 $\quad$ **23.** $\quad$ 9 $\quad$ **24.** $\quad$ 17
$\quad\quad - 9 \quad\quad\quad\quad - 9 \quad\quad\quad\quad - 7 \quad\quad\quad\quad - 1 \quad\quad\quad\quad - 5 \quad\quad\quad\quad - 8$

25. $7 - 3 =$ _____

26. $14 - 9 =$ _____

27. $5 - 1 =$ _____

28. $9 - 9 =$ _____

29. $8 - 6 =$ _____

30. $13 - 6 =$ _____

Complete.

31. $16 -$ _____ $= 8$

32. _____ $- 7 = 7$

33. $15 -$ _____ $= 9$

34. $13 -$ _____ $= 9$

35. _____ $- 3 = 2$

36. _____ $- 5 = 7$

37. $3 -$ _____ $= 0$

38. _____ $- 8 = 4$

39. $11 -$ _____ $= 10$

Write a family of facts for each group of numbers.

40. 3, 6, 9

_____

_____

_____

_____

41. 15, 8, 7

_____

_____

_____

_____

42. 11, 6, 5

_____

_____

_____

_____

Use with pages 12–13.

Write the two numbers whose sum is about

1. 50.
(45 26
  25 17)

_____

2. 50.
(19
  58 33
  27)

_____

3. 100.
(35
  89 72
  48)

_____

4. 100.
(25
  16 58
  47)

_____

5. 1,000.
(271
  912 469
  752)

_____

6. 1,000.
(191
  621 573
  789)

_____

Estimate. Write > or < for ( ).

7. 27 + 89 ( ) 100

8. 96 + 86 ( ) 200

9. 37 + 76 ( ) 100

10. 296 + 167 ( ) 400

11. 293 + 324 ( ) 600

12. 397 + 389 ( ) 800

13. 331 + 378 + 351 ( ) 1,000

14. 735 + 422 + 819 ( ) 2,000

15. 5,375 + 6,906 ( ) 10,000

16. 7,961 + 203 + 89 ( ) 10,000

Estimate. First write your rough estimate. Then write your adjusted estimate.

17.
```
   391
    85
   414
+ 120
```

18.
```
   735
   252
   176
+ 349
```

19.
```
  $8.61
   7.08
   1.95
+  3.50
```

20.
```
  4,681
  5,267
  3,408
+ 2,835
```

21. Volunteers at the summer fest want to sell 500 balloons. They have inflated 227 red, 86 orange, 192 blue, and 15 green balloons. Estimate how many balloons are inflated. Have they inflated more or less than 500 balloons?

_____

22. The lemonade vendor needs to begin the day with $20.00 in change. There are $8.75 in quarters, $3.85 in nickels, $4.30 in dimes, and $0.97 in pennies in the money box. Estimate the amount of money in the box. Does the vendor have $20.00 in change?

_____

Holt, Rinehart and Winston, Publishers • 5

Round each number to the nearest hundred and to the nearest thousand.

1. 7,468

2. 3,456

3. 4,663

4. 2,598

5. 1,553

6. 3,221

7. 5,532

8. 7,298

9. 985

10. 723

11. 12,339

12. 10,675

Estimate. Write > or < for ◯.

13. 4,679 + 4,598 ◯ 9,000

14. 8,486 + 11,783 ◯ 21,000

15. 7,395 + 2,931 ◯ 10,000

16. 4,211 + 5,724 + 2,916 ◯ 13,000

17. 8,716 + 9,831 ◯ 18,000

18. 6,327 + 2,469 + 3,782 ◯ 12,000

Estimate the total population in

19. the two largest cities. _____

20. the two smallest cities. _____

21. the six cities shown. _____

City	Population
Clovertown	7,862
Honeydale	5,041
Springmill	46,215
Beeville	8,961
Fairview	39,560
Clearland	2,319

Solve.

22. Farmer Barber harvested 27,216 bushels of wheat and 15,536 bushels of soybeans last year. He had contracted a harvest of 45,000 bushels of grain with the local market. Estimate his total grain harvest. Did he produce as much grain as he thought he would?

_____

23. Many airlines give a free trip to people who fly 100,000 miles or more within one year. The following table shows Carla's travel this year. Estimate the total number of miles flown. Will Carla win a free trip? _____

Jan.–Mar.	33,261 miles
Apr.–June	35,892 miles
July–Sept.	28,723 miles
Oct.–Dec.	17,219 miles

Holt, Rinehart and Winston, Publishers • 5

Estimate to solve.

1. The Clinton Block Association is renovating an old school for a community center. The block association needs 700 feet of lumber for some new walls. A lumber company donates 234 feet of lumber and the block association buys 352 feet and finds 210 feet of lumber in the basement of the old school. Do they have enough lumber? _____

2. The old school auditorium is being converted into a town-meeting hall. The first section of the meeting hall will have 65 seats. The second section will have 47 seats. The third and fourth sections will have 82 seats each. Estimate the minimum number of seats available in the new meeting hall. _____

3. Local residents have donated 900 books for a library at the community center. They use bookshelves from the old school to hold the books. One bookshelf holds 235 books. Another holds 315 books, and the last one they find holds 304 books. Do they have enough bookshelf space for the books? _____

4. A building-supply store donates 500 shingles to repair the old school roof, which leaks in 3 places. In one spot, 230 of the old shingles need to be replaced. In the last 2 places, 110 shingles need to be replaced in each place. Are there enough new shingles for the job? _____

5. It is going to cost $750 to build a game room in the new community center. Local children earn $110 washing cars. A bake sale raises $230, and a neighborhood street fair raises $516. Is there enough money to build the game room? _____

6. When the community center opens, residents hold a 3-day fair to celebrate and raise money for an operating fund. They make $125 the first day, $234 the second day, and $220 the last day. What is the minimum amount of money in the fund? _____

Add.

1. 178 + 15	**2.** $3.67 + 5.03	**3.** 402 + 336	**4.** 516 + 191	**5.** $2.25 + 7.37
6. 870 + 169	**7.** 441 + 386	**8.** 101 + 889	**9.** 743 + 302	**10.** 29 + 17
11. 648 + 296	**12.** 194 + 372	**13.** 64 + 17	**14.** 479 + 813	**15.** 765 + 479
16. 810 + 843	**17.** 218 + 93	**18.** 599 + 848	**19.** $6.69 + 6.69	**20.** 711 + 954
21. $5.42 + 2.24	**22.** 702 + 199	**23.** 654 + 456	**24.** 37 + 64	**25.** 735 + 211
26. 804 + 687	**27.** $6.22 + 9.54	**28.** 605 + 599	**29.** 14 + 57	**30.** 111 + 111

31. 12 + 35 = _____   **32.** 43 + 19 = _____   **33.** $5.45 + $3.32 = _____

34. 13 + 88 = _____   **35.** 73 + 58 = _____   **36.** 391 + 142 = _____

37. 108 + 63 = _____   **38.** $44 + $92 = _____   **39.** 77 + 99 = _____

Solve.

40. On Thursday, the Olympia Theater sold 173 mezzanine tickets and 258 balcony tickets. How many tickets were sold in all?

_____

Holt, Rinehart and Winston, Publishers • 5

Find the sum.

1.	$913.09 + 113.44	**2.**	11,692 + 84,241	**3.**	60,155 + 79,849	**4.**	33,003 + 10,225	**5.**	7,652 + 1,826
6.	10,697 + 39,401	**7.**	9,594 + 2,454	**8.**	1,809 + 6,869	**9.**	$78.08 + 16.03	**10.**	40,081 + 23,916
11.	$66.22 + 61.80	**12.**	10,750 + 64,325	**13.**	89,705 + 65,721	**14.**	706,656 + 197,038	**15.**	3,768 + 2,118

16. 1,001 + 3,016 = _____

17. 19,333 + 41,666 = _____

18. 11,991 + 18,492 = _____

19. 5,080 + 2,777 = _____

20. $61.33 + $49.67 = _____

21. 14,603 + 13,199 = _____

22. 7,444 + 1,611 = _____

23. $111.60 + $198.22 = _____

24. $171.44 + $186.52 = _____

25. 6,097 + 8,211 = _____

26. 11,654 + 678 = _____

27. 147,328 + 35,008 = _____

28. $345.05 + $92.04 = _____

29. $170.04 + $67.98 = _____

Solve.

30. The research ship, Watcher, travelled 3,678 miles in July. It travelled 2,452 miles in August. How many miles did the Watcher travel in two months?

_____

31. The crew of the Watcher tracked a pod of whales 1,654 miles in September. They tracked the pod 976 miles in October. For how many miles has the crew tracked the whales so far?

_____

32. After a trip to the Arctic, the Watcher needed repairs that cost $7,068.56. Painting the entire ship cost $5,456.73. How much money has been spent repairing and painting the ship?

_____

33. The crew bought new camera equipment that cost $768.39. The film for the cameras cost $98.45. How much did the cameras and film cost altogether?

_____

Holt, Rinehart and Winston, Publishers • 5

Add. Check by adding up.

1. 304
    915
    + 126

2. 1,349
    9,002
    + 542

3. 42
    24
    + 41

4. 63
    36
    + 60

5. 3,455
    600
    + 4,253

6. $1.89
    2.12
    + 5.08

7. 301
    54
    + 607

8. 1,000
    280
    + 2,151

9. 5,622
    3,325
    + 1,699

10. 456
    302
    + 111

11. 200
    300
    + 100

12. $65.54
    46.34
    + 72.04

13. 812
    769
    + 1,110

14. 1,575
    844
    + 3,709

15. $71.19
    45.95
    + 53.54

16. 15
    17
    + 23

17. 18
    16
    + 81

18. $95.44
    61.87
    + 52.09

19. 8,673
    1,303
    + 280

20. 1,357
    2,468
    + 3,051

21. 624
    1,879
    + 313

22. $95.78
    7.46
    + 56.23

23. 502
    815
    + 27

24. $0.34
    6.91
    + 4.57

25. 8,141
    1,767
    + 340

26. 250
    6,510
    + 132

27. 498
    62
    + 818

28. 1,582
    4,743
    + 1,956

29. $150.15
    150.15
    + 150.15

30. 3,537
    2,225
    + 2,568

31. 250 + 60 + 84 = _____

32. 59 + 102 + 88 + 33 = _____

33. $9.99 + $18.50 + $31.57 = _____

34. 95 + 37 + 10 = _____

Solve.

35. Bobby collected 125 space figures.
    Joann collected 423 space figures.
    Jordan collected 57 space figures.
    How many space figures did they
    collect in all?

    _____

Holt, Rinehart and Winston, Publishers • 5

Use with pages 24–25.

Solve each problem. Use the infobank on pages 415–420 if you need additional facts.

1. Kansas produced 32 million bushels of wheat in 1982. Minnesota produced 10 million bushels of wheat in the same year. How many bushels did the 2 states produce in all?

2. Texas produced 12 million bushels of wheat in 1982. Oklahoma produced even more. How many bushels of wheat were produced by both states in 1982?

3. Washington and Montana produced the same amount of wheat in 1982. How many bushels of wheat did each produce? How many bushels did they produce in all?

4. Texas, Minnesota, and Nebraska produced similar amounts of wheat. Which state produced the most? How much did all three states grow in all?

Name the reference source you would need to answer each of the questions. Write *newspaper*, *dictionary*, *encyclopedia*, or *almanac*.

5. Glen Ferris is considering buying additional cattle for his ranch. To do this, he must find out when the local stockyard is having a sale. How could he find this information?

6. Bryant Ferris is writing a report on Texas longhorn cattle. What source of information could he use to find out about them?

7. Whitney and Tillie are planning a picnic for the weekend. If it is warm, they can go to the mountains. Otherwise, they will picnic at the river. Where can they look to find out what the weather is likely to be?

8. Brandon and Bryant are going trout fishing for the first time. What single source of information can tell them about different kinds of fish and their habits?

9. Whitney is going to plant a flower garden. She needs to know about how much rain her area gets each year and the dates of the first and last frost.

10. Lela is writing a letter to her grandson in New York to tell him about a *hootenanny* she attended to celebrate Independence Day. Lela looks at the word and wonders where it came from. Where could she find out?

Subtraction of 2- and 3-Digit Numbers

Subtract.

1. 229
   − 196

2. 271
   − 162

3. 359
   − 43

4. 57
   − 46

5. $6.25
   − 4.37

6. 61
   − 26

7. 881
   − 25

8. 95
   − 49

9. 717
   − 454

10. $9.38
   − 6.73

11. 439
   − 112

12. 46
   − 25

13. 84
   − 27

14. 538
   − 77

15. $9.51
   − 8.66

16. 162 − 51 = _____

17. 776 − 549 = _____

18. 49 − 31 = _____

19. 697 − 639 = _____

20. 79 − 36 = _____

21. 27 − 11 = _____

22. 640 − 134 = _____

23. 326 − 209 = _____

24. 350 − 45 = _____

25. $5.78 − $0.96 = _____

26. $1.34 − $0.76 = _____

27. $5.64 − $3.06 = _____

Find *n*.

28. 212 − *n* = 127;

   n = _____

29. 360 − *n* = 94;

   n = _____

30. $2.35 − *n* = $1.06;

   n = _____

31. 116 − *n* = 18;

   n = _____

32. 469 − *n* = 14;

   n = _____

33. $1.10 − *n* = $0.98;

   n = _____

Solve.

34. José tagged 124 dolphins as part of his research on dolphin behavior. Maria tagged 243 dolphins. How many more dolphins did Maria tag than José?

_____

35. Philo needs 250 snails for his research project. He has already collected 97 snails. How many more snails does Philo need to collect?

_____

Holt, Rinehart and Winston, Publishers • 5

Use with pages 28–29.

Find the difference.

1.	8,462 − 6,311	2.	$891.26 − 55.77	3.	177,640 − 172,999	4.	568,981 − 398,765	5.	876,064 − 391,009

6.	7,983 − 3,194	7.	171,725 − 49,836	8.	4,506 − 1,134	9.	842,172 − 531,185	10.	$9,712.91 − 144.54

11.	9,763 − 985	12.	634,449 − 463,490	13.	79,442 − 1,693	14.	99,241 − 8,743	15.	666,666 − 135,782

16.	988,816 − 87,153	17.	9,931 − 3,778	18.	325,421 − 213,789	19.	125,575 − 100,989	20.	243,542 − 198,988

21.	679,222 − 51,325	22.	1,775 − 318	23.	43,725 − 5,839	24.	$324.58 − 83.69	25.	457,274 − 381,989

26. 2,714 − 986 = _____

27. $6.43 − $3.78 = _____

28. 922 − 157 = _____

29. 6,270 − 3,150 = _____

30. $2.37 − $1.49 = _____

31. 478 − 289 = _____

Solve.

32. Mr. Sal Delmonico, a radio and TV salesperson, has sold items to about 35,390 people. He believes he has talked to 116,896 people in his career. How many more people has he talked to than he has sold?

_____

Use with pages 30–31.

Find the difference.

1. 900,001
   − 100,009

2. $100.50
   −   29.58

3. 9,030
   − 6,001

4. 4,001
   − 3,002

5. 980,052
   − 242,578

6. 80,400
   − 78,925

7. 1,102
   −   594

8. 507,900
   − 407,700

9. $410.06
   − 329.24

10. 70,004
    − 22,228

11. $40.03
    − 19.01

12. $330.00
    − 317.67

13. 103
    − 77

14. 300,700
    − 199,999

15. 601,010
    − 573,467

16. 700,072
    − 625,849

17. 107,008
    − 99,889

18. $10.09
    − 10.08

19. 806,502
    − 512,321

20. 700,090
    − 59,102

21. $90.08
    − 16.94

22. 7,006
    − 3,943

23. 702,003
    − 225,679

24. 412,000
    − 367,451

25. 1,090
    −   564

26. 400
    − 136

27. 600,543
    − 317,624

28. $100.06
    −   96.69

29. 58,001
    − 42,828

30. 100,005
    − 99,436

31. 954,000 − 621,311 = _____

32. 2,100 − 1,414 = _____

33. 200 − 108 = _____

34. 407 − 122 = _____

35. 26,034 − 14,785 = _____

36. 3,703 − 988 = _____

Solve.

37. Mrs. Johnson went to buy new school
clothes for her daughter Sarah. She
began with $125. When she finished her
shopping, she had $18.51 left. How
much had she spent shopping?

_____

Holt, Rinehart and Winston, Publishers • 5

Write the letter of the operation that would solve the problem.

1. A herd of 31 antelope joined another herd of 27 antelope and formed a new herd. How large was this new herd?
   a. addition   **b.** subtraction

2. On the tundra, a herd of 48 caribou met another herd. They formed a new herd of 144. How many caribou were in the other herd?
   a. addition   **b.** subtraction

Choose the operation. Then solve.

3. A flock of 247 monarch butterflies migrated to the south. Of the 247, 133 headed toward Florida, and the rest headed toward Mexico. How many headed toward Mexico?

   _____

4. There was a school of 28 dolphins. One year, 8 dolphins were born. If none of the school dies, how many dolphins will be in the school at the end of the year?

   _____

5. Of a school of 751 goldfish, 323 were captured and sold as pets. How many were left?

   _____

6. While traveling south, a flock of 23 snow geese stopped near a pond. While there, 4 of the geese stood guard while the others ate. How many geese ate?

   _____

7. Prairie dogs are rodents that live in large "cities" beneath the plains. One prairie-dog city had 4,000 prairie dogs. If 435 of them were above ground at one time, how many were below ground?

   _____

8. Each year, herds of wild horses swim from Chincoteague Island in Virginia to the mainland. If 504 horses of 2,800 made the swim one year, how many were left behind?

   _____

9. A pair of penguins took turns sitting on an egg. The male sat for a total of 396 hours. If the female sat for the same number of hours, how long did it take for the egg to hatch?

   _____

10. Another pair of penguins sat on an egg for 864 hours. For how many hours more than the other pair did this pair sit on their egg?

   _____

Use with pages 34–35.

Write each as a decimal.

1.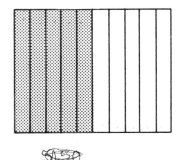

_____

2.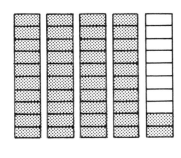

_____

3.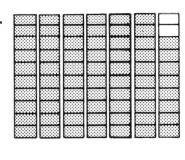

_____

4. two and seven tenths _____

5. seven and two tenths _____

6. nine and four tenths _____

7. nine tenths _____

8. nineteen and nine tenths _____

9. ninety-nine and one tenth _____

Copy and complete this place-value chart. Write each decimal on the chart.

10. 2.4   **11.** 0.3   **12.** 93.3

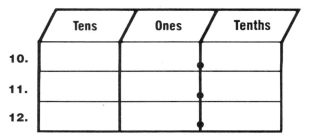

	Tens	Ones	Tenths
10.			
11.			
12.			

Write the word name for each decimal.

13. 0.5 _____

14. 3.6 _____

15. 10.4 _____

16. 15.2 _____

17. 8.7 _____

18. 13.3 _____

Solve.

19. The sailfish is a fast animal. In Florida, a sailfish was clocked at sixty-eight and one tenth mph. Write that number as a decimal.

_____

20. The giant tortoise can only travel five yards in forty-three and five tenths seconds. Write that number as a decimal.

_____

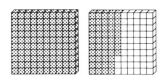

Write each as a decimal.

1.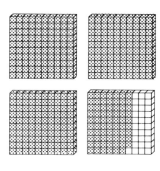

_____

2.

_____

3.

_____

4. one and twenty-five hundredths _____

5. one hundred forty and eleven hundredths _____

6. sixty-one and eight hundredths _____

7. sixty-one hundredths _____

8. twelve and five hundredths _____

Write the word name for each number.

9. 6.83 _____

10. 0.91 _____

11. 405.64 _____

12. 39.01 _____

Use the figure at the right.

13. Write the decimal for the number of squares shaded in Figure X. _____

14. Write the decimal for the number of squares shaded in Figure Y. _____

15. Write the decimal for the number of squares shaded in Figure Y and Figure Z together. _____

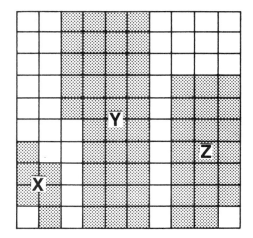

Use with pages 46–47.

Write each as a decimal.

1. ten and three hundred five thousandths _____

2. ten and thirty-five thousandths _____

3. one and three hundred fifty-one thousandths _____

4. twelve thousandths _____

Write the word name for each decimal.

5. 76.016 _____

6. 0.009 _____

7. 5.803 _____

8. 58.003 _____

Write the value of the underlined digit.

9. 0.4̲27 _____   **10.** 6,214.798 _____

11. 16.091̲ _____   **12.** 3̲.101 _____

13. 5.6̲71 _____   **14.** 8,6̲90.352 _____

15. 7.598̲ _____   **16.** 4,367.0̲51 _____

Copy and complete the chart. Write the decimal.

	Thousands	Hundreds	Tens	Ones	Tenths	Hundredths	Thousandths	
17.	1	2	3	4	0	0	0	= 1234.000
18.	0	0	2	2	3	1	0	= 0022.310
19.	4	0	1	0	6	0	0	= 4,010.600
20.	0	0	0	0	4	1	5	= 0.415
21.	5	7	0	4	3	9	7	= 5,704.397
22.	0	3	9	1	9	7	8	= 0391.978

Use with pages 48–49.

Can you use the bar graph to answer these questions?

1. Which activity uses the most calories?

_____

2. Which activity is the most popular?

_____

Solve.

3. Are more calories burned while running or walking?

_____

4. Lance ate 3 strawberries. They equaled 12.5 calories. Which activity could burn that number of calories in one minute?

_____

5. About 10 string beans equal 7 calories. How many of these activities could burn that number of calories in less than one minute?

_____

6. Which activity requires more calories, football or basketball?

_____

8. How many calories does a game of table tennis burn per minute?

_____

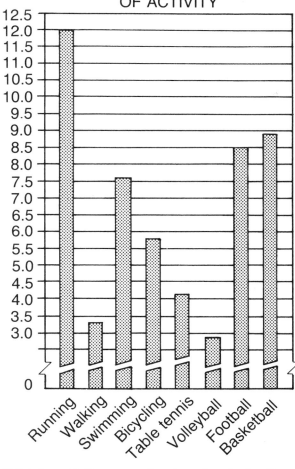

CALORIES USED PER MINUTE OF ACTIVITY

Running, Walking, Swimming, Bicycling, Table tennis, Volleyball, Football, Basketball

7. Which activity uses the least calories?

_____

9. Which uses more calories, bicycling or swimming?

_____

Compare. Write >, <, or = for ◯.

1. 0.259 ◯ 0.333   **2.** 0.33 ◯ 0.025   **3.** 0.16 ◯ 0.052

4. 0.6 ◯ 0.60   **5.** 0.093 ◯ 0.090   **6.** 2.013 ◯ 2.103

7. 6.07 ◯ 6.070   **8.** 1.56 ◯ 1.506   **9.** 2.1 ◯ 2.110

Write in order from the least to the greatest.

10. 0, 0.675, 0.009   **11.** 0.09, 0, 0.25

_____   _____

12. 0.057, 0.01, 0.052   **13.** 1.01, 2.41, 0.241

_____   _____

Write in order from the greatest to the least.

14. 0.055, 0.005, 0.55   **15.** 2.015, 2.51, 2.105

_____   _____

16. 6.14, 0.16, 0.64   **17.** 8.07, 8.083, 8.7

_____   _____

Solve.

18. If 3.■43 > 3.843, then ■ must be which digit?   _____

19. If 0.081 > 0.08■, then ■ must be which digit?   _____

20. Lara jumped 2.13 meters in the high-jump competition. Ada jumped 2.11 meters. Who jumped higher?   _____

21. Jon finished the 400-meter race in 53.23 seconds. Bob took 52.33 seconds to finish the race. Stan's time for the race was 53.32 seconds. In what order did the three runners finish?   _____

22. Daniel jumped 4.82 meters in the high jump. Pablo jumped 4.98 meters. Ryan jumped 4.28 meters. Who won the event? Who came in second?   _____

Holt, Rinehart and Winston, Publishers • 5

Round to the nearest whole number.

1. 1.3 _____

2. 13.725 _____

3. 3.7 _____

4. 21.82 _____

5. 6.54 _____

6. 72.271 _____

7. 12.15 _____

8. 3.4 _____

9. 14.15 _____

10. 5.13 _____

11. 40.45 _____

12. 18.447 _____

13. 7.105 _____

14. 7.501 _____

15. 8.86 _____

Round to the nearest tenth.

16. 40.101 _____

17. 0.146 _____

18. 2.044 _____

19. 6.40 _____

20. 6.405 _____

21. 7.09 _____

22. 0.251 _____

23. 0.215 _____

24. 2.457 _____

25. 2.15 _____

26. 26.39 _____

27. 5.707 _____

28. 23.029 _____

29. 7.054 _____

30. 8.349 _____

Round to the nearest hundredth.

31. 2.222 _____

32. 2.224 _____

33. 0.205 _____

34. 3.141 _____

35. 3.145 _____

36. 0.007 _____

37. 0.526 _____

38. 0.948 _____

39. 0.692 _____

40. 11.445 _____

41. 8.234 _____

42. 71.111 _____

43. 29.009 _____

44. 7.001 _____

45. 0.003 _____

Solve.

46. Keisha rode her bicycle 4.36 kilometers. Round this number to the nearest tenth.

_____

Estimate. Write =, > or < in the ◯.

1. 7.68 + 2.39 ◯ 9

2. 39.63 + 19.92 ◯ 60

3. 8.962 + 0.729 ◯ 10

4. 0.898 + 0.201 ◯ 1

5. 3.371 + 1.596 ◯ 6

6. 0.51 + 0.47 ◯ 1

7. 2.73 + 0.801 ◯ 3

8. 5.36 + 0.089 ◯ 6

9. 3.97 + 6.68 ◯ 10

10. 4.87 + 4.75 + 3.45 ◯ 15

11. 46.71 + 31.375 + 27.62 ◯ 100

12. 24.92 + 59.06 + 11.17 ◯ 90

Estimate. Write the letter for the range where your estimate falls.

13. 4.68 + 5.83 + 6.77 _____

a. 4–9

14. 2.98 + 2.65 + 0.89 _____

b. 10–15

15. 9.76 + 7.65 + 6.96 _____

c. 16–20

16. 7.67 + 3.89 + 2.08 _____

d. 21–25

Estimate. Write =, > or < in the ◯.

17. 36.71 − 27.85 ◯ 10

18. 78.91 − 69.34 ◯ 9

19. 47.87 − 19.9 ◯ 30

20. 51.77 − 29.6 ◯ 20

21. 8.87 − 0.968 ◯ 7

22. 11.45 − 10.55 ◯ 1

23. 73.081 − 27.6 ◯ 50

24. 97.6 − 63.911 ◯ 30

25. 27.61 − 18.09 ◯ 10

Estimate. Write the letter for the range where your estimate falls.

26. 51.7 − 27.92 _____

a. 10–19

27. 76.63 − 35.089 _____

b. 20–29

28. 69.71 − 57.8 _____

c. 30–39

29. 47.89 − 13.98 _____

d. 40–49

30. 83.59 − 27.62 _____

e. 50–59

Use with pages 56–57.

Solve. Explain why you would *overestimate* or *underestimate*.

1. Don needs to perform at least 24 hours of community service to earn his citizenship merit badge. Here is his record so far.

Week 1: 3.2 hours   **Week 5:** 3.4 hours
Week 2: 2.5 hours   **Week 6:** 5.6 hours
Week 3: 5.2 hours   **Week 7:** 2.8 hours
Week 4: 2.9 hours   **Week 8:** 2.1 hours

Has Don earned his merit badge? _____

_____

2. Jill is on the phone ordering the following items: scout manuals for $67.80; mess kits for $49.50; and day packs for $88.88. The troop has exactly $208. Do they have enough money to pay for Jill's order? _____

_____

3. The troop is going to camp out at Rottinwood Camp. The camp has room for 120 scouts. If 22 scouts go from Company *A*, 44 scouts go from Company *B*, and 36 scouts go from Company *C*, will there be enough room at the camp? _____

4. Each scout must spend 90 hours in the wilderness to earn a camping merit badge. Here are some times for the first 3 outings.

Tim: 11.2; 10.5; 30.9   Janie: 36.2; 20.7; 11.9
Carol: 20.5; 31.6; 48.1   Biff: 31.8; 23.2; 40.4
Scott: 24.9; 44.2; 51.3   Juanita: 30.5; 47.6; 30.8

Which scouts have earned their merit badges? _____

_____

5. Biff is making plaster casts of animal footprints. He has only enough equipment to make one cast at a time. It takes 3.2 hours for the plaster to dry in a bear print, 2.3 hours for it to dry in a raccoon print, and 1.2 hours for it to dry in a deer print. Will 9 hours be enough time to make all 3 casts? _____

Holt, Rinehart and Winston, Publishers • 5

Add.

1. 3.95
    + 0.350

2. 9.1
    + 4.90

3. 66.09
    + 5.099

4. 0.990
    + 7.119

5. 3.142
    + 27.008

6. 2.97
    + 0.97

7. $75.07
    +   9.99

8. $437.78
    +   6.45

9. 0.6
    0.7
    + 0.3

10. 1.5
    4.60
    + 3.63

11. 5.47
    0.08
    + 11.59

12. 9.463
    11.354
    + 15.789

13. 0.49
    + 0.56

14. $5.75
    2.47
    + 6.93

15. $45.36
    36.45
    + 17.71

16. 0.49
    + 0.38

17. 0.54
    + 7.38

18. $5.75
    3.82
    + 6.93

19. 6.42
    4.62
    + 2.46

20. $75.37
    11.55
    + 10.81

21. 4.27 + 0.55 = _____

22. 33.81 + 6.493 = _____

23. 1.08 + 4.35 + 3.87 = _____

24. 2.03 + 5.16 + 7.21 = _____

Add. Find the first digit of each sum below. Write the letter above the digit to solve the riddle.

25. 3.62
    + 4.185
        = H

26. 763.2
    + 49.8
        = N

27. 0.887
    + 9.023
        = A

28. 54.128
    + 3.2
        = T

29. 32.661
    + 33.101
        = G

30. 29.26
    + 16.98
        = I

31. 22.436
    + 187.3
        = O

32. 99.999
    + 1.001
        = W

What state name sounds like a lot of laundry?

___ ___   S   _H_ ___ ___ ___ ___ ___ ___
 1   9   7   4   8   6   5   2   8

Use with pages 60–61.

Subtract.

1. 0.2 − 0.19	**2.** 81.08 − 78.17	**3.** 91.17 − 4.29	**4.** 9.16 − 8.25	**5.** $7.45 − 5.65
6. 53.56 − 47.90	**7.** 76.70 − 67.80	**8.** 34.02 − 5.89	**9.** $65.71 − 4.65	**10.** 13.00 − 9.36
11. $76.57 − 39.24	**12.** 8.69 − 5.24	**13.** 34.7 − 16.83	**14.** 101.06 − 100.98	**15.** 135.86 − 32.45
16. 0.57 − 0.06	**17.** 0.71 − 0.66	**18.** 1.09 − 0.38	**19.** $2.00 − 1.23	**20.** 43.80 − 4.99
21. $13.03 − 4.67	**22.** $64.00 − 15.07	**23.** 79.00 − 0.43	**24.** $53.99 − 30.79	**25.** $67.89 − 0.24

26. 6.02 − 6.00 = _____

27. 120.78 − 94.96 = _____

28. 18.17 − 9.29 = _____

29. 0.5 − 0.28 = _____

30. 0.93 − 0.07 = _____

31. 3.14 − 1.99 = _____

32. 16.61 − 11.91 = _____

33. 7.05 − 4.01 = _____

Solve.

34. A bird's flying speed was measured at 106.25 mph in the U.S.S.R. Another bird in India was recorded at a speed of 171.8 mph. Which country had the faster bird and by how much?

_____

35. The fastest racehorse was recorded at a speed of 43.26 mph. Round this speed to the nearest tenth, and then to the nearest whole number.

_____

Holt, Rinehart and Winston, Publishers • 5

Write the letter of the correct answer.

1. A roll of 24-exposure color print film costs $2.60. A 36-exposure roll costs $1.80 more. How much does the 36-exposure roll cost?
   a. $n = \$1.80 + \$2.60$
   b. $n = \$2.60 - \$1.80$

2. Wallet-size reprints cost $0.30 each, and large prints cost $3.75 each. Sally orders one of each. How much does she spend?
   a. $n = \$3.75 - \$0.30$
   b. $n = \$3.75 + \$0.30$

Write an equation. Then solve.

3. Pepe bought a roll of 36-exposure color print film for $3.68. The film costs $7.75 to develop. How much did Pepe spend in all?

4. Film for 36 color slides costs $5.69. Developing the film costs $4.75. If Lulu has $11.00, will she have enough to buy the film and have it developed?

5. A 20-exposure roll of color print film costs $4.75 to develop. The same size roll of color slides costs $1.80 less to develop. How much does it cost to develop a 20-exposure roll of slides?

6. Edna found an old photo of her grandparents. She had it enlarged and framed at a cost of $14.70. She also had 2 wallet-size reprints made at a cost of $0.75 each. How much did Edna spend?

7. Jody is sending away the 2 rolls of film she shot on her vacation to be developed. Each roll costs $3.25 to be developed. For what amount should Jody make out her check?

8. Zoe took some photographs of the Greek Festival for *The Journal*. The newspaper paid her $60.00 for them. Zoe's expenses came to $26.30. What was Zoe's profit?

9. Arnold took a picture of each of his classmates and one of the teacher. He found a lab that charged $12.75 for developing and printing his roll of film. The shipping charge was $1.25. How much money will Arnold need?

★10. Al had a photo of his puppy enlarged at a cost of $11.95. The tax came to $0.94. He paid with a 20-dollar bill. How much change did Al get?

Holt, Rinehart and Winston, Publishers • 5

Use with pages 64–65.

Multiply.

1. $\begin{array}{r} 6 \\ \times\, 2 \\ \hline \end{array}$	**2.** $\begin{array}{r} 1 \\ \times\, 9 \\ \hline \end{array}$	**3.** $\begin{array}{r} 8 \\ \times\, 3 \\ \hline \end{array}$	**4.** $\begin{array}{r} 5 \\ \times\, 4 \\ \hline \end{array}$	**5.** $\begin{array}{r} 7 \\ \times\, 6 \\ \hline \end{array}$	**6.** $\begin{array}{r} 2 \\ \times\, 6 \\ \hline \end{array}$
7. $\begin{array}{r} 8 \\ \times\, 9 \\ \hline \end{array}$	**8.** $\begin{array}{r} 3 \\ \times\, 4 \\ \hline \end{array}$	**9.** $\begin{array}{r} 0 \\ \times\, 5 \\ \hline \end{array}$	**10.** $\begin{array}{r} 6 \\ \times\, 6 \\ \hline \end{array}$	**11.** $\begin{array}{r} 8 \\ \times\, 2 \\ \hline \end{array}$	**12.** $\begin{array}{r} 7 \\ \times\, 1 \\ \hline \end{array}$
13. $\begin{array}{r} 3 \\ \times\, 8 \\ \hline \end{array}$	**14.** $\begin{array}{r} 9 \\ \times\, 1 \\ \hline \end{array}$	**15.** $\begin{array}{r} 5 \\ \times\, 9 \\ \hline \end{array}$	**16.** $\begin{array}{r} 1 \\ \times\, 4 \\ \hline \end{array}$	**17.** $\begin{array}{r} 6 \\ \times\, 7 \\ \hline \end{array}$	**18.** $\begin{array}{r} 5 \\ \times\, 0 \\ \hline \end{array}$
19. $\begin{array}{r} 1 \\ \times\, 7 \\ \hline \end{array}$	**20.** $\begin{array}{r} 4 \\ \times\, 9 \\ \hline \end{array}$	**21.** $\begin{array}{r} 6 \\ \times\, 3 \\ \hline \end{array}$	**22.** $\begin{array}{r} 9 \\ \times\, 5 \\ \hline \end{array}$	**23.** $\begin{array}{r} 2 \\ \times\, 8 \\ \hline \end{array}$	**24.** $\begin{array}{r} 4 \\ \times\, 3 \\ \hline \end{array}$

25. $4 \times 7 =$ _____

26. $8 \times 3 =$ _____

27. $5 \times 4 =$ _____

28. $(8 \times 3) \times 6 =$ _____

29. $5 \times (5 \times 4) =$ _____

30. $2 \times (2 \times 7) =$ _____

Complete. Write the name of the property.

31. $6 \times (4 + 7) = (6 \times 4) + (\underline{} \times \underline{})$ _____

32. $5 \times (3 + 4) = 15 + \underline{}$ _____

33. $(2 \times 4) \times 2 = 2 \times (\underline{} \times 2)$ _____

34. $3 \times (8 + 6) = (3 \times 8) + (\underline{} \times \underline{})$ _____

35. $(1 \times 9) \times 6 = 1 \times (9 \times \underline{})$ _____

36. $4 \times (5 + 7) = (4 \times 5) + (\underline{} \times \underline{})$ _____

Solve.

37. Stephanie has a pen pal in India and another in Italy. If she receives 3 letters per year from each pen pal, how many letters will she receive in 3 years?

_____

38. Stephanie's Italian pen pal telephones her every year on her birthday. If they talk for 8 minutes per call, how many minutes will they talk over 5 years?

_____

Holt, Rinehart and Winston, Publishers • 5

Multiply.

1. 10 × 6	**2.** 30 × 4	**3.** 1,000 × 10	**4.** 200 × 2	**5.** 60 × 7
6. 2,000 × 30	**7.** 10 × 8	**8.** 100 × 9	**9.** 5,000 × 40	**10.** 70 × 5
11. 10 × 7	**12.** 8,000 × 30	**13.** 6,000 × 20	**14.** 800 × 800	**15.** 40 × 7
16. 9,000 × 40	**17.** 60 × 6	**18.** 4,000 × 70	**19.** 5,000 × 90	**20.** 3,000 × 20

21. 70 × 3,000 = _____   **22.** 500 × 500 = _____   **23.** 8 × 60 = _____

24. 4 × 4,000 = _____   **25.** 9 × 80 = _____   **26.** 2 × 1,000 = _____

Copy the answer blanks and the numbers. What do you say
when you order turtle soup?

___ ___ ___ ___   _____ _____   _____ _____ ___ _____ _____ _____
9,000 540 81,000 800   280,000 350,000   10,000 600,000 540 4,000 4,000 24,000

Multiply. Then match the letter with the answer above.

27. 1,000 × 9 = M	**28.** 7,000 × 50 = T	**29.** 30,000 × 20 = N	**30.** 800 × 5 = P	**31.** 4,000 × 6 = Y
32. 60 × 9 = A	**33.** 9,000 × 9 = K	**34.** 4,000 × 70 = I	**35.** 1,000 × 10 = S	**36.** 10 × 80 = E

Use with pages 78–79.

Holt, Rinehart and Winston, Publishers • 5

Without finding the exact answer, write the letter of the answer that is reasonable.

1. Allie plays guitar in a group called the Squealers. The group also includes a drummer, a bass player, a pianist, a singer, and one other guitarist. How many members are there in the band?
   a. 2   b. 6   c. 20

2. Each member of the Squealers received $20 for playing at the county fair. How much did the entire band earn at the county fair?
   a. $20   b. $120   c. $1,200

3. Allie bought 10 blank tapes to record the band's music. If each tape cost $2.00, how much did she spend?
   a. $20.00   b. $2.00   c. $200.00

4. The Squealers went on a nationwide tour. They went to 30 cities. They played an average of 3 shows in each city. About how many shows did they play, all total?
   a. 9   b. 90   c. 600

5. On their tour, the group spent 3 days in each of 30 cities. How many days did their tour last?
   a. 30 days
   b. 90 days
   c. 365 days

6. The Squealers earned a total of $20,750 on their tour. They spent $3,246 on expenses. How much money did they make in profit?
   a. $17,504
   b. $1,750.40
   c. $24,000

7. The group played in a school auditorium. There were 60 rows of seats and 100 seats in each row. Every seat was taken. How many people came to the concert?
   a. 60   b. 6,000   c. 600

8. One day the Squealers gave a free concert in the park. Each of the 6 members of the group put up 100 posters advertising the concert. How many posters did they put up all together?
   a. 60   b. 6,000   c. 600

9. The Squealers recorded an album on tape. It had 10 songs that lasted 3 minutes each. How long was the tape?
   a. 30 minutes
   b. 90 minutes
   c. 300 minutes

10. The group wanted 10 copies of the tape to send to 10 local radio stations. How many copies did they need?
   a. 10
   b. 60
   c. 100

Estimate.

1. $\begin{array}{r} 301 \\ \times\ 19 \\ \hline \end{array}$	**2.** $\begin{array}{r} 37 \\ \times\ 29 \\ \hline \end{array}$	**3.** $\begin{array}{r} \$7.17 \\ \times\ \ \ \ 9 \\ \hline \end{array}$	**4.** $\begin{array}{r} 532 \\ \times\ 73 \\ \hline \end{array}$

5. $\begin{array}{r} 41 \\ \times\ 21 \\ \hline \end{array}$ **6.** $\begin{array}{r} 54 \\ \times\ 13 \\ \hline \end{array}$

7. $\begin{array}{r} \$9.06 \\ \times\ \ \ \ 9 \\ \hline \end{array}$ **8.** $\begin{array}{r} 48 \\ \times\ 11 \\ \hline \end{array}$ **9.** $\begin{array}{r} 212 \\ \times\ 82 \\ \hline \end{array}$ **10.** $\begin{array}{r} 33 \\ \times\ 14 \\ \hline \end{array}$ **11.** $\begin{array}{r} 62 \\ \times\ 13 \\ \hline \end{array}$ **12.** $\begin{array}{r} \$5.88 \\ \times\ \ \ \ 8 \\ \hline \end{array}$

13. $\begin{array}{r} 481 \\ \times\ 39 \\ \hline \end{array}$ **14.** $\begin{array}{r} 86 \\ \times\ 49 \\ \hline \end{array}$ **15.** $\begin{array}{r} 952 \\ \times\ 81 \\ \hline \end{array}$ **16.** $\begin{array}{r} \$8.15 \\ \times\ \ \ \ 2 \\ \hline \end{array}$ **17.** $\begin{array}{r} 417 \\ \times\ 72 \\ \hline \end{array}$ **18.** $\begin{array}{r} 594 \\ \times\ 38 \\ \hline \end{array}$

19. $\begin{array}{r} 63 \\ \times\ 29 \\ \hline \end{array}$ **20.** $\begin{array}{r} 74 \\ \times\ 18 \\ \hline \end{array}$ **21.** $\begin{array}{r} \$7.05 \\ \times\ \ \ \ 7 \\ \hline \end{array}$ **22.** $\begin{array}{r} 366 \\ \times\ 89 \\ \hline \end{array}$ **23.** $\begin{array}{r} 67 \\ \times\ 12 \\ \hline \end{array}$ **24.** $\begin{array}{r} 875 \\ \times\ 75 \\ \hline \end{array}$

25. $\begin{array}{r} 99 \\ \times\ 41 \\ \hline \end{array}$ **26.** $\begin{array}{r} 28 \\ \times\ 36 \\ \hline \end{array}$ **27.** $\begin{array}{r} 603 \\ \times\ 25 \\ \hline \end{array}$ **28.** $\begin{array}{r} \$1.15 \\ \times\ \ \ \ 6 \\ \hline \end{array}$ **29.** $\begin{array}{r} 851 \\ \times\ 36 \\ \hline \end{array}$ **30.** $\begin{array}{r} \$4.44 \\ \times\ \ \ \ 3 \\ \hline \end{array}$

31. $39 \times 89 =$ _____

32. $22 \times \$9.16 =$ _____

33. $95 \times 266 =$ _____

34. $13 \times 184 =$ _____

35. $58 \times 364 =$ _____

36. $47 \times 333 =$ _____

Solve.

37. Every day, Jeremy crosses the Silver Gate Bridge 4 times. He crosses once to go to school, once to go home for lunch, once to go back to school, and once to return home. If Jeremy goes to school 186 days in a year, about how many times does he cross the bridge?

_____

38. When Jeremy arrives at school, he and his friend Carlos exercise before class begins. If together they do a total of 30 jumping jacks, about how many exercises do they do each year? HINT: There are 186 school days.

_____

Holt, Rinehart and Winston, Publishers • 5

Use with pages 82–83.

Solve. Find an estimate or an exact answer as needed.

1. Marvin needs to raise $500 to repair the wall to the racoon display at his game farm. The admission fee to the farm is $1.75. If 295 people visit the farm during the week, will Marvin earn enough money to repair the wall?

   _____

2. The local zoo covers 1,043 acres. The state park nearby is almost 4 times as large as the zoo. About how large is the state park?

   _____

3. The members of the Zoo Club want to buy three books about some of the animals they saw during their last trip to the zoo. They have exactly $17.50 in their budget to spend on books.

   The cost of each book is:

   Bats by Night $5.23
   Hungry Hippos $3.79
   Lions Live $9.58

   Do they have enough money?

   _____

4. The Zoo Club also has $185 to spend on new t-shirts. There are 25 members in the club. The t-shirts cost $6.95 each. Does the club have enough money to buy each member a new t-shirt?

   _____

Multiply.

1. 31×9	**2.** 151×4	**3.** 563×4	**4.** $\$0.34 \times 8$	**5.** 307×5
6. $\$3.46 \times 2$	**7.** 789×3	**8.** 50×6	**9.** 93×5	**10.** 36×6
11. 819×4	**12.** 53×6	**13.** 117×3	**14.** 648×9	**15.** $\$5.40 \times 3$
16. 68×9	**17.** $\$7.10 \times 2$	**18.** 353×4	**19.** 44×5	**20.** 254×3

21. $6 \times 32 =$ _____ **22.** $4 \times 601 =$ _____ **23.** $5 \times \$2.50 =$ _____

24. $2 \times \$10.20 =$ _____ **25.** $7 \times 17 =$ _____ **26.** $3 \times 48 =$ _____

27. $8 \times 64 =$ _____ **28.** $9 \times \$1.83 =$ _____ **29.** $7 \times 211 =$ _____

Solve.

30. Henry, Sol, and Phillippa each buy a book about the founding of New York City. Each book costs $7.35. How much did the three friends spend? _____

31. Jonas had 156 books in his library. In a few years the number of books increased 7 times. How many books does Jonas have in his library now? _____

32. Bette bought 9 new books for her library. Each book cost $9.78. How much did Bette spend on books? _____

33. Erin has 5 bookshelves in her library. Each shelf holds 45 books. How many books can Erin fit on the shelves in her library? _____

Multiply. Estimate to check your answer.

1. 2,340
    × 3

2. $62.51
    × 4

3. 5,928
    × 7

4. 1,598
    × 2

5. 12,067
    × 5

6. 4,789
    × 8

7. 7,234
    × 8

8. 9,560
    × 3

9. $85.21
    × 4

10. 5,344
    × 6

11. $26.98
    × 9

12. 15,300
    × 2

13. 1,351
    × 9

14. 6,205
    × 3

15. 3,482
    × 5

16. 24,059
    × 3

17. 7,846
    × 7

18. $52.83
    × 6

19. 4,763
    × 4

20. 9,368
    × 2

21. 5 × 8,650 = _____

22. 3 × 22,121 = _____

23. 4 × $97.14 = _____

24. 2 × 13,053 = _____

25. 7 × 5,822 = _____

26. 6 × $46.79 = _____

Solve.

27. Captain Juarez has been the skipper of the ferryboat *Isabelle* for 6 years. If he averages 3,550 trips a year across Wellington Sound, how many trips has he made during his 6 years as skipper?

_____

28. During that period, the *Isabelle* carried about 15,820 people and about 11,915 cars per year. How many people did the ship carry during Captain Juarez's time as skipper?

_____

how many cars? _____

Holt, Rinehart and Winston, Publishers • 5

Use the Infobank on page 417 to solve.

1. Jill is making a box kite and two delta kites. How many sticks will she need? How many feet of string will she need for the tails?

2. Jeff is making a flat kite, a box kite, and a delta kite. How many inches long would all three kites be if Jeff measured them from end to end?

_____

Choose the operation you would use to solve the problem. Write the letter of the correct answer.

3. Jeff has a piece of string 42 inches long. He uses 36 inches to make a kite tail. How many inches of string does he have left?

a. addition   **b.** subtraction

4. Jill has 4 feet of red paper, 5 feet of blue paper, and 8 feet of yellow paper with which to make kites. How many feet of paper has she in all?

a. addition   **b.** subtraction

Use the graph to solve.

5. How many times did Jeff fly his box kite between March and May? Was this greater than or less than the number of times he flew it between June and August?

_____

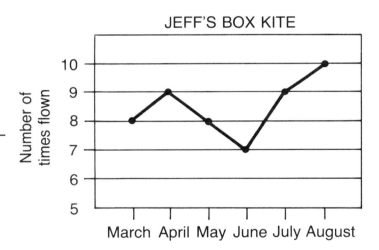

JEFF'S BOX KITE

6. In which month did Jeff fly his box kite the most? How many more times did he fly it than in the month he flew it the least?

_____

Estimate to solve.

7. Jeff has $10.00. He wants to buy a box kite that costs $4.25, a ball of string that costs $1.50, and a delta kite that costs $2.75. Does he have enough money?

_____

8. Jill wants to buy two specialty kites for $7.25 each. She has two $5 bills and three $1 bills. Does she have enough money to buy both kites?

_____

Holt, Rinehart and Winston, Publishers • 5

Use with page 90.

Write an equation to solve.

9. Jill buys paper and string for $6.75. She pays for it with a $10 bill. How much change will she get?

10. Jeff buys 4 balls of kite string for $0.75 each. How much do all 4 balls of string cost?

Solve.

11. Tom and Nicky go to the hobby shop and buy paper for $1.50, string for $0.75, and glue for $0.80. How much change do they receive from $5.00?

12. Louise buys ribbon for her kite tail and pays for it with $1.00. She receives $0.22 change. How much money did she spend on the ribbon?

13. Jennifer went to the store and bought kites for her 6 cousins. She paid with a $20 bill and received $3.73 in change. How much money did she spend?

14. Mark tangled his kite in a tree and spent $1.40 for glue and $2.60 for tape to make repairs. He paid for them with $5.00. What was his change?

15. Elspeth made a japanese-dragon kite. She spent $7.30 on paper, $5.10 on silk ribbons, $0.75 on glue, and $2.41 on glitter and sequins. What was her change from $20.00?

16. Christina decided to make a dragon kite. She paid for the supplies with $30.00. She received $8.15 as change. How much money did Christina spend?

17. Judy bought a kite for $4.50, and string for $1.25. She paid with a $10 bill and received $3.25 as change. Judy went back to the cashier to explain the mistake. What was the mistake?

18. Richard bought a box kite for $6.15. He gave the cashier $10.00. The cashier gave him $3.95. He went back to the cashier to return the extra change. How much money did he give back to the cashier?

19. Tom bought 3 sheets of kite paper for $2.10 each. What was his change from $10.00?

20. Alfie bought a kite for each of his 4 nephews. They were $3.80 each. What was his change from $20.00?

Holt, Rinehart and Winston, Publishers • 5

Multiply.

1. $\begin{array}{r} 61 \\ \times\ 10 \\ \hline \end{array}$

2. $\begin{array}{r} 137 \\ \times\ 35 \\ \hline \end{array}$

3. $\begin{array}{r} \$27.46 \\ \times\ 14 \\ \hline \end{array}$

4. $\begin{array}{r} 289 \\ \times\ 27 \\ \hline \end{array}$

5. $\begin{array}{r} 8,100 \\ \times\ 30 \\ \hline \end{array}$

6. $\begin{array}{r} \$35.28 \\ \times\ 46 \\ \hline \end{array}$

7. $\begin{array}{r} 47 \\ \times\ 80 \\ \hline \end{array}$

8. $\begin{array}{r} 511 \\ \times\ 33 \\ \hline \end{array}$

9. $\begin{array}{r} 749 \\ \times\ 25 \\ \hline \end{array}$

10. $\begin{array}{r} 1,678 \\ \times\ 69 \\ \hline \end{array}$

11. $\begin{array}{r} 2,022 \\ \times\ 50 \\ \hline \end{array}$

12. $\begin{array}{r} 94 \\ \times\ 11 \\ \hline \end{array}$

13. $\begin{array}{r} 310 \\ \times\ 20 \\ \hline \end{array}$

14. $\begin{array}{r} \$85.16 \\ \times\ 47 \\ \hline \end{array}$

15. $\begin{array}{r} 509 \\ \times\ 73 \\ \hline \end{array}$

16. $\begin{array}{r} 87 \\ \times\ 19 \\ \hline \end{array}$

17. $\begin{array}{r} 923 \\ \times\ 40 \\ \hline \end{array}$

18. $\begin{array}{r} 3,187 \\ \times\ 36 \\ \hline \end{array}$

19. $\begin{array}{r} \$56.41 \\ \times\ 50 \\ \hline \end{array}$

20. $\begin{array}{r} \$67.99 \\ \times\ 43 \\ \hline \end{array}$

21. $25 \times 7,654 =$ _____

22. $90 \times \$87.33 =$ _____

23. $17 \times 9,113 =$ _____

24. $81 \times 4,555 =$ _____

25. $96 \times 1,036 =$ _____

26. $70 \times 306 =$ _____

27. $13 \times 5,939 =$ _____

28. $43 \times 7,026 =$ _____

Solve.

29. Mara works in the mailroom of a large company. Each day she sends about 204 pieces of mail. How many pieces of mail does she send in 31 days? _____

30. Mara orders 24 boxes of envelopes. Each box costs $12.76. How much does Mara spend on envelopes? _____

Holt, Rinehart and Winston, Publishers • 5

Multiply.

1.	562 × 349	**2.**	197 × 200	**3.**	843 × 656	**4.**	$9.72 × 498	**5.**	235 × 176
6.	$8.64 × 973	**7.**	621 × 517	**8.**	743 × 459	**9.**	253 × 186	**10.**	346 × 300
11.	472 × 931	**12.**	869 × 500	**13.**	$7.42 × 610	**14.**	596 × 372	**15.**	260 × 418
16.	563 × 927	**17.**	$7.99 × 683	**18.**	348 × 297	**19.**	900 × 193	**20.**	426 × 317

21. 718 × 569 = _____

22. 201 × 462 = _____

23. 537 × $6.28 = _____

24. 343 × $1.58 = _____

25. 985 × 611 = _____

26. 257 × 316 = _____

27. 306 × 719 = _____

28. 634 × 811 = _____

Solve.

29. The novelist who has written the most books is Kathleen Lindsey. Each of her books is about 278 pages long and has about 117 words per page. About how many words does each book contain?

_____

30. About how many total pages were there in her 904 novels?

_____

Complete the plan by completing the missing step.

1. The Sioux Indians lived on the Great Plains. One day, a Sioux tribe sent out 7 parties to gather food. If each party contained four smaller groups of five Indians each, then how many Indians went on the expedition?
Step 1: Find out how many Indians were in each party.

Step 2: _____

_____

2. One Sioux village had 17 tipis. Ten of them were small tipis that housed 2 people in each. The others were large tipis that housed three people in each. How many people lived in the village?

Step 1: _____

_____

Step 2: Find out the sum of the number of people in small tipis and the number of people in large tipis.

Make a plan. Then solve.

3. Tipis were made of buffalo hide. Each small tipi was made of 4 buffalo hides. Each large tipi was made of 8 hides. In Small Foot Village, there were 14 large tipis and one small tipi. How many buffalo hides were used to make all the tipis in the village?

4. Araho Village had 20 tipis, each of which housed 2 villagers. If each villager owned two ponchos, then how many ponchos were there in the village?

5. Winter was coming soon, and so the villagers started to make winter coats. There were 12 adults and 6 children who needed coats. One buffalo hide was used to make 3 children's coats or 2 adults' coats. How many hides were needed?

6. Ten villagers traveled to their winter campsite. They brought 14 horses along. Each villager rode his or her own horse, and the remaining horses were used to carry supplies. If each horse carried 172 pounds, how many pounds of supplies did the villagers bring?

7. Presley goes to the American Indian College of Art in New Mexico. In his first year, Presley did 3 paintings on buffalo hide, 6 on canvas, and the rest on paper. If he did 18 pieces of work, how many did he paint on paper?

8. Presley went to visit his 3 younger brothers on the reservation. He brought each of them 5 packs of baseball cards as a present. If each pack cost $0.25, how much money did Presley spend?

Holt, Rinehart and Winston, Publishers • 5

Estimate. Write > or < for ◯.

1. 3.7 × 42.1 ◯ 120

2. 9.13 × $1.62 ◯ $14

3. 5.6 × 3.2 ◯ 20

4. 3.69 × 1.35 ◯ 6

5. 4.3 × $8.75 ◯ $40

6. 2.4 × 8.9 ◯ 16

7. 7.6 × $24.50 ◯ $200

8. 1.3 × 3.2 ◯ 3

9. 6.11 × 8.42 ◯ 48

10. 2.7 × 43.62 ◯ 100

11. 6.8 × $5.24 ◯ $40

12. 3.8 × 7.7 ◯ 32

Estimate.

13.   34.72
    ×   6.3

14. $6.65
    ×   4.1

15.   7.5
    × 3.6

16.   46.7
    × 1.15

17.   2.6
    × 5.3

18.   10.31
    ×   2.2

19.   5.94
    × 7.9

20. $32.89
    ×   7.3

21.   23.9
    × 11.1

22.   52.35
    ×   4.8

23.   7.3
    × 4.5

24. $6.13
    × 5.78

Solve.

25. Cal Cool usually uses 83.8 kilowatt-hours of electricity each month. After he bought an air conditioner, he estimated his use would be 1.4 times as great. Did he expect to use more or less than 130 kilowatt-hours per month? _____

26. Hal Heater's average monthly electric bill during the summer is $38.95. He uses 1.8 times as much electricity during the winter. Is his average monthly bill in winter more or less than $70? _____

Holt, Rinehart and Winston, Publishers • 5

Solve the problems below. If you have trouble, go to the Help File.

1. Playing tennis for one hour burns 444 calories. Edna played tennis for 2 hours. How many calories did she burn?

_____

2. Cycling at 14 miles per hour burns up 200 calories in 1 hour. How many calories would be burned cycling for 3 hours at that rate?

_____

3. A person consumes almost 7 pints of oxygen every 10 minutes while resting. About how many pints does a person consume while resting for one hour? (HINT: There are 60 minutes in an hour.)

_____

4. While mountaineering, a person consumes 22 pints of oxygen every four minutes. How much oxygen would a person consume mountaineering 18 times that long?

_____

5. A person takes 140 breaths in 10 minutes while shopping and almost 2 times as many while chopping wood. About how many breaths does a person take in 10 minutes while chopping wood?

_____

6. While digging a ditch, a person's heart beats about 200 times per minute. How many times would a person's heart beat digging a ditch for 1 hour? (HINT: There are 60 minutes in an hour.)

_____

7. Jogging at 5.5 miles per hour burns up 240 calories in an hour. Running burns up about 360 calories in an hour. How many more calories would you burn running for an hour than jogging?

_____

Holt, Rinehart and Winston, Publishers • 5

Multiply.

1. $7.4 \times 4 =$ _____   **2.** $3.8 \times 2 =$ _____   **3.** $0.01 \times 26 =$ _____

4. $43 \times 3.4 =$ _____   **5.** $758 \times 0.79 =$ _____   **6.** $\$0.06 \times 117 =$ _____

7. $\$6.70 \times 49 =$ _____   **8.** $0.333 \times 9 =$ _____   **9.** $114 \times 0.005 =$ _____

10. $\begin{array}{r} 5.12 \\ \times\ \ 33 \\ \hline \end{array}$ **11.** $\begin{array}{r} 0.04 \\ \times\ \ 16 \\ \hline \end{array}$ **12.** $\begin{array}{r} 0.12 \\ \times\ \ 88 \\ \hline \end{array}$ **13.** $\begin{array}{r} 0.19 \\ \times\ 459 \\ \hline \end{array}$

14. $\begin{array}{r} 39 \\ \times\ 0.01 \\ \hline \end{array}$ **15.** $\begin{array}{r} 26 \\ \times\ 0.05 \\ \hline \end{array}$ **16.** $\begin{array}{r} \$6.74 \\ \times\ \ \ 13 \\ \hline \end{array}$ **17.** $\begin{array}{r} 831 \\ \times\ 0.041 \\ \hline \end{array}$

18. $\begin{array}{r} 3.91 \\ \times\ \ 47 \\ \hline \end{array}$ **19.** $\begin{array}{r} 0.006 \\ \times\ \ \ 89 \\ \hline \end{array}$ **20.** $\begin{array}{r} 0.109 \\ \times\ \ \ 99 \\ \hline \end{array}$ **21.** $\begin{array}{r} 5.656 \\ \times\ \ \ 31 \\ \hline \end{array}$

Copy the answer blanks and the numbers.

_____	_____	_____	_____
25,493.696	1,375.992	34,703.952	11,265.06

_____	_____	_____	_____ !!
$26,260.78	$62,649.84	$13,503.27	$23,014.72

Multiply. Then copy the letter for each product.

22. $\begin{array}{r} 57.333 \\ \times\ \ \ \ 24 \\ \hline \end{array}$ **23.** $\begin{array}{r} 722.999 \\ \times\ \ \ \ \ 48 \\ \hline \end{array}$ **24.** $\begin{array}{r} \$42.98 \\ \times\ \ \ 611 \\ \hline \end{array}$ **25.** $\begin{array}{r} 563.253 \\ \times\ \ \ \ \ 20 \\ \hline \end{array}$

$\qquad$ O $\qquad\qquad\qquad$ O $\qquad\qquad\qquad$ W $\qquad\qquad\qquad$ D

26. $\begin{array}{r} \$24.07 \\ \times\ \ \ 561 \\ \hline \end{array}$ **27.** $\begin{array}{r} \$949.24 \\ \times\ \ \ \ 66 \\ \hline \end{array}$ **28.** $\begin{array}{r} 796.678 \\ \times\ \ \ \ \ 32 \\ \hline \end{array}$ **29.** $\begin{array}{r} \$1,000.64 \\ \times\ \ \ \ \ \ 23 \\ \hline \end{array}$

$\qquad$ R $\qquad\qquad\qquad$ O $\qquad\qquad\qquad$ G $\qquad\qquad\qquad$ K

Holt, Rinehart and Winston, Publishers • 5

Make an organized list. Solve.

1. Al, Bob, Carlos, and Doug enter the boy's junior division of the tennis tournament. Each boy will be matched against each other boy only once. How many matches will there be?

2. Fay, Graciela, Helen, Roy, Sam, and Ted buy box seats for the tournament. There are 3 rows of 2 seats each in the box. Each girl sits next to a boy. How many possible boy-girl pairs are there?

3. At the end of the tournament, trophies are given out for the first-place, second-place and third-place winners in each division. There are 8 divisions in all. How many trophies are awarded?

4. On the third day of the tournament, four matches are played. Joe has enough money to purchase tickets to 3 of the matches. From how many possible combinations of matches can Joe choose?

5. In the semifinals of the Girls' Junior Division, Lea plays Mindy and Nan plays Olga. The winners of those matches will play each other in the finals. How many possible combinations of players could there be for the finals?

6. As soon as one player wins 3 sets in the final match of the tennis tournament, that player is declared the winner. There can be 5 sets at most in the final match. How many different ways can the tournament final be won?

Holt, Rinehart and Winston, Publishers • 5

Use with pages 112–113.

Make an organized list. Solve.

7. There are 4 juice stands on the tournament grounds. Karl, Leroy, Melanie, Norma, and Paula take turns selling juice. How many possible combinations of juice sellers are there? On the last day of the tournament, Karl stays home. How many possible combinations of sellers are there on that day?

8. There are 3 souvenir stands on the tournament grounds. Kim, Stanley, Monica, Judy, Cindy, and Bill work at the stands in pairs. How many possible pairs are there? The souvenir stands are such a success that two stands are added. One person works in each stand. How many possible combinations of workers are there then?

9. Four trophies will be awarded after the tournament. There are 6 semifinalists. How many possible combinations of winners can there be? How many if there are only 4 semifinalists?

10. Ann, Bill, Cindy, Dan, Ed, and Fay are in the elimination round. There can be only two winners, one girl and one boy. How many possible pairs of winners can there be? How many possible pairs would there be if Fay were eliminated?

Use with pages 112–113.

Multiply.

1. 4.3 $\times$ 0.7	**2.** 0.84 $\times$ 0.6	**3.** 1.9 $\times$ 0.52	**4.** 32.95 $\times$ 0.8	**5.** 11.7 $\times$ 2.2
6. 0.56 $\times$ 0.4	**7.** 0.99 $\times$ 0.9	**8.** 0.5 $\times$ 0.37	**9.** 24.13 $\times$ 0.7	**10.** 8.1 $\times$ 0.65
11. 0.77 $\times$ 2.3	**12.** 0.8 $\times$ 0.09	**13.** 21.12 $\times$ 0.3	**14.** 0.53 $\times$ 8.2	**15.** 4.65 $\times$ 0.5

16. $0.4 \times 0.97 =$ _____ **17.** $0.39 \times 5.2 =$ _____ **18.** $0.28 \times 14.4 =$ _____

Multiply. Round the product to the nearest cent.

19. $0.47 $\times$ 0.9	**20.** $35.79 $\times$ 0.3	**21.** $6.82 $\times$ 0.5	**22.** $51.98 $\times$ 0.6	**23.** $7.23 $\times$ 0.4

Solve.

24. The Holts use an average of 287.9 kilowatt-hours of electricity each month during the winter. During the summer, they use 1.5 times as much electricity each month. What is their summer monthly average number of kilowatt-hours?

_____

25. The Fong's used 184.7 kilowatt-hours of electricity in April. If they pay $0.66 per kilowatt-hour, how much was their April bill to the nearest cent?

_____

Holt, Rinehart and Winston, Publishers • 5

Use with pages 114–115.

Multiply.

1. $5.7 \times 0.63 =$ _____

2. $8 \times \$0.01 =$ _____

3. $\$0.05 \times 0.6 =$ _____

4. $0.6 \times 0.6 =$ _____

5. $0.09 \times 35.5 =$ _____

6. $0.93 \times 0.05 =$ _____

7. $\$0.71 \times 4 =$ _____

8. $7.5 \times 0.09 =$ _____

9. $20 \times 0.63 =$ _____

10. $\$8.50 \times 32 =$ _____

11.
$$\begin{array}{r} 0.08 \\ \times\ 9.8 \\ \hline \end{array}$$

12.
$$\begin{array}{r} \$2.64 \\ \times\ \ \ 12 \\ \hline \end{array}$$

13.
$$\begin{array}{r} 0.69 \\ \times\ 3.2 \\ \hline \end{array}$$

14.
$$\begin{array}{r} 0.97 \\ \times\ 0.6 \\ \hline \end{array}$$

15.
$$\begin{array}{r} 0.15 \\ \times\ 0.3 \\ \hline \end{array}$$

16.
$$\begin{array}{r} 0.9 \\ \times\ 0 \\ \hline \end{array}$$

17.
$$\begin{array}{r} 0.721 \\ \times\ \ \ 89 \\ \hline \end{array}$$

18.
$$\begin{array}{r} 0.863 \\ \times\ \ \ 13 \\ \hline \end{array}$$

19.
$$\begin{array}{r} 0.004 \\ \times\ \ 100 \\ \hline \end{array}$$

20.
$$\begin{array}{r} 0.115 \\ \times\ 1{,}000 \\ \hline \end{array}$$

21.
$$\begin{array}{r} 0.678 \\ \times\ \ 800 \\ \hline \end{array}$$

22.
$$\begin{array}{r} 0.234 \\ \times\ \ 144 \\ \hline \end{array}$$

Solve.

23. Yoko compares the prices of "Save Energy" stickers in two stores. The first store charges $0.25 for each sticker. The second store charges 1.5 times as much. To the nearest cent, how much does the second store charge for a sticker?

_____

24. The first solar generator that Yuri built had a mass of 9.8 kilograms. Yuri's latest generator has a mass 0.08 times the mass of his first generator. What is the mass of Yuri's latest generator?

_____

Choose the information you would need to be able to solve each problem. Write the letter of the correct answer.

1. While playing tennis for one hour, a person burns up 438 calories. How many more calories would a person burn while running for an hour?
a. distance a person runs
b. calorie intake
c. calories burned while running

2. While doing strenuous work such as digging, a person breathes 5 times as often per minute as he or she does while resting. How many more breaths per minute is that?
a. breaths per minute while resting
b. breaths per minute while digging
c. both a and b

Solve. If there is not enough information, write what information you would need.

3. In 1982, Americans ate about 265 eggs per person. In the same year, the price of an egg in the state of Hawaii was $0.10. How much did the average person living in that state spend on eggs in 1982? _____

4. A pound of ground beef cost $1.49 in Hawaii in 1983. In that year, Americans bought 106.5 pounds of ground beef per person. How much did the average Hawaiian spend on ground beef? _____

5. In 1980, Americans consumed about 28.9 pounds of citrus fruits and 17.9 pounds of apples per person. Was that more than or less than all other fruits consumed per person in 1980? _____

6. In 1983, a pound of dry beans cost $0.46. Ricardo's chili recipe calls for 2.5 pounds of beans. How much did he have to spend on beans each time he prepared chili in 1983? _____

7. In 1982, the price of tuna in Honolulu was $1.17 for a 6.5 ounce can. In 1983, the price was $0.95. How much more expensive was tuna in 1982? _____

8. In 1982, a half-gallon of milk cost $0.43 more in Honolulu than it did on the mainland. Was that difference greater or smaller than in 1983? _____

9. American teenage boys eat 5.3 pounds of food per person each day. This equals a total of 1,935 pounds of food a year. What is the cost per year for feeding 2 teenage boys? _____

10. In 1984, Americans ate 250 million pounds of popcorn. One pound of popcorn costs about $0.58. About how much did the average American spend on popcorn that year? _____

Divide.

1. 3)9   2. 5)20   3. 2)4   4. 7)14   5. 6)24

6. 4)12   7. 2)12   8. 5)30   9. 4)32   10. 8)16

11. 3)21   12. 6)42   13. 7)63   14. 2)18   15. 5)45

16. 9)36   17. 6)54   18. 7)35   19. 8)56   20. 9)81

21. 24 ÷ 3 = _____   22. 32 ÷ 8 = _____   23. 28 ÷ 7 = _____

24. 45 ÷ 5 = _____   25. 48 ÷ 6 = _____   26. 63 ÷ 9 = _____

Solve.

27. The school has 21 cheerleaders. On the field, they stand in 3 equal rows. How many cheerleaders are there in each row?

_____

28. There were 45 cars in the parking lot during the game. If there were 9 cars in each row, how many rows of cars were there?

_____

Holt, Rinehart and Winston, Publishers • 5

Complete each family of facts.

1. $2 \times 3 =$ _____
   $3 \times 2 =$ _____
   $6 \div 3 =$ _____
   $6 \div 2 =$ _____

2. $5 \times 6 =$ _____
   $6 \times 5 =$ _____
   $30 \div 5 =$ _____
   $30 \div 6 =$ _____

3. $4 \times 7 =$ _____
   $7 \times 4 =$ _____
   $28 \div 4 =$ _____
   $28 \div 7 =$ _____

Write the family of facts for each set of numbers.

4. | 42 | 6 | 7 |

   _____
   _____
   _____
   _____

5. | 9 | 4 | 36 |

   _____
   _____
   _____
   _____

6. | 8 | 5 | 40 |

   _____
   _____
   _____
   _____

Divide.

7. $6\overline{)18}$ 8. $8\overline{)0}$ 9. $1\overline{)5}$ 10. $5\overline{)45}$ 11. $9\overline{)54}$ 12. $2\overline{)10}$

13. $5\overline{)30}$ 14. $4\overline{)36}$ 15. $7\overline{)42}$ 16. $8\overline{)64}$ 17. $3\overline{)0}$ 18. $9\overline{)45}$

19. $0 \div 4 =$ _____   20. $20 \div 5 =$ _____   21. $9 \div 1 =$ _____

Solve.

22. $5 \times 5 =$ _____   23. $8 \times 6 =$ _____   24. $7 \times 9 =$ _____

25. $6 \times 4 =$ _____   26. $9 \times 3 =$ _____   27. $4 \times 8 =$ _____

 Use with pages 132–133.

PRACTICE Quotients and Remainders

Divide.

1. $7 \div 2 =$ _____

2. $23 \div 4 =$ _____

3. $13 \div 3 =$ _____

4. $44 \div 5 =$ _____

5. $38 \div 6 =$ _____

6. $17 \div 4 =$ _____

7. $23 \div 3 =$ _____

8. $33 \div 9 =$ _____

9. $35 \div 8 =$ _____

10. $29 \div 4 =$ _____

11. $39 \div 7 =$ _____

12. $14 \div 4 =$ _____

13. $52 \div 8 =$ _____

14. $11 \div 3 =$ _____

15. $20 \div 7 =$ _____

16. $39 \div 5 =$ _____

17. $19 \div 2 =$ _____

18. $33 \div 5 =$ _____

19. $17 \div 3 =$ _____

20. $23 \div 6 =$ _____

21. $9 \div 2 =$ _____

22. $28 \div 5 =$ _____

23. $43 \div 9 =$ _____

24. $29 \div 6 =$ _____

25. $13 \div 8 =$ _____

26. $47 \div 7 =$ _____

27. $15 \div 2 =$ _____

28. $30 \div 4 =$ _____

29. $59 \div 9 =$ _____

30. $30 \div 8 =$ _____

Copy and complete the Input/Output table.

INPUT	OUTPUT
$10 \div 3 =$	
$27 \div 4 =$	
$44 \div 9 =$	
$37 \div 5 =$	
$34 \div 6 =$	
$17 \div 2 =$	
$74 \div 8 =$	

Holt, Rinehart and Winston, Publishers • 5

Use with pages 134–135.

Ring the letter of the operation that would solve the problem.

1. The Incan Empire existed long ago. The Inca had no written language. Instead, they tied knots in strings and sent the strings as messages. Topa was carrying 10 strings. Each string had 9 knots tied in it. How many knots were there in the strings Topa carried?
   a. multiplication   **b.** division

2. One message contained 126 knots. Each knot was part of a code that helped the runner remember the message. If there were 9 knots in each string, how many pieces of string were needed for the message?
   a. multiplication   **b.** division

Choose the operation and solve.

3. The Inca never discovered the wheel. Instead, they transported things on the backs of animals called llamas. Suppose the Incan emperor had 117 gold bricks, and each llama could carry 9 bricks. How many llamas would the emperor need to carry his load?

4. A team of 56 llamas was traveling across the Incan Empire. They came to a river, which they had to cross on a boat. The boat could hold only 7 llamas at a time. How many trips did the boat have to make in order to take all the llamas across the river?

5. The Inca built some of their temples of pure gold. If one temple had eight walls, each made of 256 gold bricks, how many bricks would it have taken to build the temple?

6. Manco earned 20 gold coins a year for 50 years. Each year, he spent 9 gold coins. If the emperor took 7 gold coins in taxes each year and Manco saved the rest, how many coins could Manco have saved in 50 years?

7. Suppose a farm cost 147 gold coins. Manco and six of his friends wanted to buy a farm to work together. Each of them had 13 gold coins. Were they able to purchase a farm?

8. Becky and Carmelita read about the Inca in their math book. They decided to make a secret knot-code in string. They each had $3. A store sold 25 feet of heavy string for $3. How many feet of string could Becky and Carmelita buy?

Holt, Rinehart and Winston, Publishers • 5

Use with pages 136–137.

Is the number divisible by 2? Write *yes* or *no*.

1. 28 _____   **2.** 67 _____   **3.** 106 _____   **4.** 849 _____

5. 390 _____   **6.** 1,121 _____   **7.** 2,643 _____   **8.** 764 _____

9. 25,312 _____   **10.** 17,736 _____   **11.** 32,451 _____   **12.** 51,750 _____

Is the number divisible by 5? Write *yes* or *no*.

13. 35 _____   **14.** 90 _____   **15.** 506 _____   **16.** 285 _____

17. 428 _____   **18.** 1,005 _____   **19.** 18,330 _____   **20.** 21,559 _____

21. 27,475 _____   **22.** 31,860 _____   **23.** 19,305 _____   **24.** 40,651 _____

Is the number divisible by 10? Write *yes* or *no*.

25. 80 _____   **26.** 645 _____   **27.** 750 _____   **28.** 1,100 _____

29. 486 _____   **30.** 3,240 _____   **31.** 12,590 _____   **32.** 20,005 _____

33. 38,370 _____   **34.** 55,550 _____   **35.** 16,321 _____   **36.** 42,794 _____

Is the first number divisible by the second? Write *yes* or *no*.

37. 72, 9 _____   **38.** 58, 7 _____   **39.** 45, 5 _____

40. 90, 10 _____   **41.** 32, 5 _____   **42.** 27, 3 _____

Solve. Write *true* or *false*.

43. If a number is divisible by 5, then it is always divisible by 10.

_____

44. If a number is divisible by 10, then it is always divisible by 5.

_____

Holt, Rinehart and Winston, Publishers • 5

Write how many digits each quotient will contain.

1. 7)1,443 _____   **2.** 5)139 _____   **3.** 8)4,793 _____   **4.** 3)736 _____

5. 6)485 _____   **6.** 2)157 _____   **7.** 9)273 _____   **8.** 8)911 _____

Write the correct estimate.

9. 4)185	4	40	400	**10.** 5)6,750	10	100	1,000

9. 4)185   4   40   400   **10.** 5)6,750   10   100   1,000

11. 6)1,985   3   30   300   **12.** 7)2,915   40   400   4,000

13. 9)826   9   90   900   **14.** 8)2,316   20   200   2,000

15. 4)219   5   50   500   **16.** 7)3,592   50   500   5,000

17. 9)28,312   30   300   3,000   **18.** 6)17,392   30   300   3,000

19. 3)89,312   300   3,000   30,000   **20.** 8)41,493   50   500   5,000

Estimate.

21. 6)3,145 _____   **22.** 9)7,316 _____   **23.** 7)4,892 _____

24. 5)2,475 _____   **25.** 4)4,019 _____   **26.** 6)3,715 _____

Solve.

27. Tour guides at the park need to separate 293 students into 8 groups. Will there be more or less than 40 students per group?

_____

28. The class was collecting fallen leaves to put into a scrapbook. They collected 119 leaves and can put 4 leaves on 1 page. Estimate to see whether 30 pages will be enough to mount 119 leaves.

_____

29. Each seat on the bus can hold 3 people. There are 131 students who must go on the last bus home. Will the bus need more or less than 40 seats to hold 131 students?

_____

Holt, Rinehart and Winston, Publishers • 5

Read the problem. Ring the number sentence that solves the problem.

1. Elmer decided to build and sell bird cages. The material for each bird cage cost $1.57. If he built 35 bird cages, how much was Elmer's total cost?
   a. $1.57 × n = 35
   b. $1.57 × 35 = n
   c. $1.57 + 35 = n

2. Julianna liked to paint. She decided to sell her paintings for $1.50 each. The material for each painting cost $0.37. How much money can she earn from each painting?
   a. $1.50 − $0.37 = n
   b. $1.50 × n = $0.37
   c. $0.37 = n × $1.50

Write a number sentence. Solve.

3. Armand's father taught him how to make wooden bookends. Armand made 44 bookends and sold them. He charged $3.50 for each bookend. How much money did Armand earn?

4. Chandra and Bobby sewed 54 shirts. They sold them for $5.95 each. If they sold nine shirts, how much money did they earn?

5. Lisa makes puppets. She sells them for $3.00 each. Last month, she made $21.00. How many puppets did Lisa sell?

6. Jeff trades baseball and football cards. Last year, he ended up with 620 baseball cards and 516 football cards. How many more baseball cards did he have?

7. John learned how to build boxes in metal shop. He sold the boxes to his friends. He made 6 boxes and sold them for a total of $27.00. How much did John charge for each box?

8. Bill helped Mr. Johnson paint his house. Mr. Johnson paid Bill $2.00 per hour. Bill made a total of $33.00 on the job. How many hours did he work?

9. Annette set up a lemonade stand outside her house. She charges $0.50 per glass. How much money will Annette earn if she sells 25 glasses?

10. Sue baked cookies for the bake sale. She made 5 dozen cookies and charged $0.15 per cookie. How much money did Sue earn?

Divide.

1. $\frac{22}{2} =$ _____

2. $\frac{45}{3} =$ _____

3. $\frac{60}{5} =$ _____

4. $\frac{40}{4} =$ _____

5. $\frac{32}{2} =$ _____

6. $\frac{39}{3} =$ _____

7. $95 \div 5 =$ _____

8. $120 \div 3 =$ _____

9. $68 \div 2 =$ _____

10. $66 \div 1 =$ _____

11. $17 \div 4 =$ _____

12. $180 \div 6 =$ _____

13. $180 \div 9 =$ _____

14. $50 \div 3 =$ _____

15. $81 \div 5 =$ _____

16. $75 \div 4 =$ _____

17. $5\overline{)145}$

18. $9\overline{)300}$

19. $4\overline{)128}$

20. $6\overline{)179}$

21. $7\overline{)345}$

22. $9\overline{)486}$

23. $3\overline{)183}$

24. $8\overline{)602}$

25. $9\overline{)855}$

26. $6\overline{)456}$

27. $8\overline{)742}$

28. $7\overline{)619}$

29. $5\overline{)325}$

30. $4\overline{)237}$

31. $9\overline{)659}$

Solve.

32. The hiking club has 171 packages of trail mix. If the packages are divided equally into 3 cartons, how many packages are there in each carton?

_____

33. The hiking club has 8 members. They must carry 112 pounds of equipment with them. If each member carries the same amount, how many pounds is that?

_____

Use with pages 144–145.

Divide.

1. $250 \div 2 =$ _____
2. $404 \div 4 =$ _____
3. $333 \div 3 =$ _____
4. $342 \div 2 =$ _____

5. $590 \div 5 =$ _____
6. $800 \div 4 =$ _____
7. $477 \div 3 =$ _____
8. $482 \div 2 =$ _____

9. $4\overline{)786}$
10. $3\overline{)603}$
11. $7\overline{)859}$
12. $7\overline{)2,845}$

13. $4\overline{)699}$
14. $5\overline{)4,090}$
15. $8\overline{)7,444}$
16. $2\overline{)1,001}$

17. $6\overline{)5,892}$
18. $7\overline{)6,252}$
19. $4\overline{)2,674}$
20. $6\overline{)1,089}$

21. $\frac{962}{7} =$ _____
22. $\frac{3,704}{4} =$ _____
23. $\frac{1,800}{8} =$ _____
24. $\frac{8,384}{9} =$ _____

Solve.

25. The Conservation Club has 1,605 members. One day each month the members form 5 groups to help pick up litter in the town's parks. How many members are in each group?

_____

26. Ralph has 924 brochures on conservation. He visits 8 schools, and passes out the same number of brochures at each school. How many brochures does Ralph pass out in each school? How many does he have left?

_____

Holt, Rinehart and Winston, Publishers • 5

Divide. Multiply to check your answer.

1. $6\overline{)7,536}$　　　　**2.** $3\overline{)8,538}$　　　　**3.** $2\overline{)3,046}$　　　　**4.** $8\overline{)9,978}$

5. $4\overline{)8,712}$　　　　**6.** $7\overline{)9,425}$　　　　**7.** $5\overline{)9,790}$　　　　**8.** $9\overline{)9,999}$

9. $2\overline{)10,946}$　　　**10.** $7\overline{)16,709}$　　　**11.** $9\overline{)21,486}$　　　**12.** $8\overline{)33,736}$

13. $5\overline{)17,935}$　　　**14.** $4\overline{)10,749}$　　　**15.** $3\overline{)17,547}$　　　**16.** $6\overline{)34,122}$

17. $2\overline{)13,795}$　　　**18.** $7\overline{)53,123}$　　　**19.** $9\overline{)84,789}$　　　**20.** $2\overline{)84,336}$

21. $4\overline{)92,704}$　　　**22.** $6\overline{)75,526}$　　　**23.** $8\overline{)99,776}$　　　**24.** $5\overline{)74,365}$

The Las Cruces Camp Scouts decide to organize a camp out. Read each statement. Then, write questions that the scouts should answer before making a decision.

1. The camp scouts have to decide where they should go for their camp out.

   _____

   _____

2. They need to set a date for the camp out.

   _____

   _____

3. The scouts need to figure out how long the camp out should be.

   _____

   _____

4. They need to decide what equipment to bring.

   _____

   _____

5. They need to plan what food they will want to take along.

   _____

   _____

6. They need to decide how they are going to get to the campsite. _____

   _____

7. What if in the middle of the camp out, raccoons eat some of the scouts' food? _____

   _____

Holt, Rinehart and Winston, Publishers • 5

Divide.

1. 3)90

2. 6)60

3. 7)285

4. 2)100

5. 4)820

6. 5)703

7. 6)642

8. 7)911

9. 4)3,212

10. 5)4,800

11. 3)1,824

12. 6)4,744

13. 9)9,612

14. 2)8,604

15. 5)20,390

16. 4)10,438

17. 980 ÷ 7 = _____

18. 616 ÷ 2 = _____

19. 1,821 ÷ 3 = _____

20. 3,650 ÷ 5 = _____

Solve.

21. The Swallow Kite Company puts 5 streamers on each kite. How many kites can the company make with 1,024 streamers? How many streamers are left?

_____

Holt, Rinehart and Winston, Publishers • 5

Divide.

1. $2.52 ÷ 6 = _____

2. $37.45 ÷ 5 = _____

3. $835.84 ÷ 8 = _____

4. 3)$2.16

5. 8)$1.68

6. 7)$4.83

7. 4)$8.40

8. 6)$6.54

9. 2)$8.96

10. 9)$9.45

11. 8)$25.60

12. 6)$43.50

13. 9)$84.33

14. 7)$42.63

15. 6)$244.50

16. 5)$345.75

17. 4)$847.24

18. 3)$421.53

19. $675.35 ÷ 5 = _____

20. $0.63 ÷ 7 = _____

21. $40.32 ÷ 8 = _____

22. $576.32 ÷ 4 = _____

23. $5.01 ÷ 3 = _____

24. $878.40 ÷ 9 = _____

Solve.

25. Harold is in charge of buying tickets for the local movie club. He spends $42.75 for 9 tickets to the Saturday afternoon show. How much does each ticket cost?

_____

26. The movie club donates $197.75 to the local library. The money is used to buy 5 copies of an educational movie video. How much does each video cost?

_____

Holt, Rinehart and Winston, Publishers • 5

Solve.

1. Brenda and John are going fishing in Maine. They will have 28 lures to share between them. How many lures will each have? How many will be left?

_____

2. John went digging for worms with his 3 friends. He found 32 worms and divided them equally among the group. How many worms did each person have?

_____

3. John and Brenda brought enough hush puppies to the camp fish fry so that each of the 31 campers could have one. John packed the hush puppies 5 per box. He only brought full boxes. How many boxes did he bring?

_____

4. Brenda's group caught 75 trout on an overnight trip. They kept the trout on stringers that would hold 9 trout each. How many full stringers did they have?

_____

5. Brenda and John spent a rainy weekend tying 37 flies. They kept them in a special fly box that had a separate little box for each fly. If the boxes were in rows of 4, how many rows of boxes contained flies? How many flies were in the last row?

_____

6. John needed 52 new fishhooks. He bought as many as he could in boxes of 8. The rest he bought separately. How many boxes did he buy? How many did he buy separately?

_____

7. John and his dad brought 27 pieces of bait. They caught 8 smallmouth bass. If it took them 3 pieces of bait to catch each fish, how many pieces did they have left? Would there be enough bait left to catch another fish?

_____

Holt, Rinehart and Winston, Publishers • 5

Divide.

1. $30\overline{)270}$

2. $40\overline{)240}$

3. $70\overline{)630}$

4. $10\overline{)80}$

5. $40\overline{)400}$

6. $80\overline{)720}$

7. $20\overline{)180}$

8. $50\overline{)400}$

9. $70\overline{)630}$

10. $10\overline{)50}$

11. $40\overline{)360}$

12. $90\overline{)810}$

13. $50\overline{)250}$

14. $90\overline{)450}$

15. $70\overline{)350}$

16. $80\overline{)400}$

17. $70\overline{)490}$

18. $60\overline{)480}$

19. $90\overline{)720}$

20. $60\overline{)180}$

21. $10\overline{)20}$

22. $20\overline{)100}$

23. $60\overline{)420}$

24. $10\overline{)30}$

25. $30\overline{)270}$

26. $250 \div 50 =$ _____

27. $450 \div 90 =$ _____

28. $\frac{80}{40} =$ _____

29. $\frac{120}{60} =$ _____

30. $\frac{720}{80} =$ _____

Write how many digits each quotient will contain.

1. 12)2,295   **2.** 23)4,578   **3.** 31)6,892   **4.** 11)3,216   **5.** 26)1,175

_____   _____   _____   _____   _____

6. 42)5,827   **7.** 53)4,895   **8.** 26)5,236   **9.** 33)15,607   **10.** 49)51,416

_____   _____   _____   _____   _____

Write the best estimate.

11. 15)1,837   10   100   1,000   **12.** 24)3,698   10   100   1,000

13. 32)9,156   20   200   2,000   **14.** 86)1,129   10   100   1,000

15. 19)214,234   1,000   10,000   100,000   **16.** 26)181,562   6,000   60,000   600,000

Estimate.

17. 74)795   **18.** 21)839   **19.** 23)675   **20.** 62)3,235

21. 14)1,569   **22.** 26)5,531   **23.** 32)9,864   **24.** 43)2,988

25. 16)3,351   **26.** 31)1,567   **27.** 42)4,456   **28.** 52)1,645

Solve.

29. A bicycle touring company put $6,350.00 into its profit-sharing fund. 12 workers are to receive equal shares of the profits. One worker wants to buy a new TV with his share. The TV costs $679.00. Will he have enough money from his share to buy the TV? Estimate to answer this question.

_____

30. An employee of the company receives $148.00 as a bonus. She decides to use her bonus to buy a book bag for each of the 27 children in the community. Each book bag costs $5.00. Will she have enough money from her bonus? Estimate to answer this question.

_____

Holt, Rinehart and Winston, Publishers • 5

Write the letter of the number sentence you could use to solve each problem.

1. The Tlingit Indians live in Alaska. In the past they traveled in large canoes. If 3 canoes were traveling from one village to another, and each canoe could hold 18 people, how many people could go?

   a. $n = 3 \times 18$ **b.** $n = 18 \div 3$

2. The Tlingit fished for salmon. If 7 people went out and caught 63 fish, and they divided them equally, what was each person's share of the fish?

   a. $n = 7 \times 63$ **b.** $n = 63 \div 7$

Write the letter of the information that you need to solve the problem.

3. The Tlingit could meet their needs by working about 30 hours a week. Is this more or less hours than Americans work today?

   a. number of hours per week Americans work today

   b. number of hours per week

4. The Tlingit held huge parties called *potlatches*. At each potlatch, the host would give most of his possessions away to his guests. If a host gave away 78 baskets, how many did each guest receive?

   a. number of guests

   b. number of baskets

Write a number sentence. Then solve.

5. One host of a potlatch gave away 35 robes of mink, 50 robes of deerskin, and 7 robes of bearskin. How many robes were given away?

6. The most prized gifts were blankets made of mountain-goat wool and cedar. To make 5 of these blankets for a potlatch took 10 months. How long did it take to make each blanket?

Make a plan. Then solve.

7. At one potlatch, there were 51 baskets of dried salmon. At the feast, 19 baskets of salmon were eaten. The remaining baskets were divided equally among 8 honored guests. How many baskets did each receive?

8. A potlatch would last 3 days. If 3 trays of smoked salmon were eaten each day, and the host had 13 trays to start with, how many trays of salmon were left to give as gifts?

Holt, Rinehart and Winston, Publishers • 5

Solve.

9. Today, the Tlingit have power-fishing boats. Each day the catch per boat is about 2,000 salmon. If 4 boats go out together, how many salmon can they bring in?

_____

10. The Tlingit deliver their catch to the cannery boat. A day's catch is worth about $900. If the 8 crew members divide that equally, how much money would each crew member make?

_____

11. Joe See lives in the Tlingit community of Sitka. He wants to visit his sister in Juneau. His boat can travel at a speed of 14 miles per hour. Joe wants to know how long the trip will take. What information does he need?

_____

12. Joe wanted to buy his sister a dress that she had seen in the window of a certain dress shop. He wants to know how much money he should bring with him. What information does he need?

_____

13. The people who live along the coastline of Alaska often travel by ferryboat. The *Tustumena* goes from Anchorage to Kodiak Island. The trip lasts overnight; so, rooms are available. Each room sleeps 2. How many rooms would a family of 5 need?

_____

14. The family brought sandwiches for lunch with them. If they brought 15 sandwiches and divided them equally, how many did each family member get?

_____

15. Joe See decided to take his family on a trip to Wrangell. The ferry left Sitka at 1:00 and arrived in Wrangell at 5:00 that same afternoon. The ferry traveled at a speed of 25 miles per hour. How many miles was the trip to Wrangell?

_____

16. Once in Wrangell, the children bought some T-shirts for a total of $8.60. Then the family went out to dinner. The dinner cost $23.50. Joe brought $70.00 with him to spend. How much money did he have left?

_____

17. Going home, Joe and his family got a ride on a fishing boat. They left Wrangell at 10:00 A.M. They stopped in Petersburg for 2 hours and 15 minutes. They arrived home at 5:00 P.M. How long was the trip home without the stop?

_____

18. On the trip home Joe spent $5.30 lunch in Petersburg, and he gave the captain of the fishing boat $18.00 for gas. How much money should Joe have left from the $37.90 he started with?

_____

Divide.

1. 14)77 **2.** 18)169 **3.** 12)84 **4.** 25)190 **5.** 16)83

6. 24)150 **7.** 36)115 **8.** 47)290 **9.** 26)60 **10.** 56)254

11. 26)78 **12.** 21)47 **13.** 31)220 **14.** 39)352 **15.** 17)140

16. $100 \div 23 =$ _____

17. $85 \div 42 =$ _____

18. $100 \div 14 =$ _____

19. $135 \div 27 =$ _____

20. $334 \div 36 =$ _____

21. $360 \div 58 =$ _____

22. $111 \div 35 =$ _____

23. $95 \div 15 =$ _____

24. $517 \div 64 =$ _____

25. $108 \div 33 =$ _____

26. $243 \div 58 =$ _____

27. $100 \div 47 =$ _____

28. $\frac{362}{63} =$ _____

29. $\frac{79}{26} =$ _____

30. $\frac{689}{30} =$ _____

Solve.

31. A small local radio station owns 126 records. About 14 records are played every hour. For how many hours can the records be played without repeating any of them? _____

Divide.

1. 22)379   **2.** 29)673   **3.** 11)283   **4.** 47)3,160

5. 25)357   **6.** 28)572   **7.** 62)982   **8.** 24)728

9. 92)1,666   **10.** 31)1,962   **11.** 26)293   **12.** 43)2,677

13. 53)925   **14.** 84)2,218   **15.** 51)1,080   **16.** 32)2,026

17. 43)3,497   **18.** 71)3,852   **19.** 82)$51.66   **20.** 47)1,557

21. $4.48 ÷ 32 = _____   **22.** 578 ÷ 94 = _____   **23.** 738 ÷ 21 = _____

Use with pages 174–175.

Read each problem. Estimate an answer.

1. If you jumped rope without stopping for 2 hours, how many times would you jump?

_____

_____

2. Name your favorite book. How long would it take to write the title 500 times? Title: _____

_____

_____

3. Think about how thick your math textbook is. How many books the size of your math book would fit on a shelf as wide as your classroom?

_____

_____

4. Imagine that you must carry enough squares of tile to cover a floor the size of your school. How many shopping bags would you need to carry all the tiles?

_____

_____

5. Think of a quart-sized milk carton. How many regular-sized paper clips would it take to fill the carton?

_____

_____

6. About how many glasses of water would a ten-year-old girl or boy drink during the 3 months of summer?

_____

_____

7. Imagine that you are walking from one end of the school building to the other. How many steps would you have to take?

_____

_____

8. Someone is bringing in enough shelled peanuts to give everyone in your class, including your teacher, a handful. How many pounds of peanuts will this be?

_____

_____

9. Imagine a table that is as big as your school playground or play area. Think of a tablecloth that could cover a table that size. How long and how wide would the cloth need to be?

_____

_____

10. Philadelphia's City Hall Tower is 548 feet high. How many shoe boxes would you have to stack on end to equal the height of that building?

_____

_____

Holt, Rinehart and Winston, Publishers • 5

Divide.

1. $75\overline{)4,367}$

2. $48\overline{)397}$

3. $34\overline{)2,834}$

4. $86\overline{)5,492}$

5. $96\overline{)4,292}$

6. $65\overline{)3,643}$

7. $54\overline{)\$41.58}$

8. $36\overline{)4,785}$

9. $68\overline{)4,635}$

10. $46\overline{)1,674}$

11. $27\overline{)\$7.83}$

12. $28\overline{)1,597}$

13. $93\overline{)3,674}$

14. $83\overline{)6,425}$

15. $35\overline{)2,279}$

16. $58\overline{)2,971}$

17. $7,413 \div 96 =$ _____

18. $811 \div 66 =$ _____

19. $5,552 \div 75 =$ _____

20. $1,926 \div 37 =$ _____

21. $\frac{1,015}{24} =$ _____

22. $\frac{340}{26} =$ _____

23. $\frac{1,539}{95} =$ _____

Holt, Rinehart and Winston, Publishers • 5

Use with pages 178–179.

Divide.

1. $16\overline{)1,646}$

2. $17\overline{)8,381}$

3. $41\overline{)14,975}$

4. $26\overline{)7,046}$

5. $23\overline{)8,114}$

6. $11\overline{)\$35.64}$

7. $18\overline{)3,100}$

8. $12\overline{)4,428}$

9. $42\overline{)5,292}$

10. $33\overline{)7,129}$

11. $59\overline{)9,314}$

12. $29\overline{)\$94.25}$

13. $6,479 \div 36 =$ _____

14. $\$364.50 \div 75 =$ _____

15. $12,952 \div 44 =$ _____

16. $9,032 \div 27 =$ _____

17. $6,562 \div 50 =$ _____

18. $\$59.75 \div 25 =$ _____

19. $\frac{48,803}{62} =$ _____

20. $\frac{\$345.03}{93} =$ _____

21. $\frac{57,753}{81} =$ _____

Solve.

22. Doris owns the Spinning Sound record store. She spends $176.04 to purchase 36 copies of a new album. How much does each album cost? _____

23. Doris uses a computer to keep track of how many customers she serves each year. Last year she served 51,272 customers. What was the average number of customers she served each week? (HINT: There are 52 weeks in a year.) _____

Divide.

1. 4,800 ÷ 8 = _____

2. 2,092 ÷ 4 = _____

3. 4,558 ÷ 9 = _____

4. 306 ÷ 3 = _____

5. 3,045 ÷ 5 = _____

6. 6,409 ÷ 8 = _____

7. 5)4,545

8. 27)13,669

9. 4)1,207

10. 8)$56.32

11. 6)607

12. 22)8,910

13. 28)$67.20

14. 33)11,221

15. 14)7,089

16. 56)19,048

17. 13)3,978

18. 17)$34.17

19. 20)4,037

20. 27)9,722

21. 30)9,067

22. 18)7,238

Holt, Rinehart and Winston, Publishers • 5

Use with pages 182–183.

Write the letter of the correct answer.

1. Pluto is the most distant planet from the sun. It takes Pluto about 248 Earth-years to complete one orbit around the sun. Americans live about 74 years. About how many American lifetimes does it take for Pluto to complete one orbit?
   a. 3.35 lifetimes
   b. 3.35 years
   c. 174 years

2. For about 20 Earth-years of each orbit, Pluto crosses the orbit of Neptune. During this time, Neptune is the most distant planet from the sun. For how many Earth-years does Pluto remain the most distant planet from the sun?
   a. 20 years
   b. 228 years
   c. 12.4 times

Solve.

3. Mercury is the closest planet to the sun. Mercury's year lasts about 88 Earth-days. About how many Earth-weeks are in each Mercury-year?

_____

4. One year on Jupiter is equal to 12 years on Earth. How old would a 72-year-old American be in Jupiter-years?

_____

5. One year on Saturn is equal to 30 Earth-years, and 60 Earth-years equals 5 Jupiter years. If Alfa is one-year-old on Saturn, how many Jupiter-years-old is he?

_____

6. It takes Earth 365 days to travel once around the sun. It takes the moon about 30 days to travel once around Earth. About how many times has the moon orbited Earth when Earth has completed one orbit of the sun?

_____

7. One Mercury-day equals about 24 weeks and 2 days on Earth. About how many Earth-days is one Mercury-day?

_____

8. One year on Jupiter is equal to 156 Earth-weeks. About how many Earth-days are in one Jupiter-year?

_____

9. Jill has a telescope on her roof. It magnifies heavenly bodies up to 125 times larger than she could see them without the telescope. How many times larger would the heavenly bodies appear if the telescope were twice as powerful?

_____

10. Jill is looking at the rings of Saturn through her telescope. They appear 50 times larger than she could see them without the telescope. Jill switches to a lens that is 4 times as powerful. How many times larger are the rings now?

_____

Holt, Rinehart and Winston, Publishers • 5

Multiply or divide.

1. $5.7 \div 10 =$ _____

2. $40. \div 100 =$ _____

3. $10 \times 0.08 =$ _____

4. $100 \times 3.971 =$ _____

5. $6 \div 10 =$ _____

6. $0.041 \div 10 =$ _____

7. $71.2 \times 1,000 =$ _____

8. $0.028 \times 100 =$ _____

9. $103.17 \div 1,000 =$ _____

10. $3.4 \times 100 =$ _____

11. $4.7 \div 100 =$ _____

12. $0.032 \times 1,000 =$ _____

Copy and complete the charts.

	x	10	100	1,000
13.	0.5			
14.	0.013			
15.	6.317			
16.	79.8			

	÷	10	100	1,000
17.	16.35			
18.	24			
19.	418			
20.	0.7			

Use the information below to answer the questions.

Child	Daily piggy-bank deposits
Ari	$0.59
Ted	$1.26
Mara	$0.31

21. How much will each have after 100 days?

Ari _____   Ted _____

Mara _____

22. Each child then withdraws the whole amount in 10 equal withdrawals. How much is each withdrawal?

Ari _____   Ted _____

Mara _____

Holt, Rinehart and Winston, Publishers • 5

Divide.

1. $37\overline{)9.176}$ **2.** $9\overline{)14.67}$ **3.** $29\overline{)3.625}$ **4.** $5\overline{)8.35}$

5. $13\overline{)49.66}$ **6.** $7\overline{)2.961}$ **7.** $3\overline{)0.1671}$ **8.** $31\overline{)12.772}$

9. $8\overline{)36.8}$ **10.** $57\overline{)407.55}$ **11.** $89\overline{)59.986}$ **12.** $11\overline{)89.452}$

13. $42\overline{)219.66}$ **14.** $17\overline{)2.091}$ **15.** $62\overline{)26.536}$ **16.** $39\overline{)121.68}$

17. $12\overline{)64.92}$ **18.** $91\overline{)240.24}$ **19.** $18\overline{)115.56}$ **20.** $80\overline{)14.880}$

21. $0.9 \div 3 =$ _____   **22.** $36.4 \div 26 =$ _____   **23.** $1.2 \div 4 =$ _____

24. $4.8 \div 8 =$ _____   **25.** $15.68 \div 7 =$ _____   **26.** $22.23 \div 19 =$ _____

27. $15.54 \div 7 =$ _____   **28.** $3.72 \div 3 =$ _____   **29.** $37.14 \div 6 =$ _____

Divide.

1. $2.7 \div 4 =$ _____

2. $1.8 \div 12 =$ _____

3. $28.21 \div 13 =$ _____

4. $3.036 \div 6 =$ _____

5. $4.035 \div 5 =$ _____

6. $83.64 \div 41 =$ _____

7. $9\overline{)0.0954}$

8. $81\overline{)2.268}$

9. $34\overline{)2.72}$

10. $44\overline{)2.552}$

11. $29\overline{)3.422}$

12. $43\overline{)45.15}$

13. $7\overline{)0.742}$

14. $30\overline{)64.02}$

15. $78\overline{)93.99}$

Solve.

16. Aileen jogged 12.2 kilometers yesterday. This is four times further than she was able to jog when she first started jogging. How far could Aileen jog when she first started?

17. Aileen decided to try bicycle riding instead of jogging. During the month of July she rode a total of 776.86 kilometers. What was the average distance she rode each day? (HINT: There are 31 days in July.)

Use with pages 200–201.

Use the guess-and-check method to solve for each blank.

1. In 1956, Lorraine Crapp was the first woman to break 5 minutes for the 400-meter freestyle swim, a record that

   stood for _____ years.

   This 2-digit number is divisible by 2, 4, and 8. The difference between its digits is 5. The number is less than 50. What is the number?

2. The Three Day Event is an equestrian competition designed to test the all-around ability of horse and rider. It includes cross-country obstacles

   _____ inches high.

   This is a 2-digit number. The sum of its digits is 11. The difference between its digits is 3. The product when doubled is a 2-digit number. What is the number?

3. In the 44 years from 1921 to 1965, which are known as the Yankee dynasty, the New York Yankees won 29 pennants and

   _____ world championships.

   This 2-digit number is divisible by 5 and 4 but *not* by 3 or 7. The number is less than 2 dozen. What is the number?

4. In basketball, the net, made of white cord, is suspended from an

   orange-painted iron ring _____ cm in diameter.

   This 2-digit number is divisible by 9 and 3. If you reverse its digits, it is divisible by 9, 6, and 3. The sum of its digits is 9, and the difference between them is 1. What is the number?

5. Tse-tung Chuang, a three-time Chinese table-tennis champion, began his training in the Children's Palace, Chingshan,

   Peking, at the age of _____ years.

   This 2-digit number is divisible by 2. The sum of its digits is less than half a dozen. When multiplied by 3, the product has a 2 in the ones place. What is the number?

6. In 1956, Betty Cuthbert, an Australian sprinter, won three Olympic gold medals

   at the age of _____.

   This is a 2-digit number less than 50. The sum of its digits is divisible by 9. The difference between its digits is divisible by 7. What is the number?

7. The track bicycle, used for sprinting, is fitted with silk-covered tubular tires

   weighing as little as _____ grams.

   This is a 3-digit number with 1 in the tens place. The sum of the other 2 digits is divisible by 2 and 4 but *not* by 6 or 8. The number is less than 300. What is the number?

8. In 1888, the Yale football team beat all its 13 opponents with a total score of

   _____ points to 0.

   This is a 3-digit number. It is divisible by 2. The sum of its first 2 digits is 15. The sum of its last 2 digits is 17. What is the number?

Use with pages 202–203.

Use the guess-and-check method to solve for each blank.

9. One of the dragonflylike species of insects is comparatively large. It has a wingspread of _____ inches.

   This 2-digit number is divisible by 2 and 3. The sum of its digits is 3. The number is greater than one dozen. What is the number?

10. If all the offspring of a pamace fly were to survive long enough to reproduce, there would be _____ generations by the end of a year.

    This is an odd 2-digit number divisible by 5. The sum of its digits is 7, and the difference between them is 3. What is the number?

11. If all its members survived, the 25th generation of flies would be so large that all the individuals packed tightly together would form a ball of flies _____ million miles in diameter.

    This even 2-digit number is divisible by 3, as is the difference between its digits. The sum of its digits is divisible by 5. What is the number?

12. An ant can lift _____ times its own weight.

    This 3-digit number is less than 500 and is divisible by 9, 5, 3, and 2. The sum of its digits is 9. The difference between its first 2 digits is one. It has a 0 in the ones place. What is the number?

13. Insects have a size range nearly _____ times greater than mammals. An Atlas moth can be almost 3,000 times as large as the smallest fly.

    This 2-digit number is divisible by 2 and 3 but *not* by 4 or 9. The difference between its digits is equal to their sum. What is the number?

14. If you added _____ to the number of times a cricket chirped in 15 seconds, you would get the temperature in degrees Fahrenheit.

    This 2-digit number is divisible by 3, as are the sum of and the difference between its digits. When multiplied by 2, the product is a 2-digit number with 8 in the ones place. What is the number?

15. Flies include some of the fastest flying insects. The horsefly has been clocked at more than _____ miles per hour.

    This is a 2-digit number. The sum of its digits is 4. The difference between its digits is 2. The number is greater than 25. What is the number?

16. When the temperature in a beehive drops below _____ degrees F, the bees form a dense ball that moves slowly about the hive, feeding on stored food.

    This 2-digit number is divisible by 3 but *not* by 2. The difference between its digits is 2. If the digits were reversed, it would be divisible by 5. What is the number?

Holt, Rinehart and Winston, Publishers • 5

Measure the length of the paper clip to the nearest

1. cm _____ **2.** mm _____

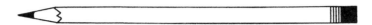

Measure the length of the pencil to the nearest

3. cm _____ **4.** mm _____

Draw a line that measures

5. 43 mm

6. 7 cm

7. 5.5 cm

8. 28 mm

Write the distance around each shape.

9.

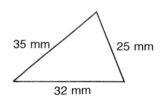

35 mm 25 mm

32 mm

_____

10.

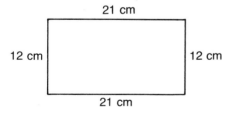

21 cm

12 cm 12 cm

21 cm

_____

11.

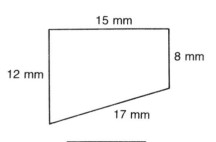

15 mm

12 mm 8 mm

17 mm

_____

12.

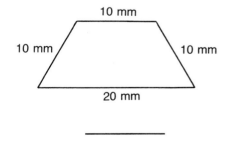

10 mm

10 mm 10 mm

20 mm

_____

Holt, Rinehart and Winston, Publishers • 5

Which unit would you use to measure the length?
Write *mm*, *cm*, *m*, or *km*.

1. distance from Texas to Iowa _____

2. height of a room _____

3. length of a teacher's desk _____

4. distance a plane travels _____

5. width of a ring _____

6. length of a ladybug _____

7. length of a car _____

8. length of a shoestring _____

Choose the appropriate unit.
Write *mm*, *cm*, *m*, or *km*.

9. A grasshopper is 30 _____ long.

10. A comb is 10 _____ long.

11. The distance from California to Pennsylvania is 3,000 _____.

12. A baseball bat is 1 _____ long.

13. A scarf is 160 _____ long.

14. Sabina's hand is 15 _____ long.

Complete.

15. 0.03 m = _____ cm

16. 3,500 m = _____ km

17. 60 mm = _____ cm

18. 7 km = _____ m

19. 78 cm = _____ m

20. 95 m = _____ km

21. 6,411 m = _____ km

22. 9.5 cm = _____ mm

23. 64.8 m = _____ cm

24. 150 cm = _____ m

25. 11,230 m = _____ km

26. 0.02 km = _____ m

Holt, Rinehart and Winston, Publishers • 5

Write the letter for the information that is not needed.

1. The Washington Market Block Association is having a block party to raise $1,000 to fix up their park. They sell 124 tickets at $4.00 each. How much money did they make selling tickets?

   a. They sold 124 tickets.

   b. They need $1,000 in all.

   c. Tickets sold for $4.00 each.

2. At the block party, Kim Lee won the beanbag toss. He scored 27.6 points in all. He threw the beanbag 3 times. About how many points did he score each time he threw the beanbag?

   a. Kim Lee won the beanbag toss.

   b. He threw the beanbag 3 times.

   c. He scored a total of 27.6 points.

List the extra information. Then solve.

3. Benches for the park cost $85.00 each. A group of 16 business men and 12 business women donated $1,360. How many benches can they buy?

4. There were 20 old benches in the park, but $\frac{3}{4}$ of them had to be replaced. The remaining 5 were repaired at a cost of $61.15. What was the cost of repairs per bench?

5. Jack Peatmoss, a volunteer, worked a total of 200 hours planting 860 plants. There were 126 shrubs and the rest were flower bulbs. How many flowers did Jack plant?

6. Jack planted borders along the park walkways for 4 days. He averaged 71.5 feet of border each day. This was 3.2 feet more than his previous average. How many feet of walkway did Jack border?

7. Nancy volunteered to paint the new benches. It took her 12 hours to paint 10 benches. It took her 3 days to do the job. How long did it take her to paint one bench?

8. Nancy can run 10 times around the park in 50 minutes. It takes Mary 3 minutes more to run the same distance. How long does it take Nancy to run around the park 1 time?

Which unit would you use to measure the capacity?
Write *mL* or *L*.

1. a soup ladle _____ **2.** an eyedropper _____

3. a large pitcher _____ **4.** a watering can _____

5. a small oil can _____ **6.** a teaspoon _____

7. a gasoline tank _____ **8.** a small glass _____

9. a rain barrel _____ **10.** a bathtub _____

11. a kitchen sink _____ **12.** a tablespoon _____

Complete.

13. 0.7 L = _____ mL **14.** 3,500 mL = _____ L

15. 1.248 L = _____ mL **16.** 624 mL = _____ L

17. 11 L = _____ mL **18.** 0.09 L = _____ mL

19. 14.6 L = _____ mL **20.** 8,000 mL = _____ L

21. 2 L = _____ mL **22.** 0.53 L = _____ mL

23. 78 mL = _____ L **24.** 8,779 mL = _____ L

25. 16 L = _____ mL **26.** 651 mL = _____ L

27. 14,300 mL = _____ L **28.** 5,000 mL = _____ L

29. 0.032 L = _____ mL **30.** 1.06 L = _____ mL

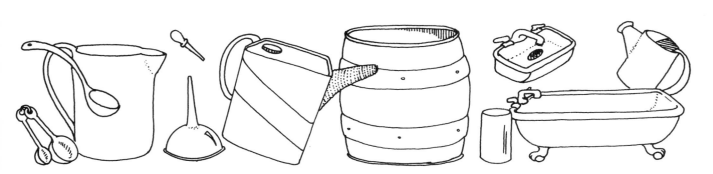

Holt, Rinehart and Winston, Publishers • 5

Use with pages 210–211.

Which unit would you use to measure the mass?
Write *mg, g,* or *kg.*

1. a spider _____

2. a dump truck _____

3. a crate of oranges _____

4. a grain of sand _____

5. a bag of cement _____

6. an apple _____

Complete.

7. 0.07 g = _____ mg

8. 860 g = _____ kg

9. 1.4 kg = _____ g

10. 63 mg = _____ g

11. 1 kg = _____ mg

12. 9 kg = _____ mg

13. 0.402 g = _____ mg

14. 139 mg = _____ g

15. 0.7 g = _____ mg

16. 969 g = _____ kg

17. 0.4 g = _____ mg

18. 45.9 g = _____ mg

19. 755 mg = _____ kg

20. 8.4 g = _____ mg

21. 0.08 kg = _____ g

22. 1,234 mg = _____ g = _____ kg

23. _____ mg = 42.6 g = _____ kg

24. 5.67 kg = _____ g = _____ mg

25. _____ kg = 139.5 g = _____ mg

Solve.

26. A ball bearing has a mass of 2 g. A box can hold 5.5 kg
of ball bearings. How many ball bearings can the box
hold?

_____

Complete the plan by writing the missing step.

1. Julio exercises 5 days a week. Each day he works on a rebounder for 10 minutes to warm up. Then, he rows for 15 minutes and lifts weights for half an hour. How much time does Julio spend exercising in one week?

   Step 1: Find Julio's total exercising time for one day.

   Step 2: _____

2. Jennifer Krall exercises 45 minutes 3 times a week. How many hours does she exercise in 6 weeks? (HINT: 60 minutes = 1 hour)

   Step 1: Find the number of minutes Jennifer exercises in 1 week.
   Step 2: Find the number of minutes Jennifer exercises in 6 weeks.

   Step 3: _____

Make a plan for each problem. Solve.

3. During the football season, Carlos gained 561 yards in 165 carries, and Aaron gained 304 yards in 95 carries. Who gained more yards per carry?

4. During the baseball season, Marty had 18 hits in 50 times at bat. Julian had 25 hits in 60 times at bat. Who had more hits per times at bat?

5. During the basketball season, Karen got 165 rebounds in 15 games. Maria got 224 rebounds in 20 games. Which girl got more rebounds per game?

6. During one 15-game soccer season, 120 liters of orange juice were drunk by the 16 members of the team. About how much juice did each member drink during one game?

7. Janice could run a kilometer twice as fast as Burt could. Burt could run a kilometer 7 seconds faster than Eliot. If Eliot could run a kilometer in 12 minutes 7 seconds, how fast could Janice run?

8. Roland could run half a kilometer in 4 minutes. At that rate, how would his time compare with Janice's?

9. Suzuki could run 2 kilometers in 10 minutes. She wanted to know whose time was better, hers or Janice's. Who had the better time?

10. One afternoon, 15 children formed teams for a 4-person relay race. One team had only 3 runners, and so one person had to run twice as far as everyone else. If the course was 300 meters long, how far did that person have to run?

Holt, Rinehart and Winston, Publishers • 5

Write the first six multiples of each number.

1. 3 _____

2. 30 _____

3. 1 _____

4. 11 _____

5. 16 _____

6. 7 _____

Write the first three common multiples.

7. 1, 7 _____

8. 4, 5 _____

9. 2, 6 _____

10. 3, 5 _____

11. 6, 8 _____

12. 15, 30 _____

Write the least common multiple.

13. 2, 3 _____

14. 2, 5 _____

15. 12, 18 _____

16. 4, 6 _____

17. 10, 25 _____

18. 5, 6 _____

19. 8, 12 _____

20. 7, 10 _____

21. 4, 9 _____

22. 10, 15 _____

23. 8, 10 _____

24. 3, 5 _____

25. 5, 15 _____

26. 9, 12 _____

27. 3, 4 _____

28. 7, 28 _____

29. 3, 7 _____

30. 12, 30 _____

31. 8, 14 _____

32. 9, 15 _____

Solve.

33. Placido needs to buy an equal number of gears, flyrods, and pistons. Use the chart to find the least number of each he could buy, and how much money he would spend.

_____

Item	Price
gears	12 for $6.50
flyrods	8 for $5.00
pistons	4 for $3.25

Holt, Rinehart and Winston, Publishers • 5

List the factors of each number.

1. 15 _____   **2.** 20 _____   **3.** 14 _____

4. 35 _____   **5.** 21 _____   **6.** 25 _____

7. 16 _____   **8.** 32 _____   **9.** 45 _____

List the common factors.

10. 2, 6 _____   **11.** 16, 24 _____   **12.** 9, 14 _____

13. 30, 75 _____   **14.** 25, 55 _____   **15.** 40, 64 _____

16. 40, 50 _____   **17.** 6, 30 _____   **18.** 36, 75 _____

Write the greatest common factor.

19. 5, 15 _____   **20.** 18, 24 _____   **21.** 7, 21 _____   **22.** 4, 16 _____

23. 3, 9 _____   **24.** 12, 44 _____   **25.** 14, 35 _____   **26.** 16, 18 _____

27. 9, 27 _____   **28.** 5, 6 _____   **29.** 12, 18 _____   **30.** 10, 24 _____

31. 3, 24 _____   **32.** 11, 33 _____   **33.** 12, 15 _____   **34.** 14, 49 _____

35. 15, 33 _____   **36.** 24, 32 _____   **37.** 15, 35 _____   **38.** 28, 42 _____

39. 2, 10 _____   **40.** 12, 20 _____   **41.** 22, 33 _____   **42.** 6, 7 _____

43. 4, 12 _____   **44.** 18, 45 _____   **45.** 16, 40 _____   **46.** 5, 20 _____

47. 8, 20 _____   **48.** 15, 25 _____   **49.** 16, 32 _____   **50.** 16, 20 _____

51. 6, 15 _____   **52.** 18, 36 _____   **53.** 7, 14 _____   **54.** 8, 12 _____

Holt, Rinehart and Winston, Publishers • 5

Use with pages 228–229.

Write *prime* or *composite* to describe each number.

1. 40 _____ **2.** 17 _____ **3.** 31 _____

4. 27 _____ **5.** 45 _____ **6.** 19 _____

7. 42 _____ **8.** 39 _____ **9.** 56 _____

10. 29 _____ **11.** 70 _____ **12.** 37 _____

13. 44 _____ **14.** 60 _____ **15.** 84 _____

Copy and complete each factor tree.

16. 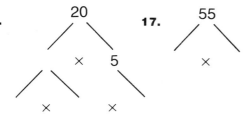 **17.** 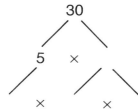 **18.** **19.**

20. 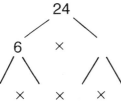 **21.** 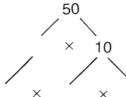 **22.** 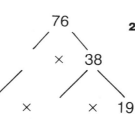 **23.**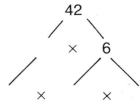

Copy and complete a factor tree to write the prime factorization of each number. Other factor trees are possible.

24. 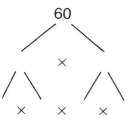 **25.** 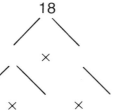 **26.**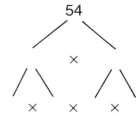

27. 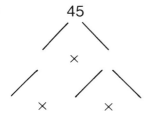 **28.** 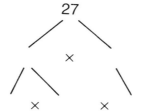 **29.**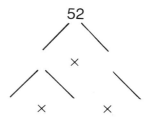

Write the fraction for the part that is shaded.

1.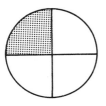

_____

2.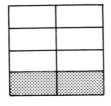

_____

3.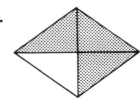

_____

4.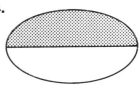

_____

5.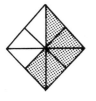

_____

6.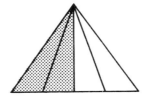

_____

7.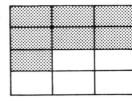

_____

8.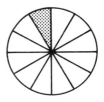

_____

9.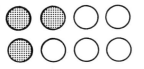

_____

10.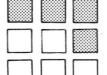

_____

11.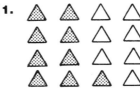

_____

12.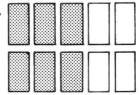

_____

Write the fraction.

13. two ninths _____

14. one twelfth _____

15. five sevenths _____

16. seven tenths _____

17. three eighths _____

18. four sixths _____

Write the decimal.

19. $\frac{8}{10}$ =

20. $\frac{6}{10}$ =

21. $\frac{9}{10}$ =

22. $\frac{1}{10}$ =

23. $\frac{2}{10}$ =

24. $\frac{7}{10}$ =

Choose the operation that you could use to solve the problem.

1. Burke and his brother caught 11 Pacific salmon at Bristol Bay, Alaska. The next week they caught 29 more. How many fish have they caught so far?

   a. multiplication   **b.** subtraction

   c. division   **d.** addition

2. In 7 days, Burke caught 21 rainbow trout in a stream near Ketchikan. On average, how many trout did he catch each day?

   a. subtraction   **b.** division

   c. multiplication   **d.** addition

Solve.

3. To catch graling, Burke used 3 fishing lines 45 feet long. How long were all 3 lines together? _____

4. Burke paid $4.50 for 6 containers of live bait. How much did each container cost? _____

5. Burke caught 4 trout that weighed an average of 2.3 pounds each. What was the weight of all 4 trout?

   _____

6. Burke went fishing with 19 pieces of bait. The fish got 7 pieces before Burke decided to try another spot. How many pieces of bait did Burke have left?

   _____

7. A coho salmon swam 2.5 km upstream one day and 2.2 km the next. How many kilometers did it swim in all?

   _____

8. Burke paddled his canoe 4.66 km one day and 5.25 km the next. How far did he paddle in all?

   _____

Complete.

1. $\frac{1}{2} = \frac{1 \times 2}{2 \times 2} = $

2. $\frac{4}{5} = \frac{4 \times 4}{5 \times 4} = $

3. $\frac{1}{4} = \frac{1 \times 5}{4 \times 5} = $

4. $\frac{1}{5} = \frac{1 \times 3}{5 \times 3} = $

5. $\frac{2}{5} = \frac{2 \times 6}{5 \times 6} = $

6. $\frac{5}{6} = \frac{5 \times 2}{6 \times 2} = $

7. $\frac{3}{4} = \frac{3 \times 6}{4 \times 6} = $

8. $\frac{1}{3} = \frac{1 \times 4}{3 \times 4} = $

9. $\frac{2}{3} = \frac{2 \times 9}{3 \times 9} = $

10. $\frac{7}{10} = \frac{}{40}$

11. $\frac{8}{12} = \frac{32}{}$

12. $\frac{10}{11} = \frac{}{66}$

13. $\frac{8}{16} = \frac{}{64}$

14. $\frac{9}{15} = \frac{45}{}$

15. $\frac{5}{8} = \frac{}{32}$

16. $\frac{3}{5} = \frac{6}{}$

17. $\frac{6}{10} = \frac{24}{}$

18. $\frac{2}{4} = \frac{}{36}$

Write the next three equivalent fractions.

19. $\frac{3}{5}, \frac{6}{10}, \frac{9}{15},$

20. $\frac{1}{6}, \frac{2}{12}, \frac{3}{18},$

21. $\frac{2}{3}, \frac{4}{6}, \frac{6}{9},$

22. $\frac{5}{7}, \frac{10}{14}, \frac{15}{21},$

Solve.

23. There are 28 students in Ivan's class. On a museum trip, $\frac{3}{4}$ of the students liked the space-exploration exhibit better than the computer exhibit. Write $\frac{3}{4}$ as an equivalent fraction that has a denominator of 28.

_____

Holt, Rinehart and Winston, Publishers • 5

Use with pages 236–237.

Complete.

1. $\dfrac{8 \div 2}{10 \div 2} =$

2. $\dfrac{14 \div 14}{28 \div 14} =$

3. $\dfrac{7 \div 7}{35 \div 7} =$

4. $\dfrac{60 \div 12}{96 \div 12} =$

5. $\dfrac{54 \div 9}{63 \div 9} =$

6. $\dfrac{10 \div 10}{40 \div 10} =$

7. $\dfrac{6 \div 6}{12 \div 6} =$

8. $\dfrac{30 \div 15}{45 \div 15} =$

9. $\dfrac{16 \div 2}{18 \div 2} =$

Is the fraction in simplest form? Write *yes* or *no*. If not, write the fraction in simplest form.

10. $\dfrac{1}{3}$ _____

11. $\dfrac{2}{4}$ _____

12. $\dfrac{2}{3}$ _____

13. $\dfrac{1}{4}$ _____

14. $\dfrac{6}{8}$ _____

15. $\dfrac{16}{18}$ _____

16. $\dfrac{6}{7}$ _____

17. $\dfrac{10}{20}$ _____

18. $\dfrac{11}{12}$ _____

19. $\dfrac{5}{6}$ _____

20. $\dfrac{12}{21}$ _____

21. $\dfrac{40}{50}$ _____

22. $\dfrac{6}{7}$ _____

23. $\dfrac{7}{14}$ _____

24. $\dfrac{15}{18}$ _____

25. $\dfrac{20}{25}$ _____

26. $\dfrac{7}{8}$ _____

27. $\dfrac{24}{40}$ _____

28. $\dfrac{17}{20}$ _____

29. $\dfrac{21}{28}$ _____

Copy the answer blanks and numbers. Write each fraction in simplest form. Write the letter above the fraction in simplest form to solve the riddle. What did Debra buy at the Alphabet Clothes Store?

$\dfrac{5}{10}$	$\dfrac{2}{8}$	$\dfrac{6}{10}$	$\dfrac{2}{6}$	$\dfrac{3}{6}$	$\dfrac{8}{10}$	$\dfrac{6}{8}$
T	I	R	H	T	A	S

___	___	-	___	___	___	___
$\dfrac{4}{5}$	$\dfrac{1}{2}$	$\dfrac{3}{4}$	$\dfrac{1}{3}$	$\dfrac{1}{4}$	$\dfrac{3}{5}$	$\dfrac{1}{2}$

Write a mixed number and a fraction for the part that is shaded.

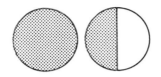

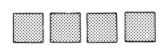

1. _____

2. _____

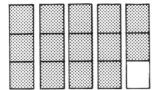

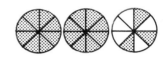

3. _____

4. _____

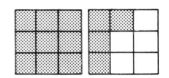

5. _____

6. _____

Write as a whole number or as a mixed number.

7. $\frac{19}{6}$ = _____   **8.** $\frac{29}{3}$ = _____   **9.** $\frac{16}{5}$ = _____   **10.** $\frac{31}{6}$ = _____

11. $\frac{11}{4}$ = _____   **12.** $\frac{41}{5}$ = _____   **13.** $\frac{37}{8}$ = _____   **14.** $\frac{63}{9}$ = _____

15. $\frac{25}{5}$ = _____   **16.** $\frac{27}{20}$ = _____   **17.** $\frac{38}{9}$ = _____   **18.** $\frac{50}{13}$ = _____

Write as a fraction.

19. $2\frac{3}{7}$ = _____   **20.** 7 = _____   **21.** $1\frac{3}{5}$ = _____   **22.** $7\frac{5}{9}$ = _____

23. $2\frac{1}{6}$ = _____   **24.** $9\frac{1}{3}$ = _____   **25.** $3\frac{3}{7}$ = _____   **26.** 25 = _____

27. $4\frac{1}{6}$ = _____   **28.** $8\frac{2}{5}$ = _____   **29.** $5\frac{1}{2}$ = _____   **30.** $16\frac{4}{5}$ = _____

Use with pages 240–241.

Compare. Write >, <, or = for $\bigcirc$.

1. $\frac{10}{12}$ $\bigcirc$ $\frac{4}{6}$

2. $\frac{1}{5}$ $\bigcirc$ $\frac{2}{5}$

3. $\frac{1}{2}$ $\bigcirc$ $\frac{6}{12}$

4. $7\frac{1}{4}$ $\bigcirc$ $7\frac{3}{4}$

5. $\frac{3}{5}$ $\bigcirc$ $\frac{5}{6}$

6. $3\frac{8}{9}$ $\bigcirc$ $6\frac{5}{9}$

7. $5\frac{1}{7}$ $\bigcirc$ $5\frac{3}{21}$

8. $\frac{7}{8}$ $\bigcirc$ $\frac{1}{4}$

9. $\frac{2}{3}$ $\bigcirc$ $\frac{10}{11}$

10. $\frac{8}{10}$ $\bigcirc$ $\frac{9}{10}$

11. $\frac{5}{15}$ $\bigcirc$ $\frac{3}{5}$

12. $1\frac{2}{6}$ $\bigcirc$ $1\frac{1}{5}$

13. $\frac{7}{8}$ $\bigcirc$ $\frac{2}{3}$

14. $\frac{1}{2}$ $\bigcirc$ $\frac{5}{10}$

15. $\frac{3}{7}$ $\bigcirc$ $\frac{1}{4}$

16. $\frac{5}{11}$ $\bigcirc$ $\frac{6}{11}$

17. $3\frac{2}{3}$ $\bigcirc$ $2\frac{2}{4}$

18. $\frac{7}{8}$ $\bigcirc$ $\frac{5}{8}$

19. $2\frac{1}{2}$ $\bigcirc$ $4\frac{1}{9}$

20. $5\frac{4}{10}$ $\bigcirc$ $4\frac{2}{5}$

Write in order from the least to the greatest.

21. $\frac{1}{2}, \frac{1}{4}, \frac{6}{8}$ _____

22. $\frac{10}{12}, \frac{4}{6}, \frac{3}{4}$ _____

23. $\frac{3}{5}, \frac{4}{7}, \frac{4}{5}$ _____

24. $\frac{7}{10}, \frac{2}{3}, \frac{5}{6}$ _____

25. $\frac{2}{3}, \frac{4}{9}, \frac{7}{9}$ _____

26. $\frac{1}{3}, \frac{1}{2}, \frac{3}{7}$ _____

Write in order from the greatest to the least.

27. $\frac{2}{5}, \frac{1}{3}, \frac{4}{15}$ _____

28. $\frac{1}{2}, \frac{3}{4}, \frac{5}{12}$ _____

29. $\frac{1}{2}, \frac{3}{5}, \frac{5}{8}$ _____

30. $\frac{2}{3}, \frac{2}{6}, \frac{5}{6}$ _____

31. $\frac{4}{12}, \frac{7}{8}, \frac{6}{12}$ _____

32. $\frac{5}{7}, \frac{3}{4}, \frac{6}{7}$ _____

Copy the fractions and letters. Cross out the fractions that are less than $\frac{1}{2}$. The remaining letters will answer the riddle.

What are fractions when they are arranged from the greatest to the least?

$\frac{3}{11}$ $\frac{9}{10}$ $\frac{1}{6}$ $\frac{8}{9}$ $\frac{3}{8}$ $\frac{6}{7}$ $\frac{1}{3}$ $\frac{1}{4}$ $\frac{10}{12}$ $\frac{3}{4}$ $\frac{2}{6}$ $\frac{5}{7}$ $\frac{4}{10}$ $\frac{7}{10}$ $\frac{5}{11}$ $\frac{3}{12}$ $\frac{6}{9}$ $\frac{2}{7}$ $\frac{7}{12}$ $\frac{3}{9}$ $\frac{4}{8}$

F A P L J L T Q I N B O K R A S D R E X R

Use with pages 242–243.

93

Write the solution that answers the question.

1. Mount Aconcagua is the tallest mountain in the Western Hemisphere. It is about 22,840 ft (6,960 meters) high. One expedition took 4 days to climb the mountain and half as long to descend. How many feet did they descend per day?
a. 2 days
b. 11,420 feet per day
c. 3,480 meters per day

2. Dale and Roy give trail rides in the Sierra Nevadas. Each customer pays $6.00 per mile for a ride that lasts about 3 hours. How much would a 10-mile ride cost?
a. 6 hours long
b. $60.00
c. Dale and Roy ride 20 miles each.

Write an equation and solve.

3. Mount Saint Helens is a volcano in the Cascade Mountains. During the 1980 eruptions, about 300 meters of its peak were blasted away. After these eruptions, the volcano's elevation was 2,549 meters. What was its height before the eruptions?

_____

4. The highest peaks in the Middle Rocky Mountains are King's Peak, 13,528 feet high, and Gannett Peak, 13,804 feet high. What is the total height of these 2 peaks?

_____

Write the letter of the best estimate.

5. New York City is approximately 60 feet above sea level. Mount Everest is about 29,000 feet above sea level. About how many times higher is Mount Everest than New York City?
a. 48   **b.** 48,000
c. 480   **d.** 4,800

6. The Amazon River in South America is about 4,000 miles long. If a ship travels an average of 19 miles a day, how many days will it take to travel the entire length of the river?
a. 100 days   **b.** 150 days
c. 200 days   **d.** 250 days

List the information that is not needed. Then solve.

7. The Zambezi River in Africa is 1,600 miles long. The Tigris River in Asia is 1,150 miles long. The Zambezi is twice as long as the St. Lawrence River. How long is the St. Lawrence River?

_____

8. Mount Fuji in Japan is approximately 12,000 feet high. It is about the same height as Mount Cook in New Zealand. If it takes a group of mountain climbers 8 days to reach the top of Mount Fuji, about how many feet did the group climb each day?

_____

Holt, Rinehart and Winston, Publishers • 5

Use with pages 244–245.

Solve.

9. Mount Rainier is 14,410 feet high. Mount Washington is 6,288 feet high. The sum of these two mountain peaks is just 378 feet more than the height of Mount McKinley. What is the height of Mount McKinley?

_____

10. Bob Simmons wants to take a group of 25 school children and 8 adult chaperones on a picnic across the river. Bob's boat can carry a total of 5 people, including Bob. How many trips will Bob have to make?

_____

11. When a mountain lion is born, it weighs about 1.1 pounds. An average adult lion weighs about 176 pounds. It takes a mountain lion $2\frac{1}{2}$ years to reach adult weight. How much weight does a lion gain a month if it gains the same amount each month? (HINT: 12 months = 1 year)

_____

12. Bay Shore Sporting Goods is having a big sale. Leather mountain-climbing boots are on sale for $89.95 a pair. Alberta Parker bought a pair for everyone in her family. The total price was $539.70. How many pairs of boots did Alberta buy?

_____

13. Mountain-climbing boots cost $105 per pair before the sale. How much would 6 pairs of boots have cost before the sale?

_____

14. Alberta saved $90.30 by buying the boots on sale. How much did she save on each pair of boots?

_____

15. Alberta also bought 2 pairs of polythermal socks for everyone in her family. The socks were on sale at 3 pairs for $14.99. How much did the 12 pairs of socks cost?

_____

16. The total price of the 12 pairs of polythermal socks before the sale was $84.00. What was the price of one pair of socks?

_____

17. The total price of the mountain-climbing boots on sale was $539.70, and the total price of the polythermal socks on sale was $59.96. If Alberta gave the cashier $600.00, how much change did she get back?

_____

18. The total price of the boots and socks on sale was $599.66. The total cost of the boots and socks before the sale was $714.00. How much did Alberta save by buying these items on sale?

_____

Holt, Rinehart and Winston, Publishers • 5

Add. Write the sum in simplest form.

1. $\frac{3}{4} + \frac{3}{4} =$ _____

2. $\frac{1}{7} + \frac{2}{7} =$ _____

3. $\frac{4}{9} + \frac{4}{9} =$ _____

4. $\frac{5}{7} + \frac{4}{7} =$ _____

5. $\frac{2}{3} + \frac{2}{3} =$ _____

6. $\frac{1}{6} + \frac{2}{6} =$ _____

7. $\frac{3}{8} + \frac{1}{8} =$ _____

8. $\frac{5}{9} + \frac{2}{9} =$ _____

9. $\frac{4}{5} + \frac{3}{5} =$ _____

10. $\begin{array}{r} \frac{3}{7} \\ + \frac{5}{7} \\ \hline \end{array}$

11. $\begin{array}{r} \frac{5}{9} \\ + \frac{5}{9} \\ \hline \end{array}$

12. $\begin{array}{r} \frac{7}{10} \\ + \frac{2}{10} \\ \hline \end{array}$

13. $\begin{array}{r} \frac{5}{12} \\ + \frac{5}{12} \\ \hline \end{array}$

14. $\begin{array}{r} \frac{4}{5} \\ + \frac{1}{5} \\ \hline \end{array}$

15. $\begin{array}{r} \frac{6}{7} \\ + \frac{5}{7} \\ \hline \end{array}$

16. $\begin{array}{r} \frac{1}{3} \\ + \frac{1}{3} \\ \hline \end{array}$

17. $\begin{array}{r} \frac{3}{15} \\ + \frac{4}{15} \\ \hline \end{array}$

Solve.

18. Joan is going shopping. She travels $\frac{7}{10}$ mile to the meat market. She travels $\frac{5}{10}$ mile further to the vegetable stand. How far has Joan traveled so far?

_____

19. Joan buys an insulated bag to carry cold meals to the beach. The bag has two layers of insulation. The inner layer is $\frac{5}{16}$ inch thick. The outer layer is $\frac{9}{16}$ inch thick. How thick is the bag's insulation?

_____

Holt, Rinehart and Winston, Publishers • 5

Write 0, $\frac{1}{2}$, or 1 to complete.

1. $\frac{9}{10}$ is close to _____. **2.** $\frac{6}{13}$ is close to _____. **3.** $\frac{2}{8}$ is close to _____.

4. $\frac{5}{30}$ is close to _____. **5.** $\frac{3}{19}$ is close to _____. **6.** $\frac{11}{20}$ is close to _____.

7. $\frac{7}{15}$ is close to _____. **8.** $\frac{1}{30}$ is close to _____. **9.** $\frac{4}{5}$ is close to _____.

10. $\frac{12}{15}$ is close to _____. **11.** $\frac{11}{12}$ is close to _____. **12.** $\frac{4}{9}$ is close to _____.

Estimate.

13. $\frac{4}{5} + \frac{4}{9} =$ _____ **14.** $\frac{1}{2} + \frac{7}{12} =$ _____ **15.** $\frac{14}{15} + \frac{7}{8} =$ _____

16. $\frac{1}{5} + \frac{1}{16} =$ _____ **17.** $\frac{9}{12} + \frac{1}{4} =$ _____ **18.** $\frac{8}{9} + \frac{9}{10} =$ _____

19. $\frac{1}{7} + \frac{1}{4} =$ _____ **20.** $\frac{5}{8} + \frac{1}{4} =$ _____ **21.** $\frac{7}{8} + \frac{1}{3} =$ _____

22. $\frac{3}{7} + \frac{2}{5} =$ _____ **23.** $\frac{1}{5} + \frac{1}{6} =$ _____ **24.** $\frac{3}{4} + \frac{1}{2} =$ _____

25. $\frac{1}{4} + \frac{1}{9} =$ _____ **26.** $\frac{1}{8} + \frac{3}{16} =$ _____ **27.** $\frac{1}{2} + \frac{1}{2} =$ _____

28. $\frac{11}{12} + \frac{2}{9} =$ _____ **29.** $\frac{10}{11} + \frac{2}{9} =$ _____ **30.** $\frac{4}{10} + \frac{1}{7} =$ _____

31. $\frac{3}{15} + \frac{9}{12} + \frac{2}{11} =$ _____ **32.** $\frac{1}{5} + \frac{6}{7} + \frac{8}{10} =$ _____

33. $\frac{13}{14} + \frac{1}{4} + \frac{9}{20} =$ _____ **34.** $\frac{6}{8} + \frac{7}{9} + \frac{5}{6} =$ _____

35. $\frac{10}{13} + \frac{7}{16} + \frac{8}{18} =$ _____ **36.** $\frac{17}{20} + \frac{2}{3} + \frac{4}{9} =$ _____

Solve.

37. Emily pours apple juice for her brother, her sister, and herself. She pours $\frac{4}{9}$ cup for her brother, $\frac{1}{3}$ cup for her sister, and $\frac{9}{10}$ cup for herself. Estimate how many cups Emily pours. _____

Holt, Rinehart and Winston, Publishers • 5

Use with pages 248–249.

PRACTICE Adding Unlike Fractions

Add. Write the sum in simplest form.

1. $\frac{3}{4}$
$+\frac{3}{8}$

2. $\frac{3}{5}$
$+\frac{1}{3}$

3. $\frac{1}{6}$
$+\frac{2}{3}$

4. $\frac{3}{10}$
$+\frac{1}{4}$

5. $\frac{2}{5}$
$+\frac{9}{10}$

6. $\frac{5}{7}$
$+\frac{1}{14}$

7. $\frac{1}{3}$
$+\frac{8}{9}$

8. $\frac{7}{8}$
$+\frac{1}{2}$

9. $\frac{5}{6}$
$+\frac{2}{9}$

10. $\frac{5}{12}$
$+\frac{9}{10}$

11. $\frac{2}{9}$
$+\frac{2}{3}$

12. $\frac{7}{10}$
$+\frac{1}{8}$

13. $\frac{1}{5}$
$+\frac{3}{10}$

14. $\frac{7}{12}$
$+\frac{7}{15}$

15. $\frac{3}{4}$
$+\frac{7}{8}$

16. $\frac{1}{6}$
$+\frac{1}{8}$

17. $\frac{1}{2}$
$+\frac{3}{16}$

18. $\frac{2}{3}$
$+\frac{4}{9}$

19. $\frac{1}{6} + \frac{2}{3} =$ _____

20. $\frac{1}{6} + \frac{5}{9} =$ _____

21. $\frac{7}{10} + \frac{2}{5} =$ _____

22. $\frac{1}{7} + \frac{3}{8} =$ _____

23. $\frac{2}{3} + \frac{7}{9} =$ _____

24. $\frac{1}{10} + \frac{3}{5} =$ _____

25. $\frac{2}{5} + \frac{7}{15} =$ _____

26. $\frac{1}{2} + \frac{1}{4} =$ _____

27. $\frac{2}{3} + \frac{5}{6} =$ _____

28. $\frac{3}{10} + \frac{1}{2} =$ _____

29. $\frac{1}{4} + \frac{5}{8} =$ _____

30. $\frac{5}{6} + \frac{7}{10} =$ _____

Solve.

31. Luis and Carolyn have 3 hours to paint a room. During that time, Luis paints $\frac{3}{10}$ of the room and Carolyn paints $\frac{3}{5}$. How much of the room is painted?

_____

32. Carolyn used $\frac{5}{6}$ gallon of paint. Luis used $\frac{1}{12}$ gallon of paint. How much paint did they use in all?

_____

Use with pages 250–251.

Subtract. Write the difference in simplest form.

1. $\dfrac{6}{9}$ $-\dfrac{4}{9}$

2. $\dfrac{2}{5}$ $-\dfrac{1}{6}$

3. $\dfrac{4}{6}$ $-\dfrac{7}{12}$

4. $\dfrac{7}{8}$ $-\dfrac{1}{4}$

5. $\dfrac{11}{15}$ $-\dfrac{2}{15}$

6. $\dfrac{3}{5}$ $-\dfrac{1}{2}$

7. $\dfrac{5}{6}$ $-\dfrac{1}{3}$

8. $\dfrac{17}{20}$ $-\dfrac{13}{20}$

9. $\dfrac{11}{12}$ $-\dfrac{1}{2}$

10. $\dfrac{5}{9}$ $-\dfrac{1}{3}$

11. $\dfrac{1}{6}$ $-\dfrac{1}{9}$

12. $\dfrac{10}{11}$ $-\dfrac{2}{11}$

13. $\dfrac{2}{9}$ $-\dfrac{1}{81}$

14. $\dfrac{3}{10}$ $-\dfrac{3}{25}$

15. $\dfrac{7}{8}$ $-\dfrac{1}{2}$

16. $\dfrac{11}{12}$ $-\dfrac{5}{12}$

17. $\dfrac{6}{10}$ $-\dfrac{2}{5}$

18. $\dfrac{16}{19}$ $-\dfrac{13}{19}$

19. $\dfrac{5}{7}$ $-\dfrac{1}{7}$

20. $\dfrac{4}{5}$ $-\dfrac{2}{15}$

21. $\dfrac{5}{6}$ $-\dfrac{2}{3}$

22. $\dfrac{11}{14}$ $-\dfrac{5}{14}$

23. $\dfrac{23}{24}$ $-\dfrac{14}{24}$

24. $\dfrac{2}{3}$ $-\dfrac{1}{3}$

25. $\dfrac{14}{15}$ $-\dfrac{1}{15}$

26. $\dfrac{15}{26}$ $-\dfrac{2}{13}$

27. $\dfrac{5}{8}$ $-\dfrac{3}{8}$

28. $\dfrac{9}{11}$ $-\dfrac{8}{11}$

29. $\dfrac{10}{27}$ $-\dfrac{7}{27}$

30. $\dfrac{3}{10}$ $-\dfrac{2}{15}$

31. $\dfrac{9}{10} - \dfrac{3}{10} =$ _____

32. $\dfrac{13}{15} - \dfrac{4}{15} =$ _____

33. $\dfrac{1}{2} - \dfrac{3}{7} =$ _____

34. $\dfrac{2}{3} - \dfrac{1}{6} =$ _____

35. $\dfrac{7}{12} - \dfrac{5}{12} =$ _____

36. $\dfrac{8}{9} - \dfrac{4}{9} =$ _____

37. $\dfrac{9}{11} - \dfrac{3}{11} =$ _____

38. $\dfrac{1}{3} - \dfrac{1}{4} =$ _____

39. $\dfrac{3}{8} - \dfrac{9}{24} =$ _____

Use with pages 252–253.

Add. Write the sum in simplest form.

1. $15\frac{1}{6}$
$+\ 9\frac{1}{4}$

2. $21\frac{1}{5}$
$+\ 6\frac{2}{3}$

3. $3\frac{2}{9}$
$+\ 5\frac{2}{9}$

4. $9\frac{6}{7}$
$+\ 12$

5. $8\frac{1}{6}$
$+\ 11\frac{3}{9}$

6. $17\frac{1}{6}$
$+\ 1\frac{7}{12}$

7. $25\frac{1}{3}$
$+\ 2\frac{2}{4}$

8. $4\frac{1}{6}$
$+\ \frac{1}{2}$

9. $1\frac{2}{3} + 1 =$ _____

10. $1\frac{1}{2} + 20\frac{1}{6} =$ _____

11. $2\frac{7}{9} + 3\frac{1}{9} =$ _____

12. $14\frac{1}{4} + 1\frac{1}{4} =$ _____

13. $5\frac{1}{3} + 15\frac{1}{8} =$ _____

14. $6\frac{2}{9} + 11\frac{1}{18} =$ _____

15. $10\frac{5}{6} + 6 =$ _____

16. $19 + 7\frac{1}{2} =$ _____

17. $3\frac{3}{7} + 4\frac{1}{3} =$ _____

18. $5 + 2\frac{1}{5} =$ _____

19. $9\frac{1}{4} + 3\frac{1}{2} =$ _____

20. $1\frac{1}{2} + 3\frac{1}{4} =$ _____

21. $4 + 4\frac{3}{8} =$ _____

22. $5\frac{1}{3} + 1\frac{1}{2} =$ _____

23. $7\frac{2}{5} + 4\frac{3}{10} =$ _____

24. $6\frac{5}{8} + 8\frac{1}{8} =$ _____

25. $16 + 5\frac{3}{8} =$ _____

26. $12\frac{4}{17} + 6\frac{8}{17} =$ _____

Solve.

27. Ari buys $2\frac{1}{4}$ pounds of apples. He also buys $1\frac{1}{2}$ pounds of grapes. How many pounds of fruit does Ari buy? _____

Holt, Rinehart and Winston, Publishers • 5

Use with pages 254–255.

Write the letter of the best estimate.

1. $5\frac{1}{10} + 3\frac{7}{8}$

  a. about 8

  b. about 9

  c. about 10

2. $8\frac{1}{4} + 4\frac{1}{9}$

  a. about 12

  b. about 13

  c. about 16

3. $9\frac{1}{8} + 2\frac{2}{7}$

  a. about 9

  b. about 10

  c. about 11

4. $3\frac{7}{12} + \frac{1}{5}$

  a. about 2

  b. about 3

  c. about 4

Add. Write the sum in simplest form.

5. $\begin{array}{r} 7\frac{3}{4} \\ + 4\frac{1}{4} \\ \hline \end{array}$

6. $\begin{array}{r} 8\frac{4}{5} \\ + 1\frac{4}{5} \\ \hline \end{array}$

7. $\begin{array}{r} 12\frac{11}{12} \\ + 3\frac{1}{4} \\ \hline \end{array}$

8. $\begin{array}{r} 6\frac{3}{10} \\ + 8\frac{9}{10} \\ \hline \end{array}$

9. $\begin{array}{r} 5\frac{9}{10} \\ + 2\frac{1}{6} \\ \hline \end{array}$

10. $\begin{array}{r} 7\frac{5}{18} \\ + 10\frac{5}{6} \\ \hline \end{array}$

11. $\begin{array}{r} 12\frac{3}{7} \\ + 3\frac{5}{7} \\ \hline \end{array}$

12. $\begin{array}{r} 4\frac{5}{6} \\ + 2\frac{1}{3} \\ \hline \end{array}$

13. $\begin{array}{r} 5\frac{1}{3} \\ + 6\frac{2}{3} \\ \hline \end{array}$

14. $\begin{array}{r} 9\frac{11}{16} \\ + 9\frac{1}{2} \\ \hline \end{array}$

15. $\begin{array}{r} 8\frac{1}{2} \\ + 10\frac{2}{3} \\ \hline \end{array}$

16. $\begin{array}{r} 6\frac{3}{4} \\ + 7\frac{1}{3} \\ \hline \end{array}$

17. $\begin{array}{r} 1\frac{7}{15} \\ + 1\frac{3}{5} \\ \hline \end{array}$

18. $\begin{array}{r} 6\frac{2}{3} \\ + 4\frac{7}{9} \\ \hline \end{array}$

19. $\begin{array}{r} 5\frac{7}{10} \\ + 5\frac{7}{20} \\ \hline \end{array}$

20. $\begin{array}{r} 11\frac{7}{8} \\ + 3\frac{3}{12} \\ \hline \end{array}$

21. $3\frac{1}{2} + 1\frac{3}{4} = $ _____

22. $2\frac{2}{3} + 2\frac{2}{3} = $ _____

23. $5\frac{9}{10} + 6\frac{2}{5} = $ _____

24. $7\frac{5}{6} + 7\frac{5}{6} = $ _____

25. $3\frac{5}{9} + 8\frac{13}{18} = $ _____

26. $4\frac{7}{8} + 3\frac{1}{6} = $ _____

Holt, Rinehart and Winston, Publishers • 5

Subtract. Write the difference in simplest form.

1. $12\frac{7}{9}$
$- \ 9\frac{2}{6}$

2. $11\frac{5}{7}$
$- \ 8\frac{1}{2}$

3. $20\frac{1}{3}$
$- \ 8\frac{2}{15}$

4. $16\frac{10}{11}$
$- \ 9$

5. $13\frac{9}{13}$
$- \ 3\frac{6}{13}$

6. $5\frac{18}{21}$
$- \ 3\frac{2}{3}$

7. $9\frac{1}{3}$
$- \ 1\frac{3}{10}$

8. $14\frac{7}{8}$
$- \ 7\frac{2}{3}$

9. $10\frac{2}{3}$
$- \ 3\frac{1}{6}$

10. $12\frac{3}{4}$
$- \ 5$

11. $8\frac{11}{14}$
$- \ 3\frac{5}{7}$

12. $9\frac{1}{2}$
$- \ 6\frac{1}{2}$

13. $5\frac{3}{4}$
$- \ 2\frac{1}{2}$

14. $14\frac{3}{4}$
$- \ 9$

15. $6\frac{2}{3}$
$- \ 1$

16. $7\frac{6}{9}$
$- \ 5\frac{1}{3}$

17. $6\frac{5}{7}$
$- \ 1\frac{2}{7}$

18. $9\frac{5}{6}$
$- \ 8\frac{1}{2}$

19. $4\frac{4}{5}$
$- \ 2\frac{1}{10}$

20. $5\frac{2}{3}$
$- \ 3\frac{4}{9}$

21. $4\frac{3}{4} - 2\frac{1}{4} =$ _____

22. $6\frac{3}{8} - 5\frac{1}{8} =$ _____

23. $10\frac{6}{7} - 8\frac{3}{14} =$ _____

24. $8\frac{5}{8} - 1 =$ _____

25. $7\frac{8}{9} - 3\frac{4}{9} =$ _____

26. $8\frac{3}{4} - 2\frac{1}{2} =$ _____

Solve.

27. Felipe wants to be on the track team. On his first day of training, he runs $6\frac{1}{4}$ times around the track. The second day, he runs $8\frac{1}{2}$ times around the track. How many more times did he run around the track on the second day? _____

102

Subtract. Write the answer in simplest form.

1. $8 - 3\frac{1}{3} =$ _____

2. $5\frac{1}{4} - 2\frac{3}{4} =$ _____

3. $7\frac{1}{4} - 2\frac{1}{3} =$ _____

4. $9\frac{5}{8} - 2\frac{6}{8} =$ _____

5. $10\frac{1}{5} - 5\frac{7}{10} =$ _____

6. $6 - 2\frac{1}{7} =$ _____

7. $3\frac{1}{4} - 1\frac{7}{8} =$ _____

8. $8\frac{1}{2} - 7\frac{11}{12} =$ _____

9. $11\frac{2}{20} - 3\frac{7}{10} =$ _____

10. $4 - 3\frac{1}{2} =$ _____

11. $4\frac{1}{4} - 2\frac{3}{4} =$ _____

12. $10\frac{1}{3} - 6\frac{1}{2} =$ _____

13. $7\frac{2}{5} - 2\frac{4}{5} =$ _____

14. $9 - 7\frac{1}{3} =$ _____

15. $8\frac{1}{5} - 3\frac{1}{4} =$ _____

16. $3\frac{2}{3} - 1\frac{6}{7} =$ _____

17. $6 - 2\frac{5}{12} =$ _____

18. $7\frac{1}{5} - 3\frac{5}{6} =$ _____

19. $8\frac{3}{4} - 2\frac{4}{5} =$ _____

20. $8\frac{5}{24} - 1\frac{11}{12} =$ _____

21. $7\frac{1}{11} - 5\frac{1}{2} =$ _____

22. $\begin{array}{r} 10 \\ -\ 8\frac{5}{6} \\ \hline \end{array}$

23. $\begin{array}{r} 5\frac{3}{7} \\ -\ 3\frac{5}{7} \\ \hline \end{array}$

24. $\begin{array}{r} 13\frac{4}{15} \\ -\ 7\frac{4}{5} \\ \hline \end{array}$

25. $\begin{array}{r} 16\frac{2}{13} \\ -\ 13\frac{13}{26} \\ \hline \end{array}$

26. $\begin{array}{r} 8 \\ -\ 6\frac{3}{4} \\ \hline \end{array}$

27. $\begin{array}{r} 6\frac{4}{9} \\ -\ 2\frac{7}{9} \\ \hline \end{array}$

28. $\begin{array}{r} 17\frac{7}{16} \\ -\ 7\frac{7}{8} \\ \hline \end{array}$

29. $\begin{array}{r} 19\frac{8}{21} \\ -\ 18\frac{6}{7} \\ \hline \end{array}$

Solve.

30. Hans brought $12\frac{1}{4}$ pounds of hamburger to the picnic. After lunch there were $3\frac{7}{8}$ pounds left. How many pounds of hamburger were used?

_____

Write the letter of the correct answer.

1. A group of 27 senior citizens are going on a hike along the Peconic River. They plan to drive to the river. If each car can hold 5 people, how many cars will they need?

   a. 5   b. $5\frac{1}{2}$ c. 6

2. The group walked 3 miles in 4 hours before stopping for lunch. How far did they walk in one hour?

   a. $\frac{3}{4}$ of a mile
   b. $1\frac{1}{3}$ miles
   c. 1 mile

Solve.

3. Sally is in charge of food for the senior citizens' river hike. Sally can put 10 sandwiches into each pack. If 38 sandwiches are needed, how many packs will Sally put together?

   _____

4. At the Bay Shore Senior Citizens Center, 39 members have signed up for a two-day hike in the Catskill Mountains. Each tent has room for 7 adults. How many tents will be needed?

   _____

5. While on a 5-hour hike, a group of 5th graders walked 12 miles. How far did they walk in 1 hour?

   _____

6. How far could twice as many 5th graders walk in 5 hours?

   _____

7. On a river-rafting trip, each raft carried a total of 9 people. If 53 people took the trip, how many rafts were used?

   _____

8. There is 1 guide for every 8 people who go on the river-rafting trip. If 55 people decide to go rafting, how many guides will be needed?

   _____

9. On a canoe trip, each canoe holds only 3 people. If 14 people want to go on the trip, how many canoes will they need?

   _____

10. If 21 sandwiches were divided equally among the 14 people, how many would each person get?

   _____

11. There are 45 people who have signed up for a canoe trip. The guide will bring 4 packs of food for each person. If 21 packs of food fit into each waterproof container, how many waterproof containers will the guide bring?

   _____

12. If the waterproof containers are divided among 15 boats, how many boats would carry containers?

   _____

Holt, Rinehart and Winston, Publishers • 5

Multiply. Write the answer in simplest form.

1. $\frac{1}{2} \times \frac{1}{4} =$ _____

2. $\frac{3}{4} \times \frac{8}{9} =$ _____

3. $\frac{1}{4} \times \frac{1}{6} =$ _____

4. $\frac{1}{5} \times \frac{1}{3} =$ _____

5. $\frac{1}{10} \times \frac{1}{3} =$ _____

6. $\frac{6}{7} \times \frac{1}{2} =$ _____

7. $\frac{3}{4} \times \frac{5}{6} =$ _____

8. $\frac{1}{3} \times \frac{1}{7} =$ _____

9. $\frac{2}{5} \times \frac{1}{5} =$ _____

10. $\frac{1}{5} \times \frac{1}{8} =$ _____

11. $\frac{1}{4} \times \frac{6}{7} =$ _____

12. $\frac{3}{8} \times \frac{2}{3} =$ _____

13. $\frac{1}{2} \times \frac{1}{9} =$ _____

14. $\frac{2}{3} \times \frac{1}{8} =$ _____

15. $\frac{7}{8} \times \frac{5}{7} =$ _____

16. $\frac{1}{9} \times \frac{1}{4} =$ _____

17. $\frac{1}{6} \times \frac{1}{7} =$ _____

18. $\frac{1}{5} \times \frac{1}{2} =$ _____

19. $\frac{1}{4} \times \frac{1}{3} =$ _____

20. $\frac{3}{10} \times \frac{1}{3} =$ _____

21. $\frac{3}{5} \times \frac{2}{3} =$ _____

22. $\frac{4}{9} \times \frac{1}{2} =$ _____

23. $\frac{1}{4} \times \frac{1}{8} =$ _____

24. $\frac{1}{8} \times \frac{4}{5} =$ _____

Copy the answer rules and fractions.
What has four wheels and flies?

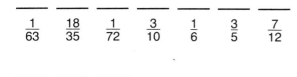

| $\frac{1}{63}$ | $\frac{18}{35}$ | $\frac{1}{72}$ | $\frac{3}{10}$ | $\frac{1}{6}$ | $\frac{3}{5}$ | $\frac{7}{12}$ |

| $\frac{1}{7}$ | $\frac{4}{7}$ | $\frac{1}{2}$ | $\frac{3}{7}$ | $\frac{1}{50}$ |

Multiply. Then match the letters with the answer.

25. $\frac{4}{5} \times \frac{3}{8} =$ _____ B

26. $\frac{1}{9} \times \frac{1}{8} =$ _____ R

27. $\frac{1}{2} \times \frac{6}{7} =$ _____ C

28. $\frac{1}{5} \times \frac{1}{10} =$ _____ K

29. $\frac{7}{8} \times \frac{2}{3} =$ _____ E

30. $\frac{4}{7} \times \frac{9}{10} =$ _____ A

31. $\frac{3}{7} \times \frac{1}{3} =$ _____ T

32. $\frac{1}{7} \times \frac{1}{9} =$ _____ G

33. $\frac{5}{6} \times \frac{3}{5} =$ _____ U

34. $\frac{1}{5} \times \frac{5}{6} =$ _____ A

35. $\frac{4}{5} \times \frac{5}{7} =$ _____ R

36. $\frac{3}{4} \times \frac{4}{5} =$ _____ G

Multiply. Write the answer in simplest form.

1. $\frac{1}{2} \times 6 =$ _____

2. $2 \times \frac{1}{2} =$ _____

3. $8 \times \frac{5}{6} =$ _____

4. $\frac{1}{4} \times 24 =$ _____

5. $\frac{1}{4} \times 30 =$ _____

6. $10 \times \frac{1}{2} =$ _____

7. $\frac{1}{7} \times 14 =$ _____

8. $\frac{1}{4} \times 32 =$ _____

9. $25 \times \frac{3}{5} =$ _____

10. $\frac{1}{9} \times 60 =$ _____

11. $33 \times \frac{2}{3} =$ _____

12. $\frac{1}{4} \times 100 =$ _____

13. $\frac{4}{7} \times 21 =$ _____

14. $64 \times \frac{1}{4} =$ _____

15. $\frac{2}{9} \times 48 =$ _____

16. $\frac{5}{6} \times 60 =$ _____

17. $\frac{4}{5} \times 15 =$ _____

18. $\frac{4}{7} \times 21 =$ _____

19. $40 \times \frac{7}{8} =$ _____

20. $96 \times \frac{1}{5} =$ _____

21. $100 \times \frac{7}{10} =$ _____

22. $20 \times \frac{4}{5} =$ _____

23. $49 \times \frac{2}{7} =$ _____

24. $\frac{1}{3} \times 3 =$ _____

Write $\frac{1}{3}$ of each number.

25. 21 _____

26. 28 _____

27. 39 _____

28. 45 _____

29. 65 _____

30. 24 _____

31. 52 _____

32. 10 _____

Write $\frac{1}{4}$ of each number.

33. 43 _____

34. 14 _____

35. 1,000 _____

36. 80 _____

37. 28 _____

38. 100 _____

39. 17 _____

40. 21 _____

Write $\frac{3}{4}$ of each number.

41. 12 _____

42. 1,000 _____

43. 28 _____

44. 16 _____

45. 50 _____

46. 100 _____

47. 25 _____

48. 20 _____

Holt, Rinehart and Winston, Publishers • 5

Use with pages 274–275.

Multiplying Fractions and Mixed Numbers

Multiply. Write each product in simplest form.

1. $\frac{3}{4} \times 1\frac{1}{3} =$ _____

2. $6 \times 10\frac{1}{2} =$ _____

3. $2\frac{1}{6} \times \frac{1}{2} =$ _____

4. $1\frac{3}{4} \times \frac{2}{5} =$ _____

5. $2\frac{2}{3} \times 1\frac{1}{4} =$ _____

6. $\frac{5}{6} \times 1\frac{2}{3} =$ _____

7. $\frac{5}{6} \times 1\frac{1}{2} =$ _____

8. $2\frac{1}{6} \times \frac{2}{5} =$ _____

9. $3\frac{1}{3} \times \frac{1}{3} =$ _____

10. $\frac{4}{5} \times 4\frac{1}{2} =$ _____

11. $\frac{2}{3} \times 6\frac{1}{4} =$ _____

12. $\frac{3}{4} \times 2\frac{1}{6} =$ _____

13. $6 \times \frac{2}{3} =$ _____

14. $3\frac{3}{5} \times 1\frac{1}{2} =$ _____

15. $\frac{2}{7} \times 9\frac{1}{2} =$ _____

16. $\frac{1}{4} \times 2\frac{5}{6} =$ _____

17. $8 \times \frac{7}{8} =$ _____

18. $\frac{3}{8} \times 1\frac{1}{7} =$ _____

19. $3\frac{3}{4} \times 1\frac{1}{2} =$ _____

20. $9 \times \frac{3}{8} =$ _____

21. $\frac{5}{6} \times 6 =$ _____

22. $9\frac{1}{2} \times \frac{2}{3} =$ _____

23. $5\frac{1}{5} \times \frac{1}{4} =$ _____

24. $3\frac{1}{3} \times \frac{1}{9} =$ _____

25. $4\frac{1}{4} \times 2\frac{1}{2} =$ _____

26. $\frac{3}{7} \times 1\frac{1}{3} =$ _____

27. $\frac{1}{10} \times 4\frac{1}{6} =$ _____

28. $\frac{1}{9} \times 8\frac{1}{2} =$ _____

29. $5\frac{1}{2} \times \frac{2}{7} =$ _____

30. $\frac{2}{3} \times 5\frac{2}{5} =$ _____

Solve.

31. The new Kiwi IVG portable computer weighs $10\frac{3}{4}$ pounds. The battery for the computer weighs $\frac{1}{5}$ as much. How much does the battery weigh?

_____

32. The Zegga VS laptop computer weighs 5 pounds. The portable printer that can be attached to the computer weighs $1\frac{3}{8}$ times as much. How much does the printer weigh?

_____

Use with pages 276–277.

Estimate to solve.

1. The Jambon Drama Club is putting on the play *Knights of the Round Table*. The club may use the auditorium from 4:30 P.M. to 6:30 P.M. They must leave no later than 6:45 P.M. Here is their rehearsal schedule:

   Act 1: $15\frac{1}{4}$ minutes   Act 3: $27\frac{1}{2}$ minutes

   Act 2: 36 minutes   Act 4: $22\frac{1}{2}$ minutes

   Will the club be finished rehearsing by 6:45 P.M.?

2. The club has a budget of $225 for the play. So far, they have spent the following amounts of money.

   $42.75: costumes $12.50: special effects

   $61.50: props $44.62: equipment rental

   $30.47: scenery   ($22.31 per day)

   $32.50: lights

   Do they have enough money to rent equipment for 2 more days?

3. The club needs a switchboard to control the lights and sound effects. A new switchboard costs $356.75 plus $57.50 for installation. Renting one costs $33.10 per day. They would need to rent a switchboard for 14 days. Would it be more economical to purchase or to rent the equipment?

4. Sal Laloco is in charge of box office sales. Before the show opens, he sells 112 tickets at $1.95 per ticket. The club has $98 in the treasury. Does the club have enough money to buy a spotlight for $305?

5. Jennifer and Patti will play the leads in *Sisters of Lucy*. Each girl will be on stage for different lengths of time.

	Jennifer	Patti
Act 1	27.8 min	22.5 min
Act 2	18.4 min	23.2 min
Act 3	26.2 min	17.4 min

   Which girl will be on stage longer?

Use with pages 278–279.

Divide.

1.

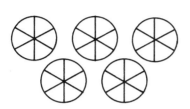

$4 \div \frac{1}{4} =$ _____

2.

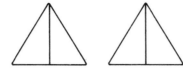

$2 \div \frac{1}{2} =$ _____

3.

$8 \div \frac{1}{2} =$ _____

4.

$5 \div \frac{1}{6} =$ _____

5.

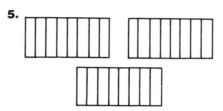

$3 \div \frac{1}{8} =$ _____

6.

$4 \div \frac{1}{5} =$ _____

7. $1 \div \frac{1}{2} =$ _____

8. $2 \div \frac{1}{5} =$ _____

9. $2 \div \frac{1}{7} =$ _____

10. $7 \div \frac{1}{8} =$ _____

11. $4 \div \frac{1}{6} =$ _____

12. $12 \div \frac{1}{3} =$ _____

13. $2 \div \frac{1}{9} =$ _____

14. $5 \div \frac{1}{5} =$ _____

15. $14 \div \frac{1}{2} =$ _____

16. $8 \div \frac{1}{5} =$ _____

17. $5 \div \frac{1}{9} =$ _____

18. $6 \div \frac{1}{3} =$ _____

19. $6 \div \frac{1}{4} =$ _____

20. $7 \div \frac{1}{6} =$ _____

21. $10 \div \frac{1}{2} =$ _____

22. $20 \div \frac{1}{5} =$ _____

23. $40 \div \frac{1}{2} =$ _____

24. $50 \div \frac{1}{2} =$ _____

25. $16 \div \frac{1}{5} =$ _____

26. $30 \div \frac{1}{5} =$ _____

27. $15 \div \frac{1}{3} =$ _____

28. $6 \div \frac{1}{5} =$ _____

29. $11 \div \frac{1}{4} =$ _____

30. $31 \div \frac{1}{2} =$ _____

Holt, Rinehart and Winston, Publishers • 5

Make a table. Solve.

1. The local ballpark can seat 1,200 people and has standing room for 300. Before a game is played, 75 people enter the stadium every minute. If everybody who enters tries to get a seat, how long would it take for 600 seats to be filled? _____

Number of minutes								
Number of people								

2. At that rate, in how much time would the standing room be filled? _____

3. If 300 people attend the game, there must be 2 hot dog vendors. If 600 people attend, there must be 4 hot dog vendors. How many people are at a game when there are 8 hot dog vendors? _____

Number of vendors				
Number of people				

4. How many vendors should there be for 750 people?

_____

5. When 450 people attend the game, 3 souvenir stands are open. When there are 900 people, 6 stands are open. How many people will 9 souvenir stands serve?

_____

Number of stands			
Number of people			

Holt, Rinehart and Winston, Publishers • 5

Use with pages 282–283.

Solve. Make a table if you need to.

6. Fritz was teaching little Sal to catch a ball. When they stood 5 feet apart, Sal caught 6 of 8 balls. At 6 feet, Sal caught 5 of 8 balls. At 7 feet, he caught every other ball. If the trend continued, how many balls would Sal have caught at a distance of 10 feet?

_____

7. Anne wants to find out whether she can shoot better fast or slowly. When she shoots fast, she makes 3 shots in 15 seconds, 6 shots after 30 seconds, and 9 shots after 45 seconds. When she shoots slowly, she makes 1 shot in 15 seconds, 5 shots after 30 seconds, and 9 shots after 45 seconds. If this trend continues, how many baskets will she have made after shooting fast for 90 seconds? How many shooting slowly?

_____

8. Thad is throwing basketballs through a hoop to improve his accuracy. When he is 1 yard away from the hoop, he throws 9 of 10 balls through the hoop. When he is 4 yards away, he throws 7 of 10 balls through the hoop and 5 of 10 balls through the hoop when he is 7 yards away. At this rate and from 16 yards away, how many of 10 throws will be good?

_____

Write *A.M.* or *P.M.*

1. Breakfast is served. _____

2. The bus brings you to school. _____

3. School ends. _____

4. The sun sets. _____

How much time has passed?

5.

from	to
12:00	**4:00**
Noon	P.M.

_____ h _____ min

6.

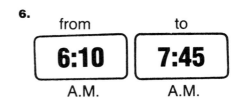

from	to
6:10	**7:45**
A.M.	A.M.

_____ h _____ min

7.

from   to

_____ h _____ min

8.

from   to

_____ h _____ min

9.

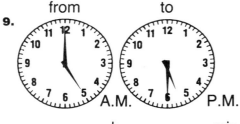

from   to

_____ h _____ min

10.

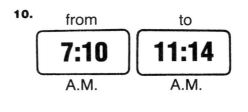

from	to
7:10	**11:14**
A.M.	A.M.

_____ h _____ min

Complete.

11. 3 y = _____ mo

12. 4 min = _____ s

13. 120 s = _____ min

14. $\frac{5}{6}$ h = _____ min

15. $\frac{2}{7}$ wk = _____ d

16. 730 d = _____ y

Holt, Rinehart and Winston, Publishers • 5

Add.

1.   3 h 10 min
  + 1 h 14 min

2.   3 h 40 min
  + 8 h 25 min

3.   6 min 32 s
  + 9 min 20 s

4.   8 h 44 min
  + 1 h 6 min

5.   12 h 12 min
  + 3 h 15 min

6.   5 h 24 min
  + 2 h 19 min

7.   7 h 22 min
  + 3 h 41 min

8.   4 min 50 s
  + 9 min 7 s

9.   22 min 16 s
  + 34 min 18 s

10.   5 min 39 s
  + 5 min 29 s

11.   9 h 14 min
  + 5 h 32 min

12.   9 h 36 min
  + 4 h 11 min

Subtract.

13.   7 h 45 min
  − 3 h 29 min

14. 18 h 59 min
  − 12 h 23 min

15.   8 min 32 s
  − 6 min 13 s

16. 18 h 39 min
  − 14 h 50 min

17.   5 h 22 min
  − 1 h 50 min

18. 28 min 18 s
  − 16 min 28 s

19. 16 min 45 s
  − 6 min 40 s

20. 10 min 10 s
  − 3 min 35 s

21.   7 min 30 s
  − 4 min 20 s

22.   2 h 51 min
  − 1 h 52 min

23.   3 h 18 min
  − 2 h 10 min

24. 48 min 25 s
  − 46 min 35 s

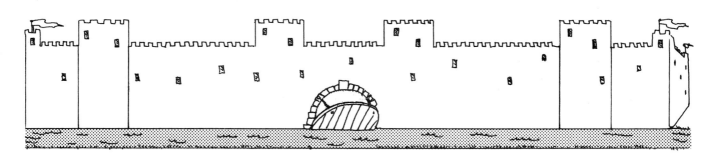

Solve.

25. Janna spent 3 h 26 min putting together a model castle on Saturday. On Monday, she spent 1 h 15 min working on it. How long did she spend in all?

26. It took Janna 15 h 18 min to complete a model bridge. The model castle took 17 h 9 min. How much longer did it take to put the castle together?

Holt, Rinehart and Winston, Publishers • 5

Use the schedule to solve.

Canoe tours	Departs	Arrives	Distance	Remarks
Riverview to Stacey	9:00 A.M.	1:00 P.M.	10 miles	Calm water
Riverview to Deep Eddy	9:00 A.M.	3:00 P.M.	14 miles	White water
Stacey to Deep Eddy	10:00 A.M.	12:30 P.M.	4 miles	White water
Stacey to Mark's Landing	2:00 P.M.	7:00 P.M.	10 miles	Sunset tour small islands
Deep Eddy to Mark's Landing	11:00 A.M.	3:30 P.M.	6 miles	Calm water small islands
Riverview to Mark's Landing	11:30 A.M.	3:30 P.M. Next day	20 miles	Calm water white water small islands overnight camp at Stacey
All trips require advance reservations. Reserve 1 week in advance for day trips, 2 weeks for overnight camping trips.				

1. Gina and Nicky are taking two trips, from Riverview to Stacey, and from Stacey to Mark's Landing. How long will they have between trips?

_____

2. Paul and Jan want to meet at Deep Eddy. If Paul leaves from Riverview, and Jan leaves from Stacey, when is the earliest they could meet?

_____

3. Gloria takes the overnight tour. The tour leaves Stacey at 11:30 A.M. At about what time did the tour reach Stacey the previous day?

_____

4. Jim is taking the bus to Stacey to go on the Stacey/Deep Eddy trip. The bus ride takes 45 minutes. When must the bus leave to reach Stacey in time?

_____

5. On March 1, Susan and Tina decided to take the overnight trip to Mark's Landing. What is the earliest day they could take the trip?

_____

6. Ralph decides to take two trips, one from Riverview to Deep Eddy, and the other from Deep Eddy to Mark's Landing. Can he take both trips the same day?

_____

Holt, Rinehart and Winston, Publishers • 5

Use with pages 288–289.

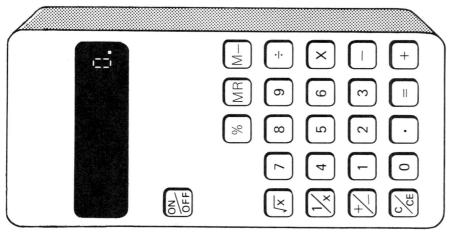

Measure this calculator to the nearest

1. inch. _____

2. $\frac{1}{2}$ in. _____

3. $\frac{1}{4}$ in. _____

4. $\frac{1}{8}$ in. _____

5. $\frac{1}{16}$ in. _____

Use a ruler to draw a line that is

6. $1\frac{1}{2}$ in.

7. $3\frac{1}{4}$ in.

8. $2\frac{7}{16}$ in.

9. $4\frac{3}{8}$ in.

Solve.

Paco is making a kite. He is using two wooden sticks and a sheet of plastic to make the kite.

10. What is the total length of the pieces of

wood? _____

11. What is the distance around the kite? _____

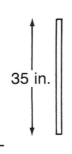

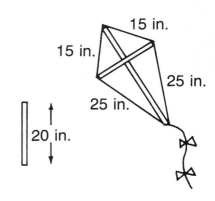

Holt, Rinehart and Winston, Publishers • 5

Write *inches*, *feet*, or *yards*.

1. A chair may be 3 _____ high.

2. A spoon may be 6 _____ long.

3. A television screen may be 21 _____ wide.

4. The distance around a jogging track may be 440 _____.

Choose the appropriate unit of measure. Write *yd* or *mi*.

5. the length of the Colorado River

_____

6. the length of a carpet

_____

7. the distance from Illinois to Mexico

_____

8. the length of an Olympic swimming pool

_____

9. the length of a football field

_____

10. the height of a window

_____

Complete.

11. 15 ft = _____ yd

12. 1 mi = _____ ft

13. 1 yd = _____ in.

14. 2 yd = _____ ft

15. 5,280 ft = _____ yd

16. 2 mi = _____ yd

Solve.

17. The *Give-Me-A-Tip* newspaper carriers all have routes which cover less than 1 mile. Copy and complete the chart to find out the distance of each carrier's route.

LENGTH OF ROUTE

	Feet	Yards	Miles
Ralph		880	$\frac{1}{2}$
Carmine	1,320	440	
Elena	1,056		$\frac{1}{5}$
Joaquin		1,320	
Masako	660		

Holt, Rinehart and Winston, Publishers • 5

Use with pages 292–293.

Write *ounces*, *pounds*, or *tons*.

1. A bag of oranges may weigh 4 _____ .

2. A tomato may weigh 5 _____ .

3. A truckload of topsoil may weigh $\frac{1}{2}$ _____ .

4. A handful of cherries may weigh 10 _____ .

Complete.

5. 3 lb = _____ oz

6. 2,000 lb = _____ T

7. 32 oz = _____ lb

8. 20 lb = _____ oz

9. 20,000 lb = _____ T

10. 20 oz = _____ lb

11. 15 T = _____ lb

12. $2\frac{1}{2}$ lb = _____ ozs

13. 2 T = _____ lb

14. 400 oz = _____ lb

15. 1,000 lb = _____ T

16. 64 oz = _____ lb

17. 8 lb = _____ oz

18. $1\frac{1}{2}$ T = _____ lb

19. 1,500 lb = _____ T

Write *cups*, *pints*, *quarts*, or *gallons*.

20. A thermos may hold 3 _____ of milk.

21. A fish tank may hold 8 _____ of water.

22. A pitcher may hold 2 _____ of juice.

23. A small carton may hold 1 _____ of cream.

Complete.

24. 2 c = _____ pt

25. 20 qt = _____ gal

26. 10 pt = _____ qt

27. 6 qt = _____ pt

28. 3 gal = _____ qt

29. 4 pt = _____ c

30. 16 qt = _____ gal

31. 6 c = _____ pt

32. 6 pt = _____ qt

Write the Fahrenheit temperature.

1.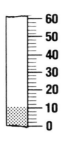

2.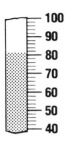

3.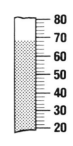

4.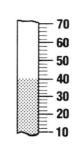

_____ _____ _____ _____

Copy and complete the chart.

	Starting temperature	Temperature change	Final temperature
5.	40°F	fell 15°	
6.	21°F	rose 12°	

Write the Celsius temperature.

7.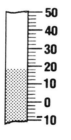

8.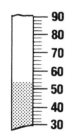

9.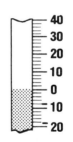

10.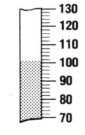

_____ _____ _____ _____

Copy and complete the chart.

	Starting temperature	Temperature change	Final temperature
11.	37°C	fell	20°C
12.		rose 6°	16°C

Use with pages 296–297.

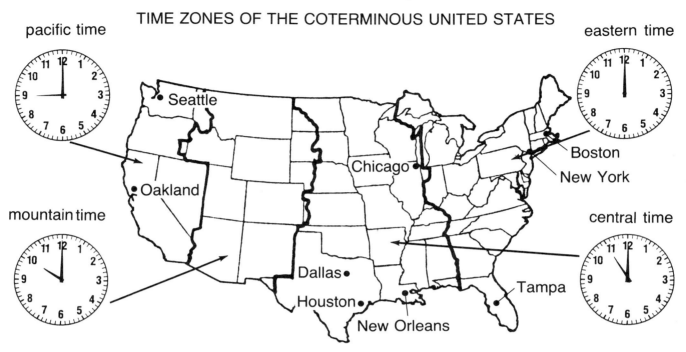

TIME ZONES OF THE COTERMINOUS UNITED STATES

pacific time

eastern time

mountain time

central time

Solve.

1. Sandy gets home from school in New York at 3:45 P.M. If his cousin in Houston also gets home at 3:45, how long does Sandy have to wait before calling her?

_____

2. A flight from Tampa, Florida, to Oakland, California, takes 6 hours. If you leave Tampa at 11:00 A.M., to what time will you have to set your watch when you arrive?

_____

3. The Chicago ball team will play a game in Seattle at 6:05 P.M., Pacific time. What time will the game begin on television in Chicago?

_____

4. If the team played in Boston at 6:00 P.M., Eastern time, what time would the game begin on television in Chicago?

_____

5. The Tra-la-la Music Company has offices in Seattle, Houston, Boston, and Chicago. If all the offices open at 9:00 A.M., what is the earliest time the manager in Boston can call all the other offices?

_____

6. All the offices of the Tra-la-la Music Company close at 5:00 P.M. nationwide. If it is 4:45 in Houston and the Houston office wants to call the Chicago office, will it still be open?

_____

Holt, Rinehart and Winston, Publishers • 5

Copy and complete the table to show each ratio three ways.

1.		5 to 6	$\frac{5}{6}$
2.	1:2		$\frac{1}{2}$
3.	15:10	15 to 10	
4.		4 to 4	$\frac{4}{4}$
5.	42:42		$\frac{42}{42}$
6.	300:500	300 to 500	

Write the ratio.

7. apples to pears _____

8. bananas to lemons _____

9. apples to lemons _____

10. pears to apples _____

11. bananas to pieces of fruit _____

12. pieces of fruit to pears _____

Write each ratio as a fraction.

13. 8 of 9

14. 2 of 5

15. 1 of 7

16. 5 of 8

_____   _____   _____   _____

17. 3 of 10

18. 9 of 25

19. 11 of 64

20. 13 of 36

_____   _____   _____   _____

21. 6 of 13

22. 4 of 11

23. 3 of 14

24. 18 of 27

_____   _____   _____   _____

What ratio am I?

25. I am the ratio of the greatest common factor of 8 and 12 to the least common multiple of 8 and 12. _____

26. I am the ratio of the greatest prime factor of 10 to the greatest prime factor of 28. _____

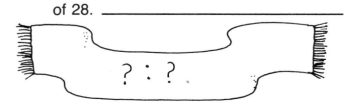

Use with pages 308–309.

Write two equal ratios.

1. $\frac{4}{5} = \frac{8}{10} =$

2. $\frac{3}{7} = \frac{6}{14} =$

3. $\frac{8}{9} = \frac{16}{18} =$

4. $\frac{7}{10} = \frac{14}{20} =$

5. $\frac{1}{2} = \frac{2}{4} =$

6. $\frac{3}{4} = \frac{6}{8} =$

Write the missing term of the equal ratio.

7. $\frac{1}{2} = \frac{}{14}$

8. $\frac{3}{8} = \frac{24}{}$

9. $\frac{5}{2} = \frac{}{10}$

10. $\frac{9}{10} = \frac{}{30}$

11. $\frac{5}{12} = \frac{}{24}$

12. $\frac{4}{6} = \frac{}{18}$

13. $\frac{7}{3} = \frac{}{21}$

14. $\frac{5}{6} = \frac{35}{}$

15. $\frac{6}{7} = \frac{}{42}$

16. $\frac{2}{9} = \frac{18}{}$

17. $\frac{1}{4} = \frac{4}{}$

18. $\frac{3}{4} = \frac{}{20}$

19. $\frac{9}{5} = \frac{}{25}$

20. $\frac{9}{4} = \frac{36}{}$

21. $\frac{5}{7} = \frac{}{63}$

22. $\frac{6}{9} = \frac{48}{}$

23. $\frac{7}{4} = \frac{}{24}$

24. $\frac{3}{2} = \frac{}{16}$

25. $\frac{8}{7} = \frac{}{35}$

26. $\frac{5}{9} = \frac{40}{}$

Write $=$ or $\neq$ for $\bigcirc$.

27. $\frac{2}{3} \bigcirc \frac{18}{24}$

28. $\frac{1}{5} \bigcirc \frac{6}{30}$

29. $\frac{7}{4} \bigcirc \frac{28}{16}$

30. $\frac{5}{8} \bigcirc \frac{40}{72}$

31. $\frac{1}{4} \bigcirc \frac{4}{16}$

32. $\frac{9}{4} \bigcirc \frac{45}{16}$

33. $\frac{1}{6} \bigcirc \frac{5}{36}$

34. $\frac{7}{21} \bigcirc \frac{1}{3}$

Write the letter of the ratio that is equal to the given ratio.

Given ratio	A	B	C	
$\frac{1}{4}$	$\frac{3}{12}$	$\frac{4}{1}$	$\frac{5}{12}$	**35.** _____
$\frac{3}{2}$	$\frac{4}{6}$	$\frac{6}{4}$	$\frac{4}{8}$	**37.** _____
$\frac{4}{7}$	$\frac{16}{28}$	$\frac{5}{8}$	$\frac{16}{21}$	**39.** _____
$\frac{8}{9}$	$\frac{18}{16}$	$\frac{13}{14}$	$\frac{72}{81}$	**41.** _____

Given ratio	A	B	C	
$\frac{2}{3}$	$\frac{14}{15}$	$\frac{8}{12}$	$\frac{3}{2}$	**36.** _____
$\frac{5}{9}$	$\frac{10}{27}$	$\frac{10}{18}$	$\frac{15}{24}$	**38.** _____
$\frac{6}{7}$	$\frac{7}{6}$	$\frac{12}{13}$	$\frac{18}{21}$	**40.** _____
$\frac{8}{5}$	$\frac{24}{15}$	$\frac{15}{10}$	$\frac{30}{25}$	**42.** _____

Solve. Write a simpler problem if you need to.

1. Irma is a postal carrier. She drives $1\frac{3}{4}$ miles to work. Her delivery route begins $\frac{1}{2}$ a mile from the post office and is $2\frac{2}{3}$ miles long. How many miles has Irma traveled when she reaches the end of her route?

2. One day, Ely's checking account shows a balance of $57.04. He writes a check for $21.50 to pay the telephone bill and a check for $15.35 to pay the electric bill. The next day, Ely deposits $243.97 in his checking account. What is his balance that day?

3. Chopin's "Waltz in C-Sharp Minor" is 3 minutes 45 seconds long. His "Waltz in E-flat" is 5 minutes 22 seconds long. His "Heroic Polonaise" is 7 minutes 3 seconds long. His "Ballade in G Minor" is 9 minutes 13 seconds long. If the 4 pieces were taped on a 30-minute cassette, how much blank time would there be left?

4. Wayne types about 55 words per minute. A typical double-spaced page contains 500 words. How long does it take Wayne to type $9\frac{1}{2}$ pages?

5. Inez earns $3.00 per hour sorting empty cans for recycling. She is saving money to buy a gift for her mother. The gift she has chosen costs $22.98. She will spend $.85 for a card and $1.25 for wrapping paper. So far, Inez has saved $6.50. How many more hours must she work in order to reach her goal?

6. Enzio bought a hunk of cheese weighing 2.64 pounds at the store. He saved half of it for the macaroni and cheese dish he will cook for dinner. He made sandwiches for himself and 5 friends with the rest. How much cheese did he use for each sandwich?

7. Ilana cut the pattern for a skirt she is sewing. The length of a panel is $28\frac{1}{2}$ inches. Of that, $\frac{5}{8}$ inch will be used for the waistband seam, $\frac{1}{4}$ inch for finishing the lower rough edge and $2\frac{1}{2}$ inches for the hem. What is the final length of the skirt?

Holt, Rinehart and Winston, Publishers • 5

Juan makes a scale drawing of Main Street.
Scale: 1 cm : 4 m

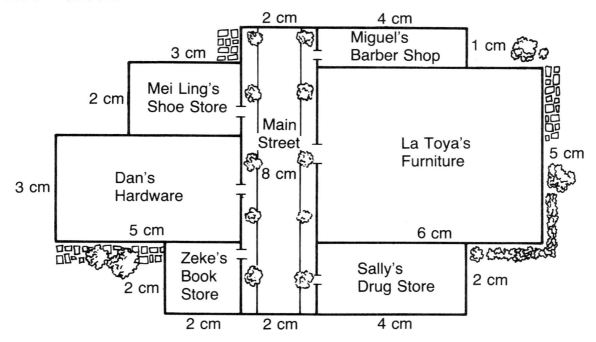

Use the scale drawing above to find the length and width of
each store.

1. Mei Ling's Shoe Store

   l = _____ ; *w* = _____

2. Miguel's Barber Shop

   l = _____ ; *w* = _____

3. La Toya's Furniture

   l = _____ ; *w* = _____

4. Sally's Drug Store

   l = _____ ; *w* = _____

5. Zeke's Book Store

   l = _____ ; *w* = _____

6. Dan's Hardware

   l = _____ ; *w* = _____

Solve.
Use the scale drawing above.

7. What is the length of the wall between
Mei Ling's Shoe Store and Dan's
Hardware?

   _____

8. The door to La Toya's Furniture is 2 m
wide. How wide would it be on the scale
drawing?

   _____

Alaskan sourdoughs were prospectors who traveled alone through the Alaskan wilderness searching for gold. They were called sourdoughs because they carried sourdough starter pots strapped to their packs. They used these pots whenever they wanted to make a batch of sourdough bread.

Alaskan Sourdough Bread

$\frac{2}{3}$ cup sourdough starter

1 pack active dry yeast

$1\frac{1}{3}$ cup warm water

$3\frac{3}{4}$ cup unsifted all-purpose flour

$2\frac{1}{8}$ teaspoon salt

$\frac{1}{2}$ teaspoon baking soda

---

1. Jenny wants to make two batches of sourdough bread. How many cups of sourdough starter will she need?

_____

2. Jenny makes two batches of the bread. How many teaspoons of salt will she need?

_____

3. Jenny has $10\frac{1}{2}$ cups of flour. Can she make 3 batches of the sourdough bread? How much more flour would she need? _____

4. Rick and Dave plan to make sourdough bread for their family-reunion picnic. They make $4\frac{1}{2}$ batches of the bread. How much flour do they need?

_____

5. Rick has a 10-lb bag of flour that equals about $18\frac{1}{2}$ cups. Will he have enough flour to make $4\frac{1}{2}$ batches of sourdough bread? _____

Holt, Rinehart and Winston, Publishers • 5

A	B	C	D

Copy the table.
Use Figures A–D to complete the table.

	Figure	Ratio of shaded part to whole	Write as "per 100"	Write using %
1.	A	26 to 100		
2.	B		7 per 100	
3.	C			58%
4.	D	83 to 100		

Write the percent.

5. $\frac{51}{100}$

_____

6. $\frac{46}{100}$

_____

7. $\frac{4}{100}$

_____

8. $\frac{19}{100}$

_____

9. 12 of 100

_____

10. 2 to 100

_____

11. 84:100

_____

12. 59:100

_____

13. 65:100

_____

14. 87 to 100

_____

15. 61 per 100

_____

16. 74 of 100

_____

17. 3 of 100

_____

18. 38:100

_____

19. 94:100

_____

20. 8 of 100

_____

21. 17 to 100

_____

22. 5:100

_____

23. 37 of 100

_____

24. 98 per 100

_____

25. a ratio of 35 to 100 _____

Write as a percent.

1. 0.42 = _____   **2.** 0.76 = _____   **3.** 0.30 = _____   **4.** 0.80 = _____

5. 0.05 = _____   **6.** 0.09 = _____   **7.** 0.1 = _____   **8.** 0.6 = _____

9. 0.62 = _____   **10.** 0.43 = _____   **11.** 0.86 = _____   **12.** 0.94 = _____

13. 0.60 = _____   **14.** 0.70 = _____   **15.** 0.5 = _____   **16.** 0.3 = _____

17. 0.04 = _____   **18.** 0.02 = _____   **19.** 0.4 = _____   **20.** 0.03 = _____

21. 0.36 = _____   **22.** 0.79 = _____   **23.** 0.07 = _____   **24.** 0.83 = _____

25. 0.73 = _____   **26.** 0.87 = _____   **27.** 0.32 = _____   **28.** 0.88 = _____

29. 0.95 = _____   **30.** 0.45 = _____   **31.** 0.18 = _____   **32.** 0.06 = _____

33. 0.8 = _____   **34.** 0.19 = _____   **35.** 0.01 = _____   **36.** 0.65 = _____

Write as a decimal or whole number.

37. 35% = _____   **38.** 76% = _____   **39.** 42% = _____   **40.** 93% = _____

41. 32% = _____   **42.** 5% = _____   **43.** 7% = _____   **44.** 10% = _____

45. 30% = _____   **46.** 52% = _____   **47.** 67% = _____   **48.** 37% = _____

49. 2% = _____   **50.** 8% = _____   **51.** 31% = _____   **52.** 20% = _____

53. 90% = _____   **54.** 14% = _____   **55.** 48% = _____   **56.** 64% = _____

57. 86% = _____   **58.** 99% = _____   **59.** 17% = _____   **60.** 24% = _____

61. 43% = _____   **62.** 53% = _____   **63.** 84% = _____   **64.** 33% = _____

Holt, Rinehart and Winston, Publishers • 5

Copy and complete the table. Write each fraction in simplest form.

	Fraction	Decimal	Percent
1.	$\frac{1}{2}$		
2.		0.25	
3.			30%
4.		0.75	
5.	$\frac{4}{5}$		
6.			60%

Write each percent as a fraction in simplest form.

7. 50% = _____   **8.** 25% = _____   **9.** 14% = _____   **10.** 60% = _____

11. 30% = _____   **12.** 11% = _____   **13.** 15% = _____   **14.** 20% = _____

Write each fraction as a percent.

15. $\frac{42}{100}$ = _____   **16.** $\frac{58}{100}$ = _____   **17.** $\frac{1}{4}$ = _____   **18.** $\frac{2}{5}$ = _____

19. $\frac{41}{50}$ = _____   **20.** $\frac{8}{25}$ = _____   **21.** $\frac{9}{20}$ = _____   **22.** $\frac{1}{2}$ = _____

23. $\frac{7}{10}$ = _____   **24.** $\frac{19}{50}$ = _____   **25.** $\frac{10}{25}$ = _____   **26.** $\frac{3}{4}$ = _____

Solve.

27. Anthony is painting his apartment. He has finished $\frac{3}{5}$ of it. What percent of his apartment has he painted?   _____

28. Fran has completed 40% of the new patio which she is building. What fraction of the patio has she completed?   _____

Holt, Rinehart and Winston, Publishers • 5

PRACTICE — Percent of a Number

Find the percent of each number.

1. 20% of 70 = _____
2. 50% of 30 = _____
3. 70% of 240 = _____

4. 40% of 100 = _____
5. 9% of 1,400 = _____
6. 4% of 200 = _____

7. 3% of 3,600 = _____
8. 10% of 250 = _____
9. 28% of 300 = _____

10. 90% of 130 = _____
11. 76% of 500 = _____
12. 1% of 1,200 = _____

13. 34% of 400 = _____
14. 70% of 20 = _____
15. 43% of 200 = _____

16. 30% of 120 = _____
17. 5% of 100 = _____
18. 8% of 300 = _____

19. 2% of 1,600 = _____
20. 52% of 400 = _____
21. 65% of 20 = _____

22. 12% of 450 = _____
23. 40% of 160 = _____
24. 6% of 150 = _____

25. 60% of 180 = _____
26. 74% of 200 = _____
27. 95% of 60 = _____

28. 300% of 100 = _____
29. 50% of 12 = _____
30. 20% of 50 = _____

Copy the answer boxes and numbers.
Which animal wouldn't you trust?

7   36   198   80   54   98   12   150

Solve. Complete each equation. Write the letter in the box
that has the same number as the equation answer to solve
the riddle.

C   30% of 120 = _____

A   10% of 70 = _____

E   40% of 200 = _____

H   75% of 200 = _____

E   60% of 90 = _____

T   70% of 140 = _____

H   99% of 200 = _____

A   20% of 60 = _____

Use with pages 324–325.

Find the percent that each part is of the whole.

1. 3 dimes
10 coins

_____% are dimes.

2. 4 red cars
16 cars

_____% are red.

3. 5 mysteries
25 books

_____% are mysteries.

4. 6 oak trees
12 trees

_____% are oak.

5. 2 roses
20 flowers

_____% are roses.

6. 4 horses
100 animals

_____% are horses.

Compute.

7. What percent
of 25 is 10?
_____

8. 14 is what
percent of
28? _____

9. What percent
of 30 is 6?
_____

10. 36 is what
percent of
48? _____

11. 27 is what
percent of
45? _____

12. What percent
of 70 is 21?
_____

13. 44 is what
percent of
55? _____

14. 23 is what
percent of
50? _____

15. What percent
of 80 is 24?
_____

16. 75 is what
percent of
300? _____

17. What percent
of 40 is 2?
_____

18. 10 is what
percent of
1,000?
_____

What percent is the first number of the second?

19. 12, 30 _____ **20.** 16, 25 _____ **21.** 19, 50 _____ **22.** 32, 40 _____

23. 16, 64 _____ **24.** 3, 60 _____ **25.** 45, 90 _____ **26.** 14, 35 _____

Solve.

27. The flag of Mathmania has 60 stars. Of these, 36 are blue. What percent of the stars are blue?

_____

28. The flag has 20 stripes. There are 6 red stripes. What percent of the stripes are not red?

_____

Answer *true* or *false*.

1. The part of a circle graph that represents $\frac{1}{3}$ is smaller than the part that represents 50%. _____

2. If a circle graph were divided into 5 unequal parts, each part would be 20% of the whole. _____

Use the circle graph to solve.

3. What proportion of the world's telephones shown in the graph are used in specific countries? _____

4. In which country are the greatest number of telephones in use?

_____

5. To the nearest million, how many more telephones are in use in the United Kingdom than in the Soviet Union?

_____

TELEPHONES IN USE WORLDWIDE

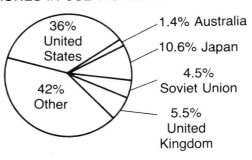

Total—508,286,000

6. Of the countries shown, which has the smallest percentage of telephones in use?

_____

Use both circle graphs to solve.

MONEY SPENT BY UNITED STATES
TOURISTS IN EUROPE

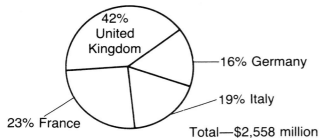

Total—$2,558 million

7. Was more money spent by American tourists visiting Europe or by Europeans visiting the United States?

_____

9. In which 2 countries combined did American tourists spend about as much as they did in the United Kingdom?

_____

MONEY SPENT BY EUROPEAN
TOURISTS IN THE UNITED STATES

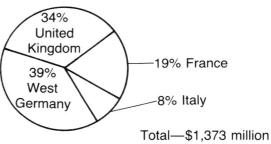

Total—$1,373 million

8. Who spent more money, American tourists visiting France or German tourists visiting the United States?

_____

10. How much more money was spent by Americans visiting Europe than by Europeans visiting the United States?

_____

Use with pages 328–329.

Identify and name each figure.

1.

_____

2.

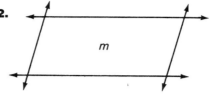

_____

3.

_____

4.

_____

5.

_____

6.

_____

7. Name all the rays. _____

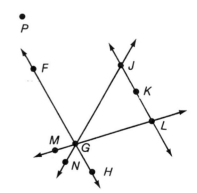

Copy points *P*, *Q*, *R*, and *S* at the right.

8. Draw $\overline{PR}$.

9. Draw $\overrightarrow{PQ}$.

10. Draw $\overleftrightarrow{PS}$ intersecting $\overleftrightarrow{QS}$.

11. Draw $\overline{QR}$.

Complete. Use the diagram to answer.

12. Name all the lines. _____

13. Name three points on $\overleftrightarrow{JL}$. _____

14. Name the point where $\overleftrightarrow{JN}$ intersects $\overleftrightarrow{LM}$.

_____

15. Name two parallel lines.

_____

16. Name two rays with endpoint *K*. _____

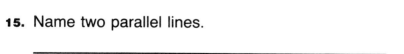

Are the lines perpendicular? Write *yes* or *no*.

1.
_____

2.
_____

3.
_____

4.
_____

Give three different names for each angle.

5.
_____
_____
_____

6.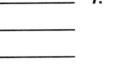
_____
_____
_____

7.
_____
_____
_____

Name the vertex, the sides, and the angle.

8.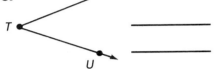
_____
_____
_____

9.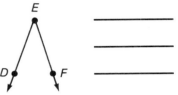
_____
_____
_____

Write whether the angle is *right, acute, obtuse,* or *straight.*

10.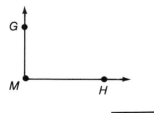
_____

11.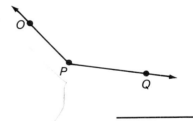
_____

12.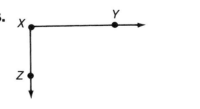
_____

13.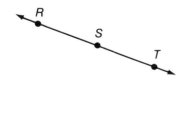
_____

14.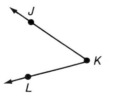
_____

15.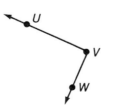
_____

Use with pages 342–343.

Use a protractor to measure the angle.

1.

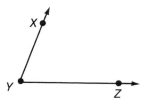

_____

2.

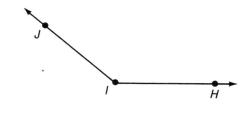

_____

3.

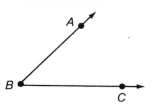

_____

4.

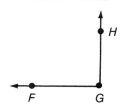

_____

5.

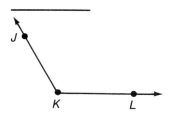

_____

6.

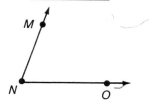

_____

7.

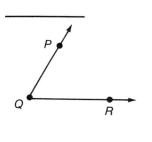

_____

8.

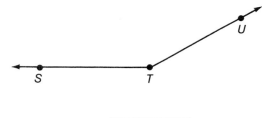

_____

Draw each angle.

9. 35°

10. 125°

Name each triangle, and write if it is *equilateral*, *isosceles*, or *scalene*.

1.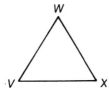

2.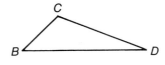

3.

_____   _____   _____

Name each triangle, and write if it is *right*, *obtuse*, or *acute*.

4.

5.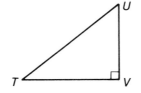

6.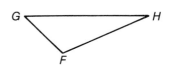

_____   _____   _____

Write the measure of the missing angle.

7.

80°   80°

8.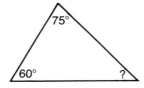

75°   60°   ?

9.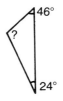

46°   ?   24°

_____   _____   _____

10. Use the figure to complete.

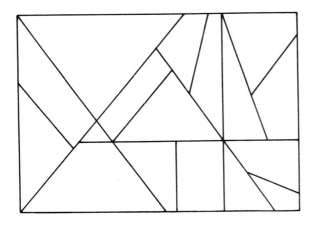

How many triangles? _____

How many are right triangles? _____

Holt, Rinehart and Winston, Publishers • 5

Use with pages 346–347.

Solve by finding the pattern.

1. Dennis and Lulu went on a trip to Mexico. They were admiring some tiles on a building in the market at Oaxaca when they noticed a pattern of yellow tiles. First, there were 2 tiles, then 4 tiles, then 6 tiles. Lulu saw that the pattern 2, 4, 6, continued. What are the next three numbers of tiles in the pattern?

2. During the trip, Dennis used a tape recorder to practice his Spanish every day for 9 days. His schedule for the first 3 days was 15, 20, and 22 minutes. He continued this pattern for 4 more days. Then, he added to the pattern 5 minutes a day for 2 more days. For how many minutes did Dennis practice on the fourth, fifth, sixth, and seventh days? For how many minutes a day did he practice on the last 2 days?

3. Lulu decided to learn how to make Spanish lace. For one pattern, she tatted 3 stitches, then 6 stitches, then 5 stitches, then 8 stitches, then 7 stitches, and so on. What are the next 5 numbers in this pattern? What is the pattern?

4. Lulu made up some lace patterns of her own. She gave each pattern a name and wrote the names in a particular order. Her first 5 patterns, listed in order, were Amour, Beau, Combo, Daisy, and Earl. Her next 2 patterns were Garland and Fancy. Add them to the list in the proper place order she most likely orginally wrote them.

5. Dennis and Lulu both took tennis lessons. Lulu could hit 5 balls for every 6 balls served. Dennis could hit 4 balls for every 6 balls served. If Lulu hit 20 balls, how many balls were served to her? How many balls could Dennis hit of the same number of balls served to Lulu?

6. Lulu and Dennis were sitting at their window watching the excursion boats leave from the harbor. A boat left at 8:15 A.M., 8:45 A.M., 9:17 A.M., and 9:51 A.M. At what times did the next two excursion boats leave? How many minutes apart did they leave?

7. Dennis kept track of when the sun set each night they spent in Acapulco. It set at 7:00 P.M., 7:03 P.M., 7:06 P.M., and 7:09 P.M. How many more nights went by before it set at 7:18 P.M.?

8. Dennis was very late for lunch, and Lulu passed the time waiting for him by eating guacamole and tortilla chips. She ate 1 chip in 5 minutes, then 3 chips in the next 5 minutes. How many chips did she eat in the following 5 minutes?

Holt, Rinehart and Winston, Publishers • 5

Solve by finding the pattern.

9. Dennis and Lulu found a diagram of an ancient Aztec ritual. The arrows show how many squares a warrior danced forward and how many squares he danced back before going forward again. Complete the diagram. What is the pattern?

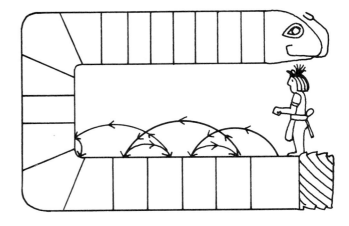

_____

_____

_____

10. In one ancient storehouse, Dennis found some markings on a wall showing the count of sacks of grain and cocoa. The first marks indicate 2 sacks of grain and 1 of cocoa. Draw the next two tallies of grain and cocoa. What was the ratio of grain to cocoa?

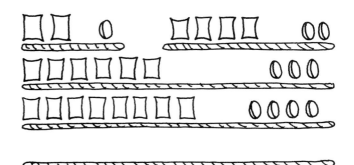

_____

11. Lulu saw an ancient tally. A friend explained that the slash marks were used to record the amount of corn harvested. The circles showed how much corn was used that year. Part of the tally was destroyed. If the pattern continued, what would the missing tally have been? Complete it. What fraction of the corn was used? What fraction was left?

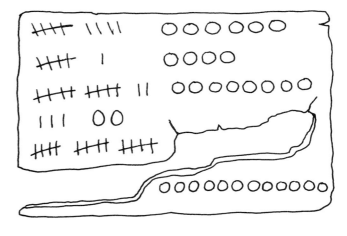

_____

Holt, Rinehart and Winston, Publishers • 5

Use with pages 348–349.

Name the polygon.

1.

2.

3.

4.

_____

_____

_____

_____

5.

6.

7.

8.

_____

_____

_____

_____

Identify the polygon.

9. a ten-sided figure _____

10. a six-sided figure that has all sides and angles equal _____

11. a quadrilateral that has four right angles and four equal sides _____

12. a three-sided figure _____

Trace each figure.
Draw all the diagonals from point *C*.

13.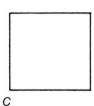

14.

15.

Trace each figure.
Draw all the diagonals from each vertex.

16.

17.

Holt, Rinehart and Winston, Publishers • 5

Write *chord*, *radius*, or *diameter* for the given segment.

1.

_____

2.

_____

3.

_____

4.

_____

5.

_____

6.

_____

7.

_____

8.

_____

Write the diameter of a circle with the given radius.

9. 1 cm   **10.** 3 cm   **11.** 5 cm   **12.** 10 cm   **13.** 28 cm

_____   _____   _____   _____   _____

Write the radius of a circle with the given diameter.

14. 6 cm   **15.** 12 cm   **16.** 20 cm   **17.** 28 cm   **18.** 60 cm

_____   _____   _____   _____   _____

Use a ruler and a compass to draw a circle that has a

19. radius of 3 cm.   **20.** diameter of 4 cm.

Use with pages 352–353.

Use the time-zone map, the circle graph, or the schedule at the right to solve.

pacific time mountain time central time eastern time

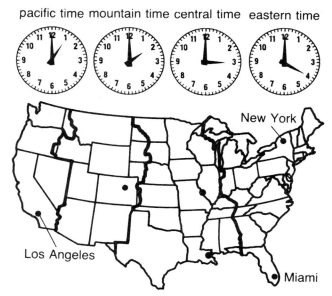

DESTINATIONS OF SKYHAPPY FLIGHTS

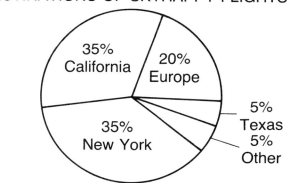

1. Maria flies from New York and arrives in Denver 4 hours later. If her watch showed 2:15 P.M. when she left New York, what time did it show when she reached Denver? For how many hours will she have to set her watch back?

_____

2. Don flies from Los Angeles, California, to Miami, Florida, in 5 hours and 15 min. He left Los Angeles at noon. What time did he arrive in Miami?

_____

3. Skyhappy Airlines plans to discontinue its flights to Europe and divert those planes to New York and California. If the flights to Europe are divided equally, what percent of all Skyhappy flights will go to New York? What percent will go to California?

_____

4. What percent of all current flights do not go to New York or California?

_____

5. If the flight from New York to Los Angeles stops in St. Louis for 45 minutes, how long is the flying time?

_____

6. How much longer does it take to fly to New Orleans than it takes to fly to St. Louis?

_____

SKYHAPPY AIRLINE FLIGHTS FROM NEW YORK

Leave New York	Arrive	Time
8:30 A.M.	St. Louis	12:00 noon
8:30 A.M.	New Orleans	1:00 P.M.
8:45 A.M.	Atlanta	12:30 P.M.
9:00 A.M.	Miami	3:30 P.M.
10:00 A.M.	Dallas	3:00 P.M.
1:00 P.M.	Phoenix	6:00 P.M.
1:00 P.M.	Denver	5:00 P.M.
1:00 P.M.	Billings	5:15 P.M.
1:15 P.M.	Los Angeles	8:15 P.M.
2:00 P.M.	Seattle	9:00 P.M.

Solve.

7. Mary is spending 2 days in Billings, Montana. She can spend $82 for food and entertainment. If she spends $20 a day for food, how much money will she have left for her entertainment?

_____

8. Mary can spend $100 during her 2 nights in Billings. She has decided to add any money that she doesn't have to pay the hotel to her entertainment fund. If the hotel costs $45 a night, how much money can she add to the fund?

_____

Use the recipe at the right to solve.

9. If Ralph wants to expand the recipe to feed 5 people, how many more carrots must he add? What fraction of a pound of beef must he add?

_____

10. If Ralph makes enough goulash to feed 9 people, how much chicken stock must he have? how many onions? how much oil?

_____

> Ralph's Hungarian Goulash (serves 3)
>
> 1 lb lean beef, cubed
> 3 carrots, sliced
> 1 cup tomato puree
> 1 pint sour cream
> 1 cup chicken stock
> 2 medium onions, chopped
> 3 tablespoons olive oil
> 1 tablespoon paprika
> salt and pepper to taste

Solve.

11. James is taking Skyhappy Airlines to Borneo. A round-trip ticket cost him $680. Instead of flying back home from Borneo, he cashes in half of his ticket and flies to Buenos Aires. If his ticket to Buenos Aires cost him $200, how much money did the airline refund to him?

_____

12. James gets a job in Buenos Aires. He makes $9 per hour. He works from 8:00 A.M. to 4:00 P.M. and takes two 45-minute breaks. How much money does he earn each night if he is not paid for his breaks?

_____

13. James finds that a plane ticket from Buenos Aires to his home costs $600. He has the $140 refund and $292.50 that he saved from his wages. How much more money does he need for his plane ticket?

_____

14. When James arrived home, he took 6 rolls of film to be developed and printed. It costs him $7.25 a roll for prints. Later, he finds a store that will develop film for $6.30 a roll. How much money would James have saved if he had taken his film to the cheaper place?

_____

Use with pages 354–355.

Is the line segment congruent to $\overline{RS}$?
Write *yes* or *no*. Use a ruler to measure. Trace to check.

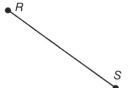 **1.** 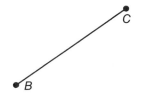 **2.**  **3.**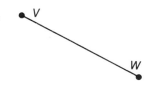

_____   _____   _____

Is the angle congruent to $\angle M$? Write *yes* or *no*.
Use a protractor to measure. Trace to check.

4. 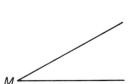 **5.**   **6.**

_____   _____   _____

Is the figure congruent to Figure *JKLM*? Write *yes* or *no*.
Use a protractor and ruler to measure the angles and sides.
Trace to check.

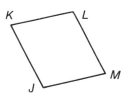 **7.**   **8.** 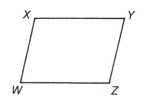 **9.**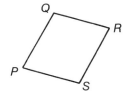

_____   _____   _____

$\triangle ABC$ is congruent to $\triangle FGH$. Write the corresponding angle
or side.

10. $\overline{AB} \cong$ _____   **11.** $\overline{BC} \cong$ _____

12. $\angle B \cong$ _____   **13.** $\overline{FH} \cong$ _____

14. $\angle H \cong$ _____   **15.** $\angle A \cong$ _____

Is the dotted line a line of symmetry? Write *yes* or *no*.

1.

_____

2.
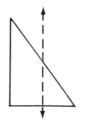
_____

3.
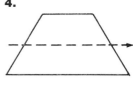
_____

4.

_____

Trace each figure. Draw all lines of symmetry for each figure.
Then count the lines.

5.

_____

6.

_____

7.

_____

8.

_____

9.
_____

10.
_____

Trace and complete each figure so that the dotted line is a
line of symmetry.

11.
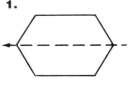

12.
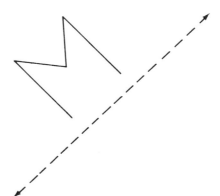

1. Name the figure that is similar to *GHIJK*. _____

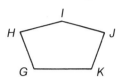 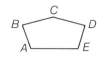 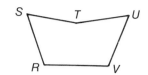

2. Name the triangle that is similar to △*QRS*. _____

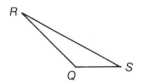 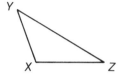 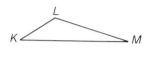 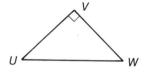

Figure *LMNO* is similar to figure *CDEF*.
Use this information to answer Questions 3–5.

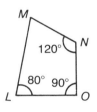 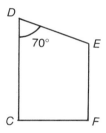

3. Find the measure of ∠*M* _____

4. Find the measure of ∠*E* _____

5. Find the measure of ∠*C* _____

Write *true* or *false*.

6. All equilateral triangles are similar. _____

7. All rectangles are similar. _____

8. All regular pentagons are similar. _____

Ari wants to carpet the den, which is the same shape as the
garage, but half the size. Trace the smaller figure and draw a
floor plan of the den.

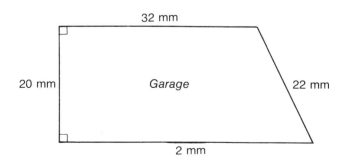

Name the ordered pair for each point.

1. G _____
2. N _____

3. L _____
4. H _____

5. S _____
6. O _____

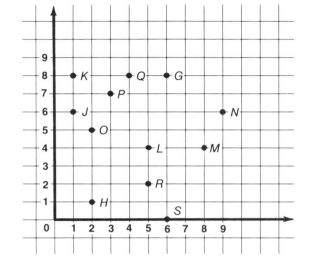

Name the point for each ordered pair.

7. (8,4) _____
8. (3,7) _____

9. (1,6) _____
10. (5,2) _____

11. (4,8) _____
12. (1,8) _____

Use graph paper to make a grid like the one on the right. Graph the points for each figure. Then connect the points in order for each figure.

Figure ABCD:
A(1,9); B(3,13); C(5,9); D(3,5)

Figure EFGH:
E(8,1); F(7,3); G(8,5); H(9,3)

Are the two figures similar?

_____

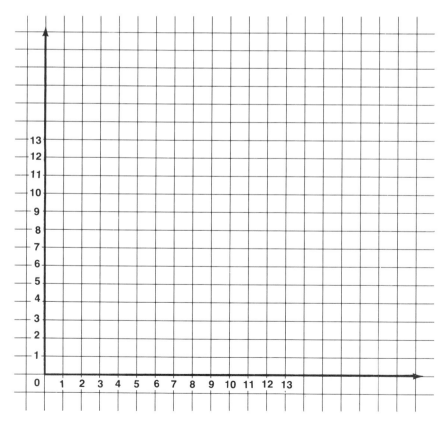

Holt, Rinehart and Winston, Publishers • 5

Use with pages 362–363.

Find the perimeter of each figure.

1.

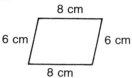

8 cm
6 cm | 6 cm
8 cm

_____

2.

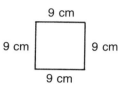

9 cm
9 cm | 9 cm
9 cm

_____

3.

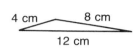

4 cm | 8 cm
12 cm

_____

4.

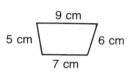

9 cm
5 cm | 6 cm
7 cm

_____

5.

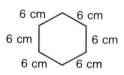

6 cm | 6 cm
6 cm | 6 cm
6 cm | 6 cm

_____

6.

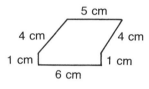

5 cm
4 cm | 4 cm
1 cm | 1 cm
6 cm

_____

Use a centimeter ruler to find the perimeter of each figure.

7.

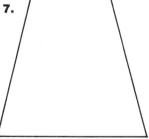

Perimeter: _____

8.

Perimeter: _____

9.

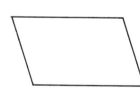

Perimeter: _____

Find the perimeter.

10. a rectangle whose sides measure 8 cm, 3 cm, 8 cm, and 3 cm

_____

11. a pentagon with each side 7 cm

_____

12. a polygon whose sides measure 6 cm, 4 cm, 8 cm, 2 cm, and 5 cm

_____

13. a triangle whose sides measure 16 cm, 18 cm, and 20 cm

_____

Count to find the area.

1.

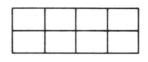

_____ square units

2.

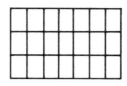

_____ square units

3.

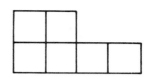

_____ square units

Multiply to find the area.

4.

4 cm

8 cm

_____ cm²

5.

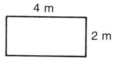

4 m

2 m

_____ m²

6.

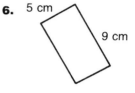

5 cm

9 cm

_____ cm²

7.

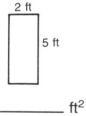

2 ft

5 ft

_____ ft²

8.

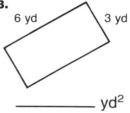

6 yd   3 yd

_____ yd²

9.

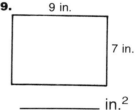

9 in.

7 in.

_____ in.²

Multiply to find the area of the rectangle or square.

10. *l* = 8 cm, *w* = 3 cm

Area = _____

11. *l* = 9 cm, *w* = 2 cm

Area = _____

12. *l* = 10 in., *w* = 10 in.

Area = _____

13. *l* = 4 ft, *w* = 2 ft

Area = _____

14. *l* = 12 in., *w* = 9 in.

Area = _____

15. *l* = 10 m, *w* = 4 m

Area = _____

Holt, Rinehart and Winston, Publishers • 5

Area of Triangles

Count to find the area.

1.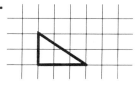

_____ square units

2.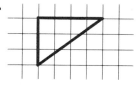

_____ square units

3.

_____ square units

Multiply to find the area.

4.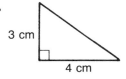

3 cm

4 cm

_____ cm²

5.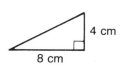

4 cm

8 cm

_____ cm²

6.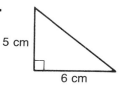

5 cm

6 cm

_____ cm²

7.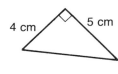

4 cm   5 cm

_____ cm²

8.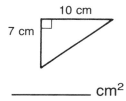

10 cm

7 cm

_____ cm²

9.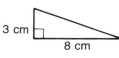

3 cm

8 cm

_____ cm²

10.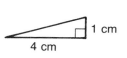

1 cm

4 cm

_____ cm²

11.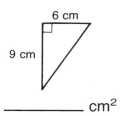

6 cm

9 cm

_____ cm²

Copy and complete the chart.

A TRIANGLE:

	Base	Height	Area
12.	5 ft	4 ft	_____ ft²
13.	3 cm	10 cm	_____ cm²
14.	7 mi	2 mi	_____ mi²
15.	3 m	12 m	_____ m²
16.	2 cm	5 cm	_____ cm²
17.	11 in.	4 in.	_____ in.²
18.	6 ft	6 ft	_____ ft²

Use with pages 368–369.

Write the letter for the correct number sentence.

1. The Nile River is 6,671 kilometers long. The Congo River is 4,667 kilometers long. How much longer is the Nile River than the Congo River?
   a. $6{,}671 + 4{,}667 = n$
   b. $6{,}671 - 4{,}667 = n$
   c. $6{,}671 \div 4{,}667 = n$

2. The Niagara River forms a border between the United States and Canada. It is only 35 miles long. The Rhine River in Europe is 20 times longer than the Niagara River. How long is the Rhine River?
   a. $35 + 20 = n$
   b. $35 - 20 = n$
   c. $35 \times 20 = n$

Write the number sentence and solve.

3. Pike's Peak in Colorado is 14,110 feet above sea level. This mountain is far inland, and its peak rises only 9,000 feet above the surface of the nearby Great Plains. How much above sea level are the Great Plains of Colorado?

_____

4. Mount Everest is the highest mountain in the world. It is 8,848 meters above sea level. It is 2,951 meters higher than Mount Cotopaxi, the highest active volcano in the world. How high is Mount Cotopaxi?

_____

5. Mount Mitchell, the highest peak in the Appalachian Mountains, is 6,684 feet. John and Mary have climbed 4,295 feet. How much farther do they have to climb to reach the top?

_____

6. Jennifer Holmes and Jeff Bunge are going to canoe down the Pine River. If they travel at a speed of 6 miles per hour, how many miles will they canoe in 3 hours?

_____

7. On a 5-day canoe trip, each person is allowed to bring 1 backpack that weighs about 65 pounds. How many people take the canoe trip if the total weight of the backpacks is 780 pounds?

_____

8. A boat takes 80 hours to go downriver from Khartoum, Sudan, to Cairo, Egypt. The trip back upriver takes 120 hours. How long will it take to complete one round trip?

_____

Holt, Rinehart and Winston, Publishers • 5

Use with pages 370–371.

Name the solid figure that is shaped like the object.

1.

_____

2.

_____

3.

_____

4.

_____

5.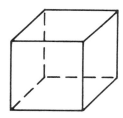

_____

6.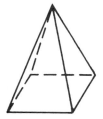

_____

7.

_____

8.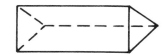

_____

Count the number of faces, edges, and vertices each figure has.

9.

_____ faces

_____ edges

_____ vertices

10.

_____ faces

_____ edges

_____ vertices

11.

_____ faces

_____ edges

_____ vertices

Copy and complete the table.

	Number of faces	Number of edges	Number of vertices
Triangular pyramid	**12.** _____	**13.** _____	**14.** _____
Rectangular prism	**15.** _____	**16.** _____	**17.** _____
Pentagonal prism	**18.** _____	**19.** _____	**20.** _____

Holt, Rinehart and Winston, Publishers • 5

PRACTICE Volume

Find the volume of each.

1.

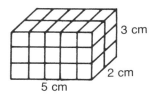

3 cm
2 cm
5 cm

_____

2.

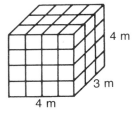

4 m
3 m
4 m

_____

3.

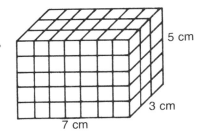

5 cm
3 cm
7 cm

_____

4.

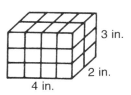

3 in.
2 in.
4 in.

_____

5.

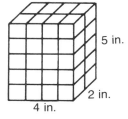

5 in.
2 in.
4 in.

_____

6.

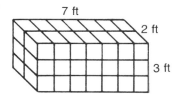

7 ft
2 ft
3 ft

_____

7.

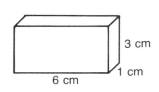

3 cm
1 cm
6 cm

_____

8.

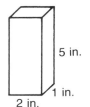

5 in.
1 in.
2 in.

_____

9.

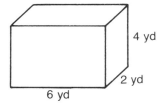

4 yd
2 yd
6 yd

_____

Copy and complete the table. Use the formula $V = l \times w \times h$.

RECTANGULAR PRISMS

Length (*l*)	Width (*w*)	Height (*h*)	Volume (*V*)
7 in.	2 in.	1 in.	**10.** _____
10 yd	4 yd	5 yd	**11.** _____
6 mi	4 mi	7 mi	**12.** _____
11 m	2 m	6 m	**13.** _____

Holt, Rinehart and Winston, Publishers • 5

Use with pages 374–375.

Solve.

1. Each year thousands of people immigrate to the United States. This table gives the number of immigrants to the United States from 1975 to 1979. Copy and complete the bar graph. Use the data in the table and round the number of immigrants to the nearest ten thousand.

IMMIGRATION

Year	Number of immigrants	Rounded numbers
1975	386,194	
1976	398,613	
1977	462,315	
1978	601,442	
1979	460,348	

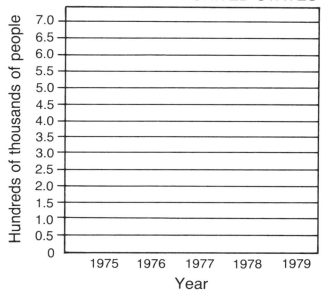

IMMIGRATION TO THE UNITED STATES

2. In 1980, the U.S. Bureau of the Census calculated the most populous cities. The table shows the four largest cities. Make a bar graph to show the data. Round the populations to a convenient place.

CITY POPULATIONS

City	Population	Rounded numbers
New York City	16,120,023	
Los Angeles	11,496,206	
Chicago	7,868,246	
Philadelphia	5,548,789	

Holt, Rinehart and Winston, Publishers • 5

Solve.

1. This table shows how many miles four people run in one week. Copy and complete the pictograph to show the number of miles each person runs in one week. Let 🚶 = 6 miles. Let 🚶 = 3 miles.

Person	Miles run in one week
Larry	30 miles
Kirk	18 miles
Lisa	36 miles
Debbie	45 miles

MILES RUN IN ONE WEEK

🚶 = 6 miles	🚶 = 3 miles
Person	**Number of miles**
Larry	🚶🚶🚶
Kirk	🚶
Lisa	🚶
Debbie	🚶

2. The Running Deer Shoe Company is designing a new line of sneakers. The Jaguar is made for basketball players, the Olympian for runners, and the Buddy Smith for tennis players. The company is also producing a sneaker called the Walking Deer for older people, and one called the Little Deer for children. Let 👟 = 100,000 sneakers produced and 👟 = 50,000. Copy and complete the pictograph to show the number of sneakers produced in one year.

SNEAKERS PRODUCED IN ONE YEAR

Jaguar	350,000
Olympian	300,000
Buddy Smith	250,000
Walking Deer	500,000
Little Deer	150,000

SNEAKERS PRODUCED IN ONE YEAR

👟 = 100,000 produced	👟 = 50,000 produced
Jaguar	
Olympian	
Buddy Smith	
Walking Deer	
Little Deer	

Holt, Rinehart and Winston, Publishers • 5

Use with pages 386–387.

1. Each year many thousands of dollars are spent to buy dogs. Copy and complete the broken-line graph to show dog sales in the United States.

UNITED STATES SALES OF DOGS

1980	$200,000
1981	$600,000
1982	$300,000
1983	$200,000
1984	$500,000
1985	$400,000
1986	$300,000

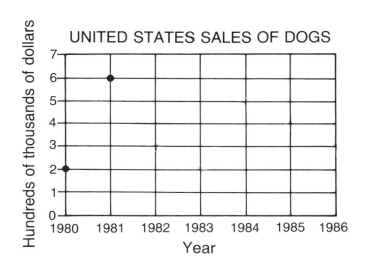

UNITED STATES SALES OF DOGS

2. Use the data in the table to make a broken-line graph to show sales at the Puppy Town Pet Store.

SALES AT PUPPY TOWN PET STORE

1980	$15,000
1981	$20,000
1982	$25,000
1983	$30,000
1984	$40,000
1985	$35,000

Use the graphs below to answer the questions.

BICYCLES SOLD BY THE CYCLORAMA CO.   BICYCLES SOLD BY THE BIKELAND CO.

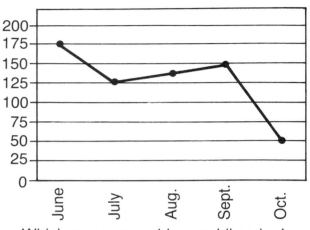
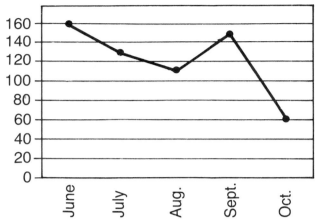

1. Which company sold more bikes in June, Cyclorama or Bikeland?

_____

2. Which company sold more bikes in August? How many more?

_____

3. Did Bikeland sell more bikes in August or September? How many more?

_____

4. Are the summer months good or bad for bicycle sales?

_____

5. In which month did Cyclorama and Bikeland have nearly the same number of sales?

_____

6. Which company had a sharper drop in sales in October?

_____

7. Which company had the sharpest increase in sales in a single month? Which month was it? How many more bikes did they sell than the month before?

_____

Holt, Rinehart and Winston, Publishers • 5

Use with pages 390–391.

First write the mean. Then write the median.

		Mean	Median			Mean	Median
1.	7, 6, 5	_____	_____	**2.**	6, 17, 26, 3, 8	_____	_____
3.	23, 11, 17, 4, 20	_____	_____	**4.**	70, 32, 68, 15, 25	_____	_____
5.	3, 7, 1, 5, 9	_____	_____	**6.**	9, 3, 12	_____	_____
7.	44, 16, 22, 8, 10	_____	_____	**8.**	5, 2, 22, 7, 19	_____	_____

First write the mode. Then write the range.

		Mode	Range			Mode	Range
9.	14, 3, 27, 62, 3, 42	_____	_____	**10.**	79, 24, 18, 24, 5, 10	_____	_____
11.	91, 86, 17, 17, 23, 59	_____	_____	**12.**	33, 66, 77, 22, 33	_____	_____
13.	203, 118, 154, 3, 203	_____	_____	**14.**	5, 25, 5, 35, 5, 75	_____	_____
15.	62, 26, 62, 216, 21, 61	_____	_____	**16.**	1, 11, 1, 11, 1, 1	_____	_____

Solve.

17. Each week, the Armstrong family reads quite a few books from the local library. This year, the Armstrongs have read 40 novels, 33 sports books, 42 science books, 67 children's books, and 33 biographies. What is the mean number of books read?

_____

18. Mrs. Armstrong works at the local library. It is her job to record the number of books borrowed each day. On Monday, 27 people checked out books. On Tuesday and Wednesday, 30 people borrowed books each day. On Thursday, 46 people borrowed books, and on Friday, 37 people borrowed books. What is the mean number of books borrowed? What is the mode?

_____

Solve. Use a tree diagram if needed.

1. The members of the Science Club decide to create a club banner. The cloth for the banner could be blue, brown, yellow, green, gold, or white. The letters for the banner could be white, black, or blue. How many combinations of cloth and letters are possible?

2. For Science Day the club wants to create an exhibit on three of the original Mercury astronauts: Scott Carpenter, John Glenn, and Gus Grissom. The exhibit will show scenes from the lives of these astronauts using a VCR, a slide projector, or a movie projector. The club decides to use a different piece of equipment for each astronaut. How many combinations are possible?

3. In addition to the exhibit, 5 members of the club want to give reports on famous American scientists and inventors. They have information on Benjamin Franklin, Thomas Jefferson, George Washington Carver, Thomas Edison, Rachel Carson, and An Wang. How many possibilities are there?

4. For the club outing, the members must decide to go to the Space Museum or to the Museum of Natural History. In either place, they can attend a lecture, see a film, or see a special exhibit. What are their choices?

Holt, Rinehart and Winston, Publishers • 5

Use with pages 394–395.

Make a tree diagram to solve each problem.

1. The Hyatt family is planning a wilderness vacation. They are thinking about going to one of three places: Yellowstone National Park, Grand Canyon National Park, or Grand Teton National Park. Once they have decided where they will go, the Hyatts must decide what they would most like to do there. They can go camping, backpacking, or white-water rafting. What are all the choices they have?

2. The Hyatts decide to go rafting. They can take a 2-day trip, a 5-day trip, or a 1-week trip down the Yellowstone River, the Lewis River, the Snake River, or the Gibbon River. What are their choices?

3. One morning, the Hyatts decide to have lunch at the Snake River Lodge. They can order one item from each group for lunch.

Group *A*	Group *B*	Group *C*
baked ham	green beans	fruit cup
veal chops	tossed salad	tapioca
chicken saute		melon medley

What combinations of food can they order from the menu?

Holt, Rinehart and Winston, Publishers • 5

Celia bought some beads at the Make-It-Yourself Jewelry
Store. In a bag, she brought home 2 orange beads, 1 yellow
bead, 3 red beads, and 2 blue beads. Suppose Celia picks a
bead from the bag without looking.

1. How many equally likely outcomes are there? _____

2. What is the probability of picking a yellow bead? _____

3. What is the probability of picking a blue bead? _____

4. What is the probability of picking a red bead? _____

Suppose you are playing a game. Imagine the cards are all
placed in a hat. You pick one card. Then you return it.

Jump up and down three times.	Get each player a glass of juice.
Get each player a glass of juice.	Each player gets you a glass of juice.
Do a household chore for the player on your right.	The player on your left does a household chore for you.
The player on your left does a household chore for you.	Jump up and down three times.
Pick the next game.	The player on your left does a household chore for you.

Find the probability for each event. Write a fraction for each
probability.

What is the probability of

5. doing a household chore? _____

6. picking the next game? _____

7. jumping up and down three times? _____

8. having someone do a household chore for you? _____

9. having another player do something for you? _____

10. getting each player a glass of juice? _____

Holt, Rinehart and Winston, Publishers • 5

Use with pages 396–397.

Predict the probability of each event below.
Write *certain* or *impossible* for each event.
There are 12 beads in a can: 6 beads are
white and 6 beads are green.
What is the probability of picking

1. a blue bead? _____

2. a white or green bead? _____

3. a green or white bead? _____

4. a yellow bead? _____

The 6 sides of this cube each have a
different letter: *A, B, C, D, E,* or *F.* Suppose
you toss the cube and note which letter
comes out on top.

5. What is the probability that the letter on
top is *C*? _____

6. What is the probability that the letter
on top is a vowel? _____

Suppose you toss the cube 60 times. Predict the number of
times the letter on top will be

7. *C* _____

8. *X* _____

9. a vowel _____

10. *E* _____

11. before *G* in the alphabet _____

Solve.

12. Hector builds a maze for his guinea pig.
The maze has 3 ways to escape and 10
ways to get lost. What is the probability
of Hector's guinea pig finding its way
through the maze?

_____

13. While Hector cleaned the cage, his
guinea pig got lost in the house. There
are 2 doors leading outside, 2 doors
leading upstairs, and 1 door to the
cellar. Is the guinea pig as likely to go
upstairs as to go outside?

_____

Holt, Rinehart and Winston, Publishers • 5

Make a list to solve.

1. Dr. Thinkhard is working on a formula for seedless raspberries. He knows the correct formula is a combination of agents W, X, Y, and Z, but he doesn't know the correct order of the agents. How many possible orders are there?

_____

2. Next weekend, Dr. Thinkhard plans to have a garage sale. He sets up a display of his old test tubes, beakers, and bunsen burners and makes a sign—"Any two for $1.00." What are all the possible pairs of objects people could buy for $1.00? (HINT: Remember that people could buy two of the same item.)

_____

Make a table to solve.

3. To test his formula for seedless raspberries, Dr. Thinkhard made a few batches. He discovered he could make a batch of formula in 0.8 hours. How long would it take him to make 3 batches? How many batches could he make in 4.8 hours?

_____

_____

4. Not every batch of the new raspberry formula was successful. Of the first 8 batches, 6 produced seedless raspberries. Of 16 batches, 12 produced seedless berries. If this trend continued, in how many batches of 48 batches would the formula produce seedless berries?

_____

Holt, Rinehart and Winston, Publishers • 5

Use with pages 400–401.

Draw a picture to solve.

5. When Dr. Thinkhard went to the Patent Office to register his formula, he had trouble finding the right room. He went to a floor that had 10 rooms on one side, numbered 1 through 10. A woman in Room 1 told him to go up 4 rooms. A man in that room told him to go back 2 rooms. Finally, a janitor told him to go up 6 rooms, and Dr. Thinkhard found the right room. Which room was it?

Make a guess, and check your answer.

6. One batch of the raspberries weighs a certain number of grams. The number has two digits and is divisible by three. The sum of the digits is 9. If you subtract the tens digit from the ones digit, you get the tens digit. How much does the batch weigh?

Make a list to solve.

7. Dr. Thinkhard made a list of chemicals he uses in many formulas. Each formula use 2 different chemicals. Using the numbers 1 through 6 to stand for the 6 chemicals, find out how many different formulas are possible.

8. Choose one problem from this lesson that you've already solved. Solve the problem in a different way.

Holt, Rinehart and Winston, Publishers • 5

Use with pages 400–401.

TO THE TEACHER:

RETEACH

This section provides additional instruction on material covered in the pupil's edition. Each page is keyed to the appropriate lesson, but could be used as instruction, extra practice, or review at any time after the lesson.

There are 431,250 fish in a school.
What is the value of the digit 4?

Match the number 431,250 with the place-value chart.

PERIODS	Thousands			Hundreds		
	hundred thousands	ten thousands	thousands	hundreds	tens	ones
	4	3	1	2	5	0

Notice that the digit 4 is in the hundred thousands place.
The value of the 4 is 4 hundred thousands or 400,000.

Complete.

The estimated population of blue whales, humpback whales,
and Bryde's whales in 58,309.

1. What is the value of the digit 3? _____

2. What is the value of the digit 5? _____

3. What is the value of the digit 8? _____

4. The digit 0 is in which place? _____

Write the value of the underlined digit.

5. 5<u>4</u>5,287 = _____

6. 835,<u>1</u>26 = _____

7. 859,<u>4</u>00 = _____

8. 706,8<u>3</u>2 = _____

9. <u>1</u>48,679 = _____

10. 2<u>6</u>5,400 = _____

11. <u>4</u>67,342 = _____

12. 3<u>2</u>8,006 = _____

13. 104,0<u>5</u>7 = _____

14. 5<u>1</u>0,608 = _____

15. 128,<u>6</u>95 = _____

16. 932,6<u>8</u>4 = _____

17. 975,4<u>2</u>3 = _____

18. <u>9</u>67,431 = _____

19. 439,6<u>1</u>2 = _____

Match the number 52,400,000 with the place-value chart.

What is the value of the digit 5?

PERIODS	Billions			Millions			Thousands			Ones		
	hundred billions	ten billions	billions	hundred millions	ten millions	millions	hundred thousands	ten thousands	thousands	hundreds	tens	ones
				5	2	4	0	0	0	0	0	

Notice that the digit 2 is in the millions place.

The value of the digit 5 is 50 millions or 50,000,000.

Complete.

The estimated population of emperor penguins in Antarctica is 71,950.

1. What is the value of the digit 9? _____

2. What is the value of the digit 7? _____

3. What is the value of the digit 5? _____

4. The digit 1 is in which place? _____

Write the value of the underlined digit.

5. 603,822,000 _____

6. 431,557,000 _____

7. 400,374,564 _____

8. 744,901,500,000 _____

9. 187,601,282,000 _____

10. 976,723,900,540 _____

The area of the Atlantic Ocean is 81,729,000 square kilometers, while the combined area of the Indian Ocean and the Arctic Ocean is 83,800,000 square kilometers. Is the combined area of the Indian and Arctic oceans greater than the area of the Atlantic Ocean?

Remember

Number lines help you to compare two numbers. Draw a number line with units large enough to accommodate 81,729,000 and 83,800,000.

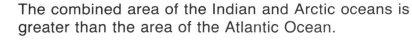

81 million   82 million   83 million   84 million   85 million

Mark the numbers on the number line. Notice that 83 million is to the right of 81 million. Therefore, 83,800,000 is greater than 81,729,000. Write 83,800,000 > 81,729,000.

The combined area of the Indian and Arctic oceans is greater than the area of the Atlantic Ocean.

Compare. Use > or < for $\bigcirc$.

1. 74 $\bigcirc$ 71   **2.** 104 $\bigcirc$ 105   **3.** 26 $\bigcirc$ 260

4. 208 $\bigcirc$ 28   **5.** 46,580 $\bigcirc$ 49,590   **6.** 9,301 $\bigcirc$ 9,830

7. 72,867 $\bigcirc$ 68,821   **8.** 878,405 $\bigcirc$ 678,405   **9.** 129,801 $\bigcirc$ 65,420

Order from the least to the greatest.

10. 501; 474; 987; 417 _____

11. 5,690; 281; 7,511; 5,201 _____

12. 103; 8,961; 1,300; 5,870 _____

13. 4,252; 1,060; 452; 215 _____

14. 858; 891; 582 _____

15. 4,191; 7,512; 7,652 _____

Connie's father told her to put on her shoes and socks. She did what he told her. First she put on her shoes. Then she put on her socks. You can see how silly the result is.

Sometimes the order in which we do things is important. At other times, it is not. Look at the results of doing one thing in two different ways. If the results are the same, the order is not important. If the results are different, the order is important.

Remember

Addition has special properties.

Commutative Property: If the order of the addends is changed, the sum remains the same.

$$5 + 2 = 7$$
$$2 + 5 = 7$$

Zero Property: If one of the addends is zero, the sum is equal to the other addend.

$$6 + 0 = 6$$
$$0 + 3 = 3$$

Associative Property: If the grouping of the addends is changed, the sum remains the same.

$$(1 + 4) + 2 = 1 + (4 + 2)$$
$$(5) + 2 = 1 + (6)$$
$$7 = 7$$

Add.

| 1. | 8
 +6 | 2. | 5
 +4 | 3. | 3
 +2 | 4. | 7
 +1 | 5. | 9
 +4 |

| 6. | 1
 +7 | 7. | 0
 +5 | 8. | 4
 +9 | 9. | 4
 +5 | 10. | 2
 +3 |

11. $(6 + 1) + 3 =$ _____

12. $8 + (2 + 4) =$ _____

13. $(5 + 0) + 6 =$ _____

14. $(7 + 2) + 9 =$ _____

15. $(0 + 9) + 7 =$ _____

16. $6 + (1 + 3) =$ _____

Holt, Rinehart and Winston, Publishers • 5

Peter has 8 tropical fish in his aquarium. He received 3 more fish for his birthday. How many fish does Peter have altogether?

To find how many, you can add.

$$8 + 3 = 11 \longleftarrow \text{sum}$$
Peter has 11 fish.

Peter gave 3 of his fish to his brother. How many fish does he have left?

To find how many fish he has left, you can subtract.

$$11 - 3 = 8 \longleftarrow \text{difference}$$
Peter has 8 fish.

You can see that the addition problem

$$8 + 3 = \boxed{11}$$

can be changed to the subtraction problem

$$\boxed{11} - 3 = 8.$$

These are related facts.

Change each subtraction problem into an addition problem.

1. $6 - 2 = \square$

2. $9 - 5 = \square$

3. $7 - 1 = \square$

_____

4. $5 - 3 = \square$

5. $8 - 5 = \square$

6. $9 - 7 = \square$

_____

7. $4 - 1 = \square$

8. $9 - 0 = \square$

9. $6 - 6 = \square$

_____

Holt, Rinehart and Winston, Publishers • 5

The chart given lists the membership of various clubs at Bedrock Elementary. There are 700 students in the school. Would you say that every student belongs to a club?

Club	Membership
Science	123
Math	158
Reading	178
Art	45
Sports	109

To answer this question, estimate the number of students that belong to a club.

Remember

When using front-end estimation to estimate a sum, first add all the numbers in the greatest place; then group pairs of numbers in order to adjust the estimate.

Add the numbers in the greatest place.

①23
①58
①78
45
+ ①09
___
4

Rough estimate: 400.
$123 + 158 + 178 + 45 + 109 < 700$

Adjust by grouping the other amounts.

$\left.\begin{matrix}123\\158\end{matrix}\right\}$ about 100

$\left.\begin{matrix}178\\45\end{matrix}\right\}$ about 100

109

Adjustment: $100 + 100 = 200$.

Adjusted estimate: $400 + 200 = 600$.

So, you would not say that every student belongs to a club.

Estimate. Write > or < for ◯.

1. $77 + 29 ◯ 100$

2. $167 + 58 ◯ 200$

3. $273 + 319 ◯ 600$

4. $1,298 + 3,916 ◯ 5,000$

5. $\$7.62 + \$8.13 ◯ \$16.00$

6. $\$16.52 + \$15.29 ◯ \$32.00$

Estimate. First write your rough estimate. Then write your adjusted estimate.

7.	**8.**	**9.**	**10.**	**11.**
238	509	$40.25	4,811	$8.87
119	247	7.56	2,362	0.26
82	198	1.72	1,708	3.39
+ 361	+ 59	+ 1.05	+ 216	+ 1.70

Holt, Rinehart and Winston, Publishers • 5

When you round to a specific place value, you need to take a close look at the digits of the number.

Round 2,359 to the nearest hundred.

Remember

Look at the digit to the right of the place to which you are rounding.

- Find the place to which you are rounding. 2 ,③5 9

- If the digit to the right is 5 or greater than 5, round up.

- If the digit to the right is less than 5, round down.

- The digit to the right is 5. Round up.   2 , 3⑤9

So, 2,359 to the nearest hundred is 2,400.

Round each number to the nearest hundred, thousand, and ten thousand.

1. 24,358 _____

2. 87,927 _____

3. 37,728 _____

4. 93,476 _____

5. 55,984 _____

6. 79,383 _____

7. 20,079 _____

8. 93,397 _____

Round to the nearest ten dollars.

9. $83.50 = _____   **10.** $75.02 = _____   **11.** $19.38 = _____   **12.** $42.93 = _____

Estimate. Write > or < for ◯.

13. 326 + 386 ◯ 800

14. 317 + 242 ◯ 500

15. 537 + 420 ◯ 1,000

16. 857 + 172 ◯ 1,000

17. 4,638 + 3,286 ◯ 7,000

18. 3,286 + 7,397 ◯ 11,000

Estimate.

19. 374
      + 486

20. 439
      + 235

21. 3,487
      + 2,562

22. 4,836
      + 6,349

23. 45,845
      + 34,704

A giant aquarium in a pet store contains 175 fish. Another aquarium contains 118 fish. How many fish are there in both aquariums?

Find 175 + 118.

Remember

When a sum in one place is 10 or more, regroup.

Add the ones	Regroup the ones.	Add the tens.	Add the hundreds.

175   5
 +118   +8
 ———   ——
       13
	1
	 175
	 +118
	 ———
	    3
		1 1
		 175 7
		 +118 +1
		 ——— ——
		   93 9
			1
			 175
			 +118
			 ———
			 293

There are 293 fish in both aquariums.

Add.

1. 358
   + 154

2. 463
   + 308

3. 677
   + 515

4. 706
   + 377

5. $3.39
   + 2.33

6. 48
   + 31

7. 13
   + 65

8. 32
   + 35

9. 53
   + 43

10. $0.66
    + 0.34

11. 27
   + 667

12. 83
   + 291

13. 29
   + 284

14. 587
   + 75

15. $1.85
    + 0.76

Holt, Rinehart and Winston, Publishers • 5

Use with pages 20–21.

There are 1,935 people who live in a small town in California. A few miles away, another small town has a population of 2,578. What is the total population of the two towns?

Add 1,935 + 2,578.

Remember

You must regroup to the next place when a sum is 10 or more.

Add the ones.	Add the tens.	Add the hundreds.	Add the thousands.
Regroup the 13 ones.	Regroup the 11 tens.	Regroup the 15 hundreds.	
$\begin{array}{r} 1 \\ 1,935 \\ +2,578 \\ \hline 3 \end{array}$	$\begin{array}{r} 11 \\ 1,935 \\ +2,578 \\ \hline 13 \end{array}$	$\begin{array}{r} 1\ 11 \\ 1,935 \\ +2,578 \\ \hline 513 \end{array}$	$\begin{array}{r} 1\ 11 \\ 1,935 \\ +2,578 \\ \hline 4,513 \end{array}$

The population of the two towns is 4,513.

Find the sum.

1. $\begin{array}{r} 5,561 \\ +7,371 \\ \hline \end{array}$

2. $\begin{array}{r} 2,315 \\ +9,659 \\ \hline \end{array}$

3. $\begin{array}{r} 8,467 \\ +6,078 \\ \hline \end{array}$

4. $\begin{array}{r} 1,588 \\ +7,148 \\ \hline \end{array}$

5. $\begin{array}{r} \$34.84 \\ +\ 8.52 \\ \hline \end{array}$

6. $\begin{array}{r} 96,949 \\ +\ 2,953 \\ \hline \end{array}$

7. $\begin{array}{r} 14,923 \\ +\ 9,484 \\ \hline \end{array}$

8. $\begin{array}{r} 46,833 \\ +24,672 \\ \hline \end{array}$

9. $\begin{array}{r} 62,780 \\ +61,621 \\ \hline \end{array}$

10. $\begin{array}{r} \$677.74 \\ +\ 94.27 \\ \hline \end{array}$

11. $\begin{array}{r} 33,426 \\ +25,629 \\ \hline \end{array}$

12. $\begin{array}{r} \$142.79 \\ +236.52 \\ \hline \end{array}$

13. $\begin{array}{r} \$310.00 \\ +725.96 \\ \hline \end{array}$

14. $\begin{array}{r} 73,295 \\ +63,428 \\ \hline \end{array}$

15. $\begin{array}{r} \$456.76 \\ +210.89 \\ \hline \end{array}$

Holt, Rinehart and Winston, Publishers • 5

A family traveling cross-country covered 151 miles on the first day, 78 miles on the second day, and 243 miles on the third day of their trip. How many miles did they travel during the three days?

You can add to find how many miles they traveled.

Find 151 + 78 + 243.

Remember

Line up the numbers so that the ones are correctly aligned in a column.

Hundreds	Tens	Ones
1	5	1
	7	8
2	4	3

$$\begin{array}{r} 151 \\ 78 \\ +243 \\ \hline \end{array}$$

Now add.

$$\begin{array}{r} {\scriptstyle 1\,1} \\ 151 \\ 78 \\ +243 \\ \hline 472 \end{array}$$

They traveled 472 miles in the three days.

Add.

1.
$$\begin{array}{r} 92 \\ 13 \\ +28 \\ \hline \end{array}$$

2.
$$\begin{array}{r} 13 \\ 11 \\ +31 \\ \hline \end{array}$$

3.
$$\begin{array}{r} 21 \\ 29 \\ +96 \\ \hline \end{array}$$

4.
$$\begin{array}{r} 44 \\ 39 \\ +58 \\ \hline \end{array}$$

5.
$$\begin{array}{r} 12 \\ 23 \\ +85 \\ \hline \end{array}$$

6.
$$\begin{array}{r} \$5.35 \\ 2.51 \\ +1.45 \\ \hline \end{array}$$

7.
$$\begin{array}{r} 260 \\ 701 \\ +627 \\ \hline \end{array}$$

8.
$$\begin{array}{r} 941 \\ 38 \\ +724 \\ \hline \end{array}$$

9.
$$\begin{array}{r} \$8.21 \\ 1.41 \\ +2.39 \\ \hline \end{array}$$

10.
$$\begin{array}{r} 717 \\ 460 \\ +928 \\ \hline \end{array}$$

11.
$$\begin{array}{r} 943 \\ 202 \\ +655 \\ \hline \end{array}$$

12.
$$\begin{array}{r} 749 \\ 23 \\ +308 \\ \hline \end{array}$$

Holt, Rinehart and Winston, Publishers • 5

A rancher had 84 sheep in his flock. He sold 25 sheep. How many sheep does the rancher have left? To find how many sheep are left, you can subtract.

Find 84 – 25.

Remember

When you subtract, sometimes you must regroup.

Not enough ones.	8 tens and 4 ones is 7 tens and 14 ones.	Regroup. 7 tens 14 ones.	Subtract the ones.	Subtract the tens.
84 – 25		7 14 8̸ 4̸ – 2 5	7 14 8̸ 4̸ – 2 5 ‾‾‾‾‾ 9	7 14 8̸ 4̸ – 2 5 ‾‾‾‾‾ 5 9

There are 59 sheep left.

Subtract.

1. 64
    – 35

2. 271
    – 225

3. 840
    – 136

4. 98
    – 59

5. 290
    – 112

6. 925
    – 74

7. 340
    – 250

8. 516
    – 470

9. 488
    – 269

10. $8.19
    – 3.48

11. 731
    – 492

12. 554
    – 376

13. 591
    – 19

14. 520
    – 87

15. $2.82
    – 1.96

16. There were 14 coyotes in a pack. Ranchers scared 8 of them away. How many coyotes remained?

_____

17. A rancher had 825 sheep in his flock. He sheared 537 of them. How many sheep remained unsheared?

_____

A farmer harvested 4,583 bushels of wheat in one day. Because of mechanical trouble, he harvested only 2,894 bushels of wheat the second day. How many more bushels of wheat did he harvest the first day than he did the second day? To find how many more bushels, you subtract.

Find 4,583 − 2,894.

| **Remember** |
| Sometimes when you subtract, you have to regroup more than once. |

Regroup. Subtract the ones.	Regroup. Subtract the tens.	Regroup. Subtract the hundreds.	Subtract the thousands.
7 13	4 17 13	3 14 17 13	3 14 17 13
4,5 8̸ 3̸	4,5̸ 8̸ 3̸	4̸,5̸ 8̸ 3̸	4̸,5̸ 8̸ 3̸
− 2,8 9 ④	− 2,8 ⑨ 4	− 2,⑧ 9 4	− ②,8 9 4
⑨	⑧ 9	⑥ 8 9	①,6 8 9

He harvested 1,689 more bushels of wheat the first day.

Find the difference.

1. 324
   − 246

2. 453
   − 187

3. 473
   − 278

4. 560
   − 238

5. $8.53
   − $4.59

6. 8,632
   − 5,742

7. 5,312
   − 4,167

8. 3,420
   − 2,357

9. 5,734
   − 4,678

10. $63.47
   − 61.89

Solve.

11. Farmer Green harvested 56,480 bushels of wheat last year. This year, he harvested 72,350 bushels of wheat. How much more wheat did he harvest this year than last year?

_____

Holt, Rinehart and Winston, Publishers • 5

A farmer in North Dakota planted 4,304 acres of wheat. Bad weather ruined 285 acres of the wheat. How many acres of wheat remained for the farmer to harvest?

To find how many acres of wheat remained, you can subtract.

Subtract 4,304 – 285.

Remember

You must regroup when subtracting a number from zero.

Regroup tens. There are no tens to regroup. So regroup hundreds.	Regroup tens.	Subtract.
$\begin{array}{r} \overset{2\ 10}{4,\cancel{3}\cancel{0}4} \\ -\ \ \ 2\ 8\ 5 \end{array}$	$\begin{array}{r} \overset{9}{2\ \cancel{10}\ 14} \\ 4,\cancel{3}\cancel{0}\cancel{4} \\ -\ \ \ \ 2\ 8\ 5 \end{array}$	$\begin{array}{r} \overset{9}{2\ \cancel{10}\ 14} \\ 4,\cancel{3}\cancel{0}\cancel{4} \\ -\ \ \ \ 2\ 8\ 5 \\ \hline 4,0\ 1\ 9 \end{array}$

There are 4,019 acres of wheat to be harvested.

Find the difference.

1. $\begin{array}{r} 200 \\ -172 \\ \hline \end{array}$	**2.** $\begin{array}{r} 609 \\ -257 \\ \hline \end{array}$	**3.** $\begin{array}{r} 700 \\ -275 \\ \hline \end{array}$	**4.** $\begin{array}{r} 800 \\ -723 \\ \hline \end{array}$	**5.** $\begin{array}{r} \$3.00 \\ -\$1.78 \\ \hline \end{array}$
6. $\begin{array}{r} 7,403 \\ -2,934 \\ \hline \end{array}$	**7.** $\begin{array}{r} 57,001 \\ -16,708 \\ \hline \end{array}$	**8.** $\begin{array}{r} 72,301 \\ -59,171 \\ \hline \end{array}$	**9.** $\begin{array}{r} \$150.00 \\ -\ 119.47 \\ \hline \end{array}$	**10.** $\begin{array}{r} \$600.40 \\ -\ 387.48 \\ \hline \end{array}$

Solve.

11. A farmer planted 5,063 acres of grain. During the first week in August, he harvested 3,430 acres of grain. How many acres remain to be harvested?

_____

Holt, Rinehart and Winston, Publishers • 5

Two hikers begin a 10-mile walk on a trail through the Grand Canyon. After walking 3 miles, they stop for a picnic lunch. Write a decimal that shows the portion of the hike that they have completed.

Remember

You can draw a picture to show the portion of the hike that the hikers have completed. Divide a square into 10 equal parts. Each part stands for one tenth. Since the hikers have walked 3 miles, shade 3 of the parts.

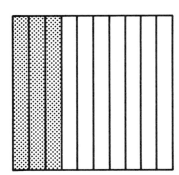

The shaded part of the picture shows three tenths. Read: *three tenths.*
The decimal is written as 0.3.

The hikers have walked 0.3 of the distance.

Write each as a decimal.

1. five tenths _____

2. seven tenths _____

3. nine tenths _____

4. six tenths _____

5. eight tenths _____

6. one tenth _____

7. two and three tenths _____

8. five and six tenths _____

9. four and nine tenths _____

10. nine and eight tenths _____

Write the word name for each decimal.

11. 0.3 _____

12. 4.5 _____

13. 6.7 _____

14. 9.6 _____

15. 7.2 _____

16. 0.8 _____

17. 3.9 _____

18. 9.9 _____

Holt, Rinehart and Winston, Publishers • 5

Use with pages 44–45.

An Indianapolis racer can make one lap at the Indy track in forty-seven and seventy-five hundredths of a second. Write this number as a decimal.

Remember

Match the number with the place-value chart.

Hundreds	Tens	Ones	Tenths	Hundredths
	4	7	7	5

decimal point

The number is read as forty-seven and seventy-five hundredths. It is written as 47.75.

Copy the place-value chart. Write each decimal on the chart.

1. 0.06

2. 1.29

3. 14.21

4. 313.41

5. 780.04

6. 10.02

Hundreds	Tens	Ones	.	Tenths	Hundredths

Write the word name.

7. 0.02 _____

8. 0.83 _____

9. 8.25 _____

10. 71.36 _____

11. 42.82 _____

12. 753.42 _____

Solve.

13. An Indy-500 race-car driver completed the first 10 miles of the race in 3.84 minutes. Write the time in words.

_____

Holt, Rinehart and Winston, Publishers • 5

The average speed for a driver at the Indianapolis Speedway was 119.026 miles per hour. Can you write the word name for this number?

Remember

You can use a place-value chart to write the number.

Thousands	Hundreds	Tens	Ones	.	Tenths	Hundredths	Thousandths
	1	1	9	.	0	2	6

The digit 6 is in the thousandths place. The number is read as *one hundred nineteen and twenty-six thousandths.*
It is written as 119.026.

Write as a decimal.

1. Three and sixty-one thousandths _____

2. One hundred thirty-seven thousandths _____

3. One hundred and thirty-seven thousandths _____

4. Fifteen and thirty-one thousandths _____

5. Five hundred forty-three and two hundred thousandths _____

Write the word name for each decimal

6. 54.31

_____

7. 6.060

_____

8. 2.009

_____

9. 0.102

_____

10. 3.002

_____

11. 0.550

_____

12. 25.026

_____

13. 1.006

_____

16

Holt, Rinehart and Winston, Publishers • 5

Use with pages 48–49.

Each pound of brass alloy used to make brass nameplates contains 0.58 lb of copper, 0.405 lb of zinc, and 0.015 lb of lead. Arrange these numbers in order from the least to the greatest.

Remember

Before comparing numbers, each number must have the same number of digits after the decimal point.

0.58	Write a zero.———————▶	0.580
0.405	———————————————▶	0.405
0.015	———————————————▶	0.015

Now each number has the same number of digits after the decimal point, and the decimal points are lined up. Begin to compare the digits from left to right.

The first digit in each number is zero.	The second digits are 0, 4, 5.	Since $0 < 4 < 5$, we can order the decimals.
0.580	0.580	0.015
0.405	0.405	0.405
0.015	0.015	0.580

From the least to the greatest, the decimals are 0.015, 0.405, 0.580.

Compare. Write $>$, $<$, or $=$ for $\bigcirc$.

1. 9.35 $\bigcirc$ 0.496   **2.** 0.52 $\bigcirc$ 0.532   **3.** 0.053 $\bigcirc$ 0.095

4. 1.20 $\bigcirc$ 0.120   **5.** 0.589 $\bigcirc$ 0.598   **6.** 25.2 $\bigcirc$ 25.9

7. 0.01 $\bigcirc$ 0.001   **8.** 1.567 $\bigcirc$ 1.568   **9.** 3.001 $\bigcirc$ 3.100

10. 1.040 $\bigcirc$ 1.004   **11.** 0.23 $\bigcirc$ 0.230   **12.** 1.740 $\bigcirc$ 1.704

Write in order from the greatest to the least.

13. 25.06, 2.56, 5.026   **14.** 2.528, 0.58, 2.5

15. 0.123, 0.132, 0.312   **16.** 0.765, 7.065, 7.650

A rectangular drip pan is placed under a printing press to keep ink and solvent off the floor. The pan covers an area of 1.765 square meters. Round 1.765 to the nearest tenth.

| Remember |

To round to the nearest tenth, look at the digit in the hundredths place.

1.765
└─hundredths position

Because the digit in the hundredths position is greater than 5, increase the digit in the tenths position by 1.

┌──5 or greater than 5 so
1.765
└──increase by 1

Rounded to the nearest tenth, 1.765 is 1.8.

Round to the nearest whole number.

1. 5.43 **2.** 42.41 **3.** 17.91 **4.** 19.20 **5.** 83.5

_____ _____ _____ _____ _____

6. 3.41 **7.** 19.37 **8.** 12.60 **9.** 34.04 **10.** 79.8

_____ _____ _____ _____ _____

Round to the nearest tenth.

11. 23.41 **12.** 1.39 **13.** 9.47 **14.** 35.62 **15.** 4.45

_____ _____ _____ _____ _____

16. 0.57 **17.** 0.29 **18.** 3.57 **19.** 33.34 **20.** 0.47

_____ _____ _____ _____ _____

Round to the nearest hundredth.

21. 1.239 **22.** 45.501 **23.** 6.941 **24.** 14.555 **25.** 43.009

_____ _____ _____ _____ _____

26. 19.115 **27.** 0.393 **28.** 0.487 **29.** 0.548 **30.** 18.986

_____ _____ _____ _____ _____

Holt, Rinehart and Winston, Publishers • 5

Margo wants to buy a stereo from Andy's Hi-Fi. The stereo costs $145.50. She has $193.37 in her savings account but has to pay a debt of $37.93. After she pays her debt, will Margo be able to afford the stereo?

Estimate $193.37 − $37.93.

Remember

When estimating sums or differences, round to the place where you can mentally compute the rounded numbers.

Decide to which place value you will round.
To the nearest whole number: $193.37 ⟶ $193
　　　　　　　　　　　　　　　 − 37.93 ⟶ 38

$193 − $38 is difficult to compute mentally; so, round to the nearest ten. $193.37 ⟶ $190
　　　　　　　　　　　　　　　　　　　　 − 37.93 ⟶ 40

You can see that $190 − $40 is easier to compute. So, the estimated difference of $193.37 − $37.93 is about $150.

Since Margo will have about $150 left after she pays her debt, she will be able to afford the stereo.

Estimate. Write > or < for ◯.

1. $3.6 + 3.92 ◯ 7$

2. $7.098 + 5.77 ◯ 12$

3. $\$9.44 + \$4.65 ◯ \$13.00$

4. $\$11.71 + \$8.54 ◯ \$20.00$

5. $10.4 - 8.84 ◯ 2$

6. $3.901 - 1.816 ◯ 1$

Estimate.

7.	**8.**	**9.**	**10.**	**11.**
9.307 − 4.691	84.47 − 69.73	13.34 + 12.63	83.42 + 27.93	65.43 − 34.78

12.	**13.**	**14.**	**15.**	**16.**
4.9 4.3 + 7.5	26.7 14.6 + 17.8	6.718 5.9 + 4.66	27.938 13.483 + 9.240	4.866 4.701 + 4.078

An Indy racer completed his first lap around the racetrack in 1.58 minutes. It took him 1.6 minutes to complete the second lap. How much time did it take the driver to complete two laps?

Remember

Line up the decimal points. Then add. Regroup if necessary.

$$
\begin{array}{r}
1\\
1.58\\
+\,1.6\\
\hline
3.18
\end{array}
$$

The two-lap time was 3.18 minutes.

Add.

1. 9.13
   + 3.19

2. 75.480
   + 2.743

3. 4.635
   + 1.9

4. $8.94
   + 9.35

5. 12.10
   + 26.32

6. 3.40
   + 50.473

7. 23.251
   + 51.036

8. 81.113
   + 54.341

9. 0.1
    0.3
   + 8.9

10. 6.00
    9.67
   + 8.52

11. 6.751
    9.421
   + 6.489

12. $2.47
    1.39
   + 3.87

Solve.

13. A United States penny weighs 48 grains, a quarter weighs 96.45 grains, and a half-dollar weighs 192.9 grains. What is the total weight of a collection of one of each of these coins?

_____

Use with pages 60–61.

A quarter weighs 96.45 grains, and a half-dollar weighs
192.9 grains. How much heavier is a half-dollar than a
quarter?

Remember

Write equivalent decimals so both numbers have the same amount of decimal
places; then line up the decimals.

Regroup. Subtract the hundredths.	Subtract the tenths.	Regroup. Subtract the ones.	Regroup. Subtract the tens.
$$\begin{array}{r} \overset{8\ 10}{192.9\cancel{0}} \\ -\ 96.45 \\ \hline 5 \end{array}$$	$$\begin{array}{r} \overset{8\ 10}{192.9\cancel{0}} \\ -\ 96.45 \\ \hline .45 \end{array}$$	$$\begin{array}{r} \overset{8\ 12\quad 8\ 10}{19\cancel{2}.9\cancel{0}} \\ -\ 96.45 \\ \hline 6.45 \end{array}$$	$$\begin{array}{r} \overset{18}{\underset{}{\cancel{1}}}\overset{8\ 12\quad 8\ 10}{\cancel{9}\cancel{2}.9\cancel{0}} \\ -\ 96.45 \\ \hline 96.45 \end{array}$$

A half-dollar is 96.45 grains heavier than a quarter.

Subtract.

1.   7.98
   − 5.59

2.   7.43
   − 2.36

3.   76.31
   − 25.17

4.   27.12
   − 16.42

5. $752.29
   − 338.49

6.   9.87
   − 2.65

7.   7.97
   − 4.15

8.   8.69
   − 5.24

9.   29.34
   − 1.14

10. $92.97
   − 1.93

11.   52.04
   − 7.65

12.   45.08
   − 5.90

13.   26.24
   − 7.90

14.   63.00
   − 5.56

15. $464.00
   − 5.59

It takes 7 minutes to put 1 horseshoe on a horse. How long
will it take to put shoes on all 4 feet of the horse?

> **Remember**
>
> You can multiply to find how long it will take. Since a horse has 4 feet, and it takes 7
> minutes to shoe each foot, you can write
>
> $$7 + 7 + 7 + 7 = 28,$$ or $$4 \times 7 = 28,$$ or $$\begin{array}{r} 7 \\ \times 4 \\ \hline 28. \end{array}$$
>
> 4 sevens

It will take 28 minutes.

Multiply.

1. $\begin{array}{r}2\\ \times 5\\ \hline\end{array}$	**2.** $\begin{array}{r}3\\ \times 6\\ \hline\end{array}$	**3.** $\begin{array}{r}7\\ \times 8\\ \hline\end{array}$	**4.** $\begin{array}{r}6\\ \times 7\\ \hline\end{array}$	**5.** $\begin{array}{r}1\\ \times 3\\ \hline\end{array}$	**6.** $\begin{array}{r}9\\ \times 0\\ \hline\end{array}$
7. $\begin{array}{r}6\\ \times 9\\ \hline\end{array}$	**8.** $\begin{array}{r}0\\ \times 4\\ \hline\end{array}$	**9.** $\begin{array}{r}4\\ \times 1\\ \hline\end{array}$	**10.** $\begin{array}{r}1\\ \times 2\\ \hline\end{array}$	**11.** $\begin{array}{r}9\\ \times 8\\ \hline\end{array}$	**12.** $\begin{array}{r}7\\ \times 9\\ \hline\end{array}$
13. $\begin{array}{r}7\\ \times 6\\ \hline\end{array}$	**14.** $\begin{array}{r}7\\ \times 8\\ \hline\end{array}$	**15.** $\begin{array}{r}9\\ \times 8\\ \hline\end{array}$	**16.** $\begin{array}{r}6\\ \times 9\\ \hline\end{array}$	**17.** $\begin{array}{r}9\\ \times 6\\ \hline\end{array}$	**18.** $\begin{array}{r}8\\ \times 7\\ \hline\end{array}$

19. A rancher has 9 horses. Every 6 weeks, he must replace
the shoes on his horses. How many shoes are needed
each time the rancher replaces the shoes on his horses?

_____

It is not unusual for a tree to grow to a height of 60 feet. The World Trade Center in New York City is over 20 times as high as a 60-foot tree. How high is the World Trade Center?

You can multiply to find the height of the World Trade Center. Multiply 20×60.

Remember

Use a pattern.

$2 \times 6 = 12$	$20 \times 6 = 120$
$2 \times 60 = 120$	$20 \times 60 = 1,200$
$2 \times 600 = 1,200$	$20 \times 600 = 12,000$
$2 \times 6,000 = 12,000$	$20 \times 6,000 = 120,000$

The World Trade Center is over 1,200 feet high.

Multiply.

1. $\begin{array}{r} 10 \\ \times\ 2 \\ \hline \end{array}$

2. $\begin{array}{r} 10 \\ \times\ 5 \\ \hline \end{array}$

3. $\begin{array}{r} 200 \\ \times\ 7 \\ \hline \end{array}$

4. $\begin{array}{r} 20 \\ \times 90 \\ \hline \end{array}$

5. $\begin{array}{r} 30 \\ \times 60 \\ \hline \end{array}$

6. $\begin{array}{r} 100 \\ \times\ 30 \\ \hline \end{array}$

7. $\begin{array}{r} 200 \\ \times\ 40 \\ \hline \end{array}$

8. $\begin{array}{r} 100 \\ \times 800 \\ \hline \end{array}$

9. $\begin{array}{r} 200 \\ \times 100 \\ \hline \end{array}$

10. $\begin{array}{r} 3,000 \\ \times\ 7 \\ \hline \end{array}$

11. $\begin{array}{r} 1,000 \\ \times\ 6 \\ \hline \end{array}$

12. $\begin{array}{r} 3,000 \\ \times\ 50 \\ \hline \end{array}$

13. $\begin{array}{r} 4,000 \\ \times\ 30 \\ \hline \end{array}$

14. $\begin{array}{r} 5,000 \\ \times\ 700 \\ \hline \end{array}$

15. $\begin{array}{r} 8,000 \\ \times\ 600 \\ \hline \end{array}$

Solve.

16. The owners of an apple orchard wanted to expand the size of their orchard by planting trees. In the spring, they marked off 20 rows for planting and planned to plant 70 trees in each row. How many trees did the owners plan to add to their orchard?

Use with pages 78–79.

Adeline is a professional photographer. In 1985, she shot 417 rolls of film. Each roll of film has 36 pictures. About how many pictures did Adeline take in 1985?

Estimate 36×417.

Remember

To estimate a product, you need to round each factor to its greatest place, and then multiply.

$$417 \longrightarrow 400$$
$$\underline{\times\ 36} \longrightarrow \underline{\times\ 40}$$
$$1{,}600$$

In 1985, Adeline took about 1,600 pictures.

Estimate.

1. 17 $\times 23$	**2.** 98 $\times 33$	**3.** 49 $\times 45$	**4.** 19 $\times 76$	**5.** 79 $\times 68$	**6.** 44 $\times 45$

7. 383 $\times\ 6$	**8.** 674 $\times\ 9$	**9.** 845 $\times\ 77$	**10.** 493 $\times\ 43$	**11.** $4.86 $\times\ 4$	**12.** $7.51 $\times\ 6$

13. $22 \times 873 =$ _____

14. $18 \times 93 =$ _____

15. $15 \times 835 =$ _____

16. $97 \times 24 =$ _____

17. $89 \times 644 =$ _____

18. $95 \times 98 =$ _____

Solve.

19. The Payola Crayon Company's best-selling box of crayons is the ColorBuster. The ColorBuster has 25 crayons. If an order is placed for 39 boxes of ColorBusters, about how many crayons would it take to fill the order?

_____

20. The EarAche Audio Company makes blank cassettes for tape recorders. The cassettes are shipped in boxes of 78. If 621 boxes are sent to Oswald's Audio Outlet, about how many cassettes will be sent?

_____

Some kinds of bamboo grow as much as 36 inches per day.
How much will those kinds of bamboo grow in one week?

Remember

You must regroup if a product is 10 or more.

| Multiply the ones. | Multiply the tens. | |
| Regroup the 4 tens. | Add the 4 tens. | |

$$
\begin{array}{r} 4 \\ 36 \\ \times\ 7 \\ \hline 2 \end{array}
\qquad
\boxed{\begin{array}{r} 6 \\ \times 7 \\ \hline 42 \end{array}}
\qquad\qquad
\begin{array}{r} 4 \\ 36 \\ \times\ 7 \\ \hline 252 \end{array}
\qquad
\boxed{\begin{array}{r} 3 \\ \times 7 \\ \hline 21 \\ +\ 4 \\ \hline 25 \end{array}}
$$

Those kinds of bamboo will grow 252 inches in one week.

Multiply.

1. $\begin{array}{r} 24 \\ \times\ 2 \\ \hline \end{array}$
2. $\begin{array}{r} 51 \\ \times\ 5 \\ \hline \end{array}$
3. $\begin{array}{r} 84 \\ \times\ 2 \\ \hline \end{array}$
4. $\begin{array}{r} 82 \\ \times\ 4 \\ \hline \end{array}$
5. $\begin{array}{r} 40 \\ \times\ 5 \\ \hline \end{array}$

6. $\begin{array}{r} 76 \\ \times\ 4 \\ \hline \end{array}$
7. $\begin{array}{r} 68 \\ \times\ 5 \\ \hline \end{array}$
8. $\begin{array}{r} 45 \\ \times\ 3 \\ \hline \end{array}$
9. $\begin{array}{r} \$0.78 \\ \times\ \ 4 \\ \hline \end{array}$
10. $\begin{array}{r} \$0.97 \\ \times\ \ 2 \\ \hline \end{array}$

11. $\begin{array}{r} 416 \\ \times\ \ 3 \\ \hline \end{array}$
12. $\begin{array}{r} 702 \\ \times\ \ 9 \\ \hline \end{array}$
13. $\begin{array}{r} 708 \\ \times\ \ 6 \\ \hline \end{array}$
14. $\begin{array}{r} \$3.47 \\ \times\ \ 2 \\ \hline \end{array}$
15. $\begin{array}{r} \$6.91 \\ \times\ \ 4 \\ \hline \end{array}$

Solve.

16. The tallest recorded species of bamboo is native to southern Burma. The growth rate of this bamboo is as much as 18 inches in 24 hours. How much will this bamboo grow in a week?

The largest living thing on Earth is a California sequoia tree named the General Sherman. It is estimated that this tree weighs 1,190 tons. How much would 3 of these trees weigh?

> **Remember**
>
> Multiply the ones, then the tens, then the hundreds, and then the thousands. Regroup if products are 10 or more.
>
> | Multiply. the ones. | Multiply the tens. Regroup. | Multiply the hundreds. | Multiply the thousands. |
> |---|---|---|---|
> | 1,190
 × 3
 0 | 2
 1,190
 × 3
 70   9 ×3 27 | 2
 1,190
 × 3
 570   1 ×3 3 +2 5 | 2
 1,190
 × 3
 3,570 |

The weight of 3 of these trees would be 3,570 tons.

Multiply.

1. 2,523
    ×   3

2. 3,702
    ×   3

3. 6,512
    ×   4

4. 5,201
    ×   8

5. $23.51
    ×   3

6. 4,370
    ×   2

7. 3,126
    ×   3

8. 1,205
    ×   4

9. 3,242
    ×   3

10. $43.35
    ×   2

Solve.

11. The total weight of the General Sherman tree, including the root system, is 1,309 tons. What would be the total weight of 4 such trees, including the root systems?

_____

Holt, Rinehart and Winston, Publishers • 5

Use with pages 88–89.

There are 365 days in a year, and each day is 24 hours
long. How many hours are there in a year?
To find how many hours, you can multiply. Find 24 × 365.

Remember

Multiply 365 by 2 tens and 4 ones. Make sure you place
your answers in the right columns.

Multiply by ones.   Multiply by tens.   Add.

$$\begin{array}{r} 365 \\ \times\ 24 \\ \hline 1460 \end{array}$$
$$\begin{array}{r} {\scriptstyle 2\ 2} \\ 365 \\ \times\quad 4 \\ \hline \mathbf{1{,}460} \end{array}$$

$$\begin{array}{r} 365 \\ \times\ 24 \\ \hline 1460 \\[4pt] 7{,}300 \end{array}$$

  ↑—tens

$$\begin{array}{r} {\scriptstyle 1\ 1} \\ 365 \\ \times\quad 20 \\ \hline \mathbf{7{,}300} \end{array}$$

$$\begin{array}{r} 365 \\ \times\ 24 \\ \hline 1460 \\ 7300 \\ \hline 8{,}760 \end{array}$$

There are 8,760 hours in a year.

Multiply.

1. $\begin{array}{r} 22 \\ \times\,30 \\ \hline \end{array}$
2. $\begin{array}{r} 23 \\ \times\,40 \\ \hline \end{array}$
3. $\begin{array}{r} 53 \\ \times\,60 \\ \hline \end{array}$
4. $\begin{array}{r} 82 \\ \times\,73 \\ \hline \end{array}$
5. $\begin{array}{r} 91 \\ \times\,24 \\ \hline \end{array}$

6. $\begin{array}{r} 65 \\ \times\,21 \\ \hline \end{array}$
7. $\begin{array}{r} 46 \\ \times\,13 \\ \hline \end{array}$
8. $\begin{array}{r} 278 \\ \times\ \ 13 \\ \hline \end{array}$
9. $\begin{array}{r} 289 \\ \times\ \ 82 \\ \hline \end{array}$
10. $\begin{array}{r} 4{,}763 \\ \times\qquad 32 \\ \hline \end{array}$

Solve.

11. If there are 8,760 hours in one year, how many minutes
are there in one year? There are 60 minutes in one hour.

_____

A typical piece of cheese pizza contains 275 calories. If 134 fifth-grade students each ate one piece of pizza, how many calories would they consume altogether?

You can multiply to find how many calories they would consume. Find 275×134.

Remember

Multiply 275 by 4 ones, 3 tens, and 1 hundreds. Place the answers in the right columns.

Multiply by ones.
```
  275
× 134
 1100
```

Multiply by tens.
```
   275
 × 134
  1100 ◄── ones
  8250 ◄── tens
```

Multiply by hundreds.
```
    275
  × 134
   1100 ◄── ones
   8250 ◄── tens
  27500 ◄── hundreds
```

Add.
```
    275
  × 134
   1100
   8250
  27500
  36,850
```

The fifth-grade students would consume 36,850 calories.

Multiply.

1. 343
    × 500

2. 421
    × 200

3. 233
    × 400

4. 505
    × 300

5. $2.31
    × 800

6. 414
    × 278

7. 392
    × 146

8. 238
    × 615

9. 247
    × 303

10. $2.06
    × 485

Solve.

11. A typical chocolate milk shake contains 335 calories. If each of the 134 fifth-grade students drank a chocolate milk shake, how many calories would they consume altogether?

_____

Holt, Rinehart and Winston, Publishers • 5

At the Futon Fish Market, squid sells for $2.75/lb. If Yukio buys 8.7 lb of squid, about how much must he pay?

Estimate $2.75 × 8.7.

Remember

Decimal products may be estimated in the same way as whole-number products are.

Round both factors to their greatest place.	Multiply the factors.
$2.75 ⟶ **3** × 8.7 ⟶ **9**	$3 × 9 $27

Yukio pays about $27 for the squid.

Estimate. Write > or < for ◯.

1. 6.8 × 3.5 ◯ 21

2. 5.4 × 7.8 ◯ 42

3. 5.9 × 2.1 ◯ 13

4. 3.4 × 46.6 ◯ 151

5. 7.3 × 74.4 ◯ 480

6. 7.4 × 9.73 ◯ 69

7. 3.57 × 8.19 ◯ 33

8. 3.85 × 53.5 ◯ 179

9. 47.85 × $8.37 ◯ $401

Estimate.

10. 4.6
   × 6.4

11. 17.7
   × 4.38

12. 64.38
   × 7.89

13. $7.27
   ×   5.4

14. $44.39
   ×   9.91

Solve.

15. Julia buys 3.6 oz of Beluga caviar. Each ounce sells for $17.85. About how much does Julia pay for the caviar?

_____

16. Jay ate 97.3 g of swordfish. 1g of swordfish contains about 7.98 g of protein. About how much protein was there in Jay's swordfish?

_____

17. Mr. Furnbach sells fishing supplies. He charges $3.98 for each square yard of netting he sells. If he sells Rona 62.5 yd² of netting, about how much does

he charge? _____

18. Julian bought 6.25 lb of sturgeon. The sturgeon was on sale at $3.75/lb. About how much did Julian pay for the

sturgeon? _____

Mrs. Evans raises sugar beets on her farm in the Red River Valley. In a normal year, her crop yields 17 tons of sugar beets an acre.

Dry weather will cause this year's crop to be 0.9 of a normal crop. How many tons of beets an acre does Mrs. Evans expect this year?

Remember

Multiply 17 by 0.9 as if you were multiplying whole numbers. Then put the decimal point in the proper place.

Multiply as you would with whole numbers.

The product has the same number of decimal places as the decimal factor. Place the decimal point in the product.

$$\begin{array}{r} 17 \\ \times\,0.9 \\ \hline 15\ 3 \end{array}$$

$$\begin{array}{r} 17 \\ \times\,0.9 \longrightarrow \text{one place} \\ \hline 15.3 \longleftarrow \text{one place} \end{array}$$

Mrs. Evans expects 15.3 tons an acre.

Multiply

1. $\begin{array}{r}53\\\times0.4\\\hline\end{array}$	**2.** $\begin{array}{r}46\\\times0.5\\\hline\end{array}$	**3.** $\begin{array}{r}63\\\times0.8\\\hline\end{array}$	**4.** $\begin{array}{r}86\\\times0.4\\\hline\end{array}$	**5.** $\begin{array}{r}94\\\times0.8\\\hline\end{array}$
6. $\begin{array}{r}12\\\times0.9\\\hline\end{array}$	**7.** $\begin{array}{r}9\\\times0.3\\\hline\end{array}$	**8.** $\begin{array}{r}43\\\times0.7\\\hline\end{array}$	**9.** $\begin{array}{r}84\\\times0.9\\\hline\end{array}$	**10.** $\begin{array}{r}78\\\times0.3\\\hline\end{array}$
11. $\begin{array}{r}1.2\\\times\ 7\\\hline\end{array}$	**12.** $\begin{array}{r}2.6\\\times58\\\hline\end{array}$	**13.** $\begin{array}{r}5.4\\\times63\\\hline\end{array}$	**14.** $\begin{array}{r}9.7\\\times37\\\hline\end{array}$	**15.** $\begin{array}{r}9.5\\\times73\\\hline\end{array}$

Holt, Rinehart and Winston, Publishers • 5

Use with pages 110–111.

Orlando runs 35.4 miles each week in Center City Park. How many miles does he run in 6.5 weeks?

Remember

Multiply as with whole numbers. Place the decimal point in the product.

Multiply as you would with whole numbers.

Add the number of decimal places in the factors. Then move the decimal point that number of places to the left.

$$
\begin{array}{r}
35.4 \\
\times\ 6.5 \\
\hline
1770 \\
21240 \\
\hline
23010
\end{array}
$$

$35.4 \longrightarrow 1$ place
$\times\ 6.5 \longrightarrow +1$ place

$$
\begin{array}{r}
1770 \\
21240 \\
\hline
230.10
\end{array}
$$
— 2 places

Orlando runs 230.1 miles in 6.5 weeks.

Multiply.

1. 0.53
× 0.5

2. 0.75
× 0.4

3. 0.8
× 0.52

4. 0.25
× 0.6

5. 0.56
× 0.2

6. 0.45
× 0.8

7. 0.29
× 1.3

8. 0.42
× 5.4

9. 0.26
× 4.1

10. 0.49
× 8.3

11. 52.78
× 0.2

12. 41.01
× 9.3

13. 0.44
× 7.6

14. 0.5
× 0.4

15. 16.37
× 0.8

16. 0.85
× 1.9

17. 11.4
× 6.3

18. 1.07
× 5.3

19. 1.67
× 0.05

20. 1.96
× 0.12

Use with pages 114–115.

Jill has a box of balloons that weighs 0.037 pounds. She
wants to know how much 2.5 boxes weigh.

Remember

Multiply as with whole numbers. Put the decimal point in the proper place. Write zeros
if necessary.

Multiply as you would with
whole numbers.

$$
\begin{array}{r}
2.5 \\
\times\,0.037 \\
\hline
175 \\
750 \\
\hline
925
\end{array}
$$

Count the decimal places in each factor.

2.5 $\longrightarrow$ 1 place
$\times\,0.037$ $\longrightarrow$ 3 places
0.0925 $\longleftarrow$ 4 places

Write a zero to place the decimal point 4
places to the left. Then insert the decimal
point.

The 2.5 boxes of balloons weigh 0.0925 pounds.

Multiply.

1. $\begin{array}{r}0.06\\ \times\ 0.4\\\hline\end{array}$	**2.** $\begin{array}{r}0.13\\ \times\ 0.2\\\hline\end{array}$	**3.** $\begin{array}{r}0.61\\ \times\ 0.4\\\hline\end{array}$	**4.** $\begin{array}{r}0.52\\ \times\ 0.3\\\hline\end{array}$	**5.** $\begin{array}{r}0.82\\ \times\ 0.3\\\hline\end{array}$
6. $\begin{array}{r}0.06\\ \times\ 1.3\\\hline\end{array}$	**7.** $\begin{array}{r}0.05\\ \times\ 2.2\\\hline\end{array}$	**8.** $\begin{array}{r}0.07\\ \times\ 1.4\\\hline\end{array}$	**9.** $\begin{array}{r}0.02\\ \times\ 2.3\\\hline\end{array}$	**10.** $\begin{array}{r}0.03\\ \times\ 4.2\\\hline\end{array}$
11. $\begin{array}{r}5.02\\ \times\ 0.2\\\hline\end{array}$	**12.** $\begin{array}{r}0.09\\ \times\ 2.3\\\hline\end{array}$	**13.** $\begin{array}{r}9.2\\ \times\,0.04\\\hline\end{array}$	**14.** $\begin{array}{r}0.07\\ \times\ 4.3\\\hline\end{array}$	**15.** $\begin{array}{r}5.5\\ \times\,0.2\\\hline\end{array}$

16. $7.7 \times 0.1 =$ _____

17. $0.06 \times 0.6 =$ _____

18. $6.3 \times 0.04 =$ _____

Holt, Rinehart and Winston, Publishers • 5

Matt went to the beach and collected 42 seashells to give to 7 of his friends. Matt wants to give each friend the same number of shells. How many shells will each friend receive?

Remember

Since Matt is dividing his shells among his friends, this is a division problem. You want to know how many sevens there are in 42. There are 6 sevens in 42 since $6 \times 7 = 42$.

Division can be shown in three ways.

quotient →6
divisor →7)42
dividend

dividend
42 ÷ 7 = 6 ←quotient
divisor

dividend
$\frac{42}{7} = 6$ ←quotient
divisor

Each friend will receive 6 shells.

Divide

1. 8)56

2. 9)63

3. 8)40

4. 7)42

5. 3)27

6. 4)28

7. 6)54

8. 9)72

9. $72 \div 8 =$ _____

10. $81 \div 9 =$ _____

11. $63 \div 7 =$ _____

12. $54 \div 9 =$ _____

13. $45 \div 5 =$ _____

14. $28 \div 7 =$ _____

15. $\frac{36}{6} =$ _____

16. $\frac{49}{7} =$ _____

17. $\frac{48}{6} =$ _____

18. $\frac{25}{5} =$ _____

19. $\frac{54}{6} =$ _____

20. $\frac{63}{9} =$ _____

Solve.

21. At Camp Meadow Lane, Martha drew 28 pictures. When she returned home, she divided them equally among her 4 brothers. How many pictures did she give to each brother?

_____

Holt, Rinehart and Winston, Publishers • 5

Kim keeps her horse, Clipper, at a stable. She feeds Clipper 6 pounds of oats each day. For how many days will 54 pounds of oats last?

Remember
Divide to find how many sixes there are in 54. You divide 54 into groups of 6 pounds each.

$54 \div 6 = 9$

Using 6, 9, and 54, you can write four number sentences. The number sentences make up a family of facts.

$$6 \times 9 = 54 \qquad 54 \div 6 = 9$$
$$9 \times 6 = 54 \qquad 54 \div 9 = 6$$

The oats will last for 9 days.

Divide

1. $7\overline{)42}$ **2.** $6\overline{)30}$ **3.** $5\overline{)20}$ **4.** $7\overline{)21}$

5. $8\overline{)56}$ **6.** $7\overline{)35}$ **7.** $9\overline{)63}$ **8.** $4\overline{)24}$

9. $6\overline{)54}$ **10.** $8\overline{)48}$ **11.** $4\overline{)32}$ **12.** $7\overline{)28}$

13. $36 \div 6 =$ _____   **14.** $42 \div 6 =$ _____   **15.** $72 \div 8 =$ _____

16. $49 \div 7 =$ _____   **17.** $54 \div 9 =$ _____   **18.** $12 \div 6 =$ _____

19. $\frac{25}{5} =$ _____   **20.** $\frac{18}{2} =$ _____   **21.** $\frac{28}{4} =$ _____

22. $\frac{15}{3} =$ _____   **23.** $\frac{21}{7} =$ _____   **24.** $\frac{54}{6} =$ _____

Solve.

25. Martin sells hay to the Run Free Stable. The stable uses 8 bales of hay each week. Martin delivers 72 bales of hay. For how many weeks will this hay last?

_____

Holt, Rinehart and Winston, Publishers • 5

Use with pages 132–133.

Kristine invited 6 friends to spend the weekend at her summer home. For lunch, Kristine's father made 15 tacos. Each guest ate 2 tacos. Kristine ate the remaining tacos. How many tacos did Kristine eat?

Remember

Divide and write the remainder next to the quotient.

$$\begin{array}{r} 2 \text{ R3} \leftarrow \text{quotient} \\ \text{divisor} \rightarrow 6\overline{)15} \leftarrow \text{dividend} \\ \underline{12} \\ 3 \leftarrow \text{remainder} \end{array}$$

The quotient times the divisor plus the remainder equals the dividend. This is a way to check your answer.

$$6 \times 2 = 12$$
$$12 + 3 = 15$$

Kristine ate 3 tacos.

Divide.

1. $4\overline{)35}$ **2.** $6\overline{)32}$ **3.** $5\overline{)18}$ **4.** $3\overline{)17}$

5. $6\overline{)28}$ **6.** $9\overline{)47}$ **7.** $8\overline{)50}$ **8.** $6\overline{)45}$

9. $4\overline{)37}$ **10.** $3\overline{)29}$ **11.** $7\overline{)68}$ **12.** $8\overline{)58}$

13. $62 \div 8 =$ _____   **14.** $73 \div 9 =$ _____

15. $58 \div 7 =$ _____   **16.** $53 \div 6 =$ _____

Holt, Rinehart and Winston, Publishers • 5

Is 30 divisible by 2, 5, or 10?

Remember

The following rules help you decide when a number is divisible by 2, 5, or 10.

Even numbers have 0, 2, 4, 6, or 8 in the ones place. They are divisible by 2.

Odd numbers have 1, 3, 5, 7, or 9 in the ones place. They are not divisible by 2.

Numbers that have 0 or 5 in the ones place are divisible by 5.

Numbers that have 0 in the ones place are divisible by 10.

Number	Rule	Division Sentences
30	It has 0 in the ones place.	$30 \div 2 = \underline{\quad 15 \quad}$ $30 \div 5 = \underline{\quad 6 \quad}$ $30 \div 10 = \underline{\quad 3 \quad}$

So, 30 is divisible by 2, 5, and 10.

Is the number divisible by 2? Write *yes* or *no*.

1. 3 _____   **2.** 5 _____   **3.** 6 _____   **4.** 10 _____   **5.** 15 _____

6. 7 _____   **7.** 12 _____   **8.** 13 _____   **9.** 20 _____   **10.** 22 _____

Is the number divisible by 5? Write *yes* or *no*.

11. 10 _____   **12.** 14 _____   **13.** 7 _____   **14.** 20 _____   **15.** 45 _____

16. 30 _____   **17.** 25 _____   **18.** 32 _____   **19.** 11 _____   **20.** 55 _____

Is the number divisible by 10? Write *yes* or *no*.

21. 20 _____   **22.** 25 _____   **23.** 30 _____   **24.** 33 _____   **25.** 45 _____

26. 50 _____   **27.** 55 _____   **28.** 23 _____   **29.** 31 _____   **30.** 80 _____

José Martín, star slugger for the Miami Maulers, has had
2,325 at bats in the last 4 seasons. If José batted about the
same number of times each season, about how many at bats
did he have two years ago?

Estimate 2,325 ÷ 4.

Remember

When estimating quotients, decide on the number of
digits in the quotient, and write zeros for the other digits
after you have found the first digit.

Divide the thousands. Think: $4\overline{)2}$. Not enough
thousands.
Divide the hundreds. Think: $4\overline{)23}$.
So, the quotient begins in the hundreds place.

It will have 3 digits. $4\overline{)2,325}$

Think: $5 \times 4 = 20$. $\overset{5}{4\overline{)2,325}}$
         $6 \times 4 = 24$.   Too great. So, use 5.

Write zeros for the other digits. $4\overline{)2,325}$ 500

José had about 500 at bats two years ago.

Write the number of digits the quotient will contain.

1. $3\overline{)483}$ _____   **2.** $5\overline{)3,162}$ _____   **3.** $6\overline{)7,016}$ _____   **4.** $2\overline{)1,982}$ _____

5. $9\overline{)1,106}$ _____   **6.** $7\overline{)7,386}$ _____   **7.** $8\overline{)5,486}$ _____   **8.** $3\overline{)9,722}$ _____

Estimate.

9. $7\overline{)637}$ **10.** $8\overline{)387}$ **11.** $5\overline{)8,486}$ **12.** $6\overline{)3,472}$ **13.** $9\overline{)8,203}$

14. $5\overline{)3,439}$ **15.** $4\overline{)8,264}$ **16.** $8\overline{)9,376}$ **17.** $2\overline{)7,387}$ **18.** $2\overline{)1,297}$

19. $7\overline{)54,486}$ **20.** $5\overline{)54,386}$ **21.** $9\overline{)38,475}$ **22.** $4\overline{)96,697}$ **23.** $3\overline{)18,927}$

Holt, Rinehart and Winston, Publishers • 5

Sue Ann delivers newspapers 7 days per week. She delivers 182 newspapers each week to the customers on her route. Each customer receives 1 paper per day. How many customers are there on Sue Ann's route?

Remember

Divide to find out how many sevens there are in 182.

Divide the hundreds.

$7)\overline{182}$

Not enough hundreds.

Divide the tens.

$$\begin{array}{r} 2 \\ 7)\overline{182} \\ 14 \\ \hline 42 \end{array}$$

Multiply. Subtract. Compare.

2 tens

Divide the ones.

$$\begin{array}{r} 26 \\ 7)\overline{182} \\ 14 \\ \hline 42 \\ 42 \\ \hline 0 \end{array}$$

Multiply. Subtract. Compare.

6 ones

2 tens 6 ones equal 26.

There are 26 customers on Sue Ann's route.

Divide.

1. $2)\overline{46}$

2. $3)\overline{81}$

3. $4)\overline{92}$

4. $6)\overline{72}$

5. $9)\overline{99}$

6. $2)\overline{47}$

7. $6)\overline{82}$

8. $6)\overline{75}$

9. $124 \div 7 =$ _____

10. $221 \div 5 =$ _____

11. $132 \div 3 =$ _____

12. $456 \div 9 =$ _____

Solve.

13. Sue Ann's brother, David, delivers the Sunday paper to 8 customers. How many Sundays will it take him to deliver 208 papers?

_____

Use with pages 144–145.

Paul works for the Good Sounds Record company. He has 5,262 records to sell to 8 stores. He wants each store to have the same number of records. Any records left over he will give to the local radio station. How many records does he sell to each store? How many records does he give to the radio station?

Remember

Divide to find how many eights there are in 5,262.

Divide the thousands.	Divide the hundreds.	Divide the tens.	Divide the ones.

Divide the thousands.

$$8)\overline{5,262}$$

Not enough thousands.

Divide the hundreds.

$$\begin{array}{r} 6 \\ 8)\overline{5,262} \\ \underline{4\ 8} \\ 4 \end{array}$$

Multiply. Subtract. Compare.

6 hundreds

Divide the tens.

$$\begin{array}{r} 65 \\ 8)\overline{5,262} \\ \underline{4\ 8} \\ 46 \\ \underline{40} \\ 62 \end{array}$$

Multiply. Subtract. Compare.

5 tens

Divide the ones.

$$\begin{array}{r} 657\ \text{R}6 \\ 8)\overline{5,262} \\ \underline{4\ 8} \\ 46 \\ \underline{40} \\ 62 \\ \underline{56} \\ 6 \end{array}$$

Multiply. Subtract. Compare. Write the Remainder.

7 ones

There are 6 hundreds, 5 tens, 7 ones and a remainder of 6.

Paul sold 657 records to each store and gave 7 records to the radio station.

Divide.

1. $2)\overline{340}$

2. $3)\overline{891}$

3. $2)\overline{560}$

4. $3)\overline{468}$

5. $4)\overline{648}$

6. $6)\overline{792}$

7. $5)\overline{975}$

8. $7)\overline{2,464}$

9. $324 \div 2 =$ _____

10. $489 \div 4 =$ _____

11. $951 \div 4 =$ _____

12. $\frac{878}{3} =$ _____

13. $\frac{328}{2} =$ _____

14. $\frac{672}{4} =$ _____

Holt, Rinehart and Winston, Publishers • 5

Mr. Noce works in Bertha's Bird Zoo. He delivers 28,514 pounds of birdseed to feed all the birds. The zoo has 8 buildings that contain birds. Mr. Noce delivers the same amount of birdseed to each building. How many pounds does he deliver to each building? How many pounds are left?

Remember

Place the first digit of the quotient in the proper place.

Divide the ten thousands.

$8\overline{)28,514}$

Not enough ten thousands.

Divide the thousands.

$$8\overline{)28,514} \quad \underline{24} \quad 4$$
3

| Multiply. |
| Subtract. |
| Compare. |

3 thousands

Divide the hundreds.

$$8\overline{)28,514} \quad \underline{24} \quad 45 \quad \underline{40} \quad 5$$
3 5

| Multiply. |
| Subtract. |
| Compare. |

5 hundreds

Divide the tens.

$$8\overline{)28,514}$$
356
24
45
40
51
48
3

| Multiply. |
| Subtract. |
| Compare. |

6 tens

Divide the ones.

$$8\overline{)28,514}$$
3,564 R2
24
45
40
51
48
34
32
2

| Multiply. |
| Subtract. |
| Compare. |

4 ones Remainder 2

Mr. Noce delivers 3,564 pounds of bird seed to each building. There are 2 pounds of birdseed left.

Divide.

1. $3\overline{)1,676}$

2. $2\overline{)9,452}$

3. $4\overline{)8,440}$

4. $6\overline{)7,860}$

Holt, Rinehart and Winston, Publishers • 5

The Build-It-Better Construction Company will build an apartment complex for 8,072 people. If each apartment is designed to house 4 people, how many apartments will the complex contain?

Remember

Keep the digits in the proper places.

Divide the thousands.	Divide the hundreds.	Divide the tens.	Divide the ones.

Divide the thousands.

```
    2
4)8,072
  8
```
Multiply.
Subtract.
Compare.

2 thousands

Divide the hundreds.

```
   2 0
4)8,072
  8
  ̄ ̄
   0
   0
```
Multiply.
Subtract.
Compare.

0 hundreds

Divide the tens.

```
   2 01
4)8,072
  8
   0
   0
   7
   4
   3
```
Multiply.
Subtract.
Compare.

1 ten

Divide the ones.

```
  2,018
4)8,072
  8
   0
   0
   7
   4
   32
   32
    0
```
Multiply.
Subtract.
Compare.

8 ones

There are no hundreds. So, we must place a zero in the quotient.

The complex will contain 2,018 apartments.

Divide.

1. 3)315

2. 4)820

3. 5)530

4. 6)1,236

5. 6)1,010

6. 9)5,680

7. 8)4,343

8. 5)3,994

9. 864 ÷ 8 = _____

10. 1,047 ÷ 7 = _____

11. 1,836 ÷ 9 = _____

Toby, Bernie, and Eleanor went to Hill's Hot-Dog Shop. The bill for the 3 of them amounted to $12.81. They split the bill evenly. How much did each person pay?

Remember

Put the dollar sign and the cents point in the proper place.

$$
\begin{array}{r}
\$\ 4.27 \\
3\overline{)\$12.81} \\
\underline{12} \\
8 \\
\underline{6} \\
21 \\
\underline{21} \\
0
\end{array}
$$

**Multiply.
Subtract.
Compare.**

Use multiplication to check.

$$
\begin{array}{r}
\$4.27 \\
\times\quad 3 \\
\hline
\$12.81
\end{array}
$$

Each person paid $4.27.

Divide.

1. $6\overline{)\$9.60}$

2. $3\overline{)\$4.23}$

3. $5\overline{)\$12.50}$

4. $7\overline{)\$6.37}$

5. $6\overline{)\$178.20}$

6. $4\overline{)\$864.52}$

7. $8\overline{)\$922.40}$

8. $3\overline{)\$940.68}$

9. $\$29.13 \div 3 = $ _____

10. $\$58.86 \div 9 = $ _____

Use with pages 154–155.

Trevor has a pony named Sassy that weighs 720 pounds. Trevor weighs 80 pounds. How many times as heavy as Trevor is Sassy?

Remember

Divide 720 by 80. Use division facts.

Think: (7 2) ÷ (8) = 9.
So, (7 2)0 ÷ (8)0 = 9.

Sassy is 9 times as heavy as Trevor.

Divide.

1. 10)‾90‾

2. 20)‾60‾

3. 40)‾80‾

4. 30)‾90‾

5. 20)‾80‾

6. 30)‾60‾

7. 40)‾80‾

8. 10)‾50‾

9. 50)‾50‾

10. 20)‾100‾

11. 40)‾120‾

12. 80)‾320‾

13. 70)‾210‾

14. 90)‾270‾

15. 20)‾120‾

16. 30)‾180‾

17. 20)‾100‾

18. 50)‾350‾

19. 20)‾120‾

20. 30)‾120‾

Solve

21. Trevor went fishing with his father. They caught 30 fish that weighed a total of 60 pounds. What was the average weight of each fish?

Holt, Rinehart and Winston, Publishers • 5

The students at the Hammon Elementary School sold 5,387 raffle tickets for their fair. The students sold the tickets in a period of 22 days. On the average, how many tickets did they sell each day?

Estimate $22\overline{)5{,}387}$.

Remember

When estimating quotients, decide on the number of digits in the quotient.

Divide the hundreds. Think: $22\overline{)53}$.
The quotient begins in the hundreds place.

It will have 3 digits. $22\overline{)5{,}387}$

Think: $2 \times 22 = 44$. Write 2. $22\overline{)5{,}387}^{\,2}$

Write zeros for the other digits. $22\overline{)5{,}387}$ ⟶ 200

The students sold about 200 tickets each day.

Write how many digits the quotient will contain.

1. $74\overline{)838}$ _____   **2.** $32\overline{)983}$ _____   **3.** $27\overline{)837}$ _____   **4.** $56\overline{)578}$ _____

5. $15\overline{)1{,}827}$ _____   **6.** $83\overline{)3{,}374}$ _____   **7.** $28\overline{)3{,}369}$ _____   **8.** $69\overline{)6{,}729}$ _____

9. $46\overline{)3{,}386}$ _____   **10.** $38\overline{)9{,}503}$ _____   **11.** $84\overline{)3{,}747}$ _____   **12.** $30\overline{)1{,}927}$ _____

Estimate. Write the letter of the correct answer.

13. $17\overline{)388}$ **a.** 2   **b.** 20   **c.** 200

14. $89\overline{)930}$ **a.** 1   **b.** 10   **c.** 100

15. $29\overline{)3{,}275}$ **a.** 10   **b.** 100   **c.** 1,000

Estimate.

16. $33\overline{)537}$ **17.** $12\overline{)973}$ **18.** $47\overline{)992}$ **19.** $14\overline{)739}$ **20.** $31\overline{)937}$

21. $93\overline{)7{,}473}$ **22.** $47\overline{)2{,}198}$ **23.** $71\overline{)3{,}343}$ **24.** $38\overline{)3{,}486}$ **25.** $12\overline{)1{,}098}$

The 21 members of the Maple Valley girls' basketball team scored 147 points during their first game. How many points did each girl score if they each scored an equal number of points?

Remember

Divide the total number of points by the number of girls.

Divide the hundreds. Think: $21\overline{)1}$. Not enough hundreds.
Divide the tens. Think: ②1$\overline{)14}$1 or $2\overline{)14}$.
Estimate 7.

| Multiply. |
| Subtract and compare. |

Each girl scored 7 points.

Divide.

1. $32\overline{)96}$
2. $24\overline{)72}$
3. $14\overline{)56}$
4. $22\overline{)66}$

5. $12\overline{)36}$
6. $31\overline{)65}$
7. $25\overline{)77}$
8. $31\overline{)67}$

9. $30\overline{)65}$
10. $27\overline{)85}$
11. $43\overline{)301}$
12. $65\overline{)260}$

13. $96 \div 11 =$ _____
14. $163 \div 18 =$ _____
15. $38 \div 16 =$ _____

Solve.

16. Mary Ann scored a total of 108 points during the first 12 games of the season. If she scored an equal number of points in each game, how many points did she score in each?

_____

Use with pages 172–173.

Becky did a science project on rainfall. She recorded the rainfall for her city. The rainfall amounted to 676 centimeters during the year. What was the average weekly rainfall?

Remember

Divide the total rainfall by the number of weeks.
Divide the hundreds. Think: $52\overline{)6}$. Not enough hundreds.

Divide the tens. Think: $52\overline{)67}$.

Divide the ones. Think: $52\overline{)156}$ or $5\overline{)15}$

Estimate ①.

```
      ①
 52)6 7 6
   5 2
   1 5     Multiply.
     6     Subtract and compare.
```

Estimate ③.

```
      1③
 52)6 7 6
   5 2 0
   1 5 6     Multiply.
   1 5 6     Subtract and compare.
```

The average weekly rainfall was 13 centimeters.

Divide.

1. $31\overline{)899}$

2. $65\overline{)780}$

3. $24\overline{)744}$

4. $76\overline{)\$12.16}$

5. $65\overline{)\$9.75}$

6. $43\overline{)767}$

7. $26\overline{)342}$

8. $45\overline{)747}$

9. $12\overline{)265}$

10. $27\overline{)899}$

11. $33\overline{)2,673}$

12. $97\overline{)5,917}$

13. $\frac{2,394}{57} = $ _____

14. $\frac{2,173}{41} = $ _____

15. $\frac{2,814}{67} = $ _____

Holt, Rinehart and Winston, Publishers • 5

Use with pages 174–175.

Mr. Bill owns a balloon factory. He sells balloons to 24 stores. He has 1,181 balloons to sell. How many balloons will each store receive? How many balloons will be left?

Remember

If the estimate of a digit in the quotient is incorrect, it needs to be corrected.

Divide the thousands. Think: $24\overline{)1}$. Not enough thousands.
Divide the hundreds. Think: $24\overline{)11}$. Not enough hundreds.
Divide the tens. Think: $24\overline{)118}$. Estimate 5.

Multiply. Too great.

$$\begin{array}{r} 5 \\ 24\overline{)1,181} \\ 120 \end{array}$$

You need to correct the estimate.

Estimate 4.
Multiply. Subtract.

$$\begin{array}{r} 4 \\ 24\overline{)1,181} \\ \underline{96} \\ 221 \end{array}$$

Divide the ones. Think: $24\overline{)221}$. Estimate 9.
Multiply. Subtract. Write the remainder.

$$\begin{array}{r} 49 \text{ R5} \\ 24\overline{)1,181} \\ 96 \\ \overline{221} \\ \underline{216} \\ 5 \end{array}$$

Mr. Bill can sell 49 balloons to each store. There will be 5 balloons left.

Find the quotient.

1. $12\overline{)547}$ **2.** $21\overline{)1,451}$ **3.** $33\overline{)793}$ **4.** $13\overline{)329}$

5. $67\overline{)3,757}$ **6.** $51\overline{)\$44.88}$ **7.** $76\overline{)4,792}$ **8.** $92\overline{)\$38.64}$

The Schobels ate 6,864 ounces of potatoes last year. What was the average number of ounces of potatoes they ate each week?

Remember

Divide the total number of ounces by the number of weeks.

Divide the thousands. Think: $52\overline{)6}$. Not enough thousands.

Divide the hundreds.
Think: $\boxed{5}2\overline{)\boxed{6}8}$ or $5\overline{)6}$.
Try ①.

```
      ①
52)6,864
   5 2
   1 6
```
Multiply.
Subtract.
Compare.

Divide the tens.
Think: $\boxed{5}2\overline{)\boxed{16}6}$ or $5\overline{)16}$.
Try ③.

```
       1③
52)6,864
   5 2
   1 66
   1 56
      1 0
```
Multiply.
Subtract.
Compare.

Divide the ones.
Think: $\boxed{5}2\overline{)\boxed{10}4}$ or $5\overline{)10}$.
Try ②.

```
       13②
52)6,864
   5 2
   1 66
   1 56
      1 04
      1 04
         0
```
Multiply.
Subtract.
Compare.

The Schobels ate an average of 132 ounces each week.

Divide.

1. $63\overline{)7,812}$

2. $14\overline{)2,338}$

3. $32\overline{)3,872}$

4. $36\overline{)\$92.52}$

5. $35\overline{)\$40.25}$

6. $75\overline{)9,912}$

7. $62\overline{)7,629}$

8. $42\overline{)6,153}$

9. $30\overline{)5,467}$

10. $31\overline{)7,553}$

11. $56\overline{)17,472}$

12. $56\overline{)14,168}$

Use with pages 180–181.

Mrs. Osland took her 23 grandchildren on a trip to an apple orchard. Her grandchildren picked 2,461 apples. What was the average number of apples picked by each grandchild?

Remember

Divide the thousands, the hundreds, the tens, and then the ones. At each step, multiply; then subtract and compare.

Divide the thousands.	Divide the hundreds.	Divide the tens. Not enough tens. Write ⓪.	Divide the ones.
$23)\overline{2,461}$ Not enough thousands.	① 23)2 , 4 6 1 ② 3 1	1 ⓪ 23)2 , 4 6 1 2 3 ↓ 1 6 0 1 6	1 0 ⑦ 23)2 , 4 6 1 2 3 ↓ 1 6 ↓ 0 ↓ 1 6 1 1 6 1 0

Each grandchild picked an average of 107 apples.

Divide.

1. $16)\overline{1,648}$ **2.** $46)\overline{9,338}$ **3.** $44)\overline{4,708}$ **4.** $67)\overline{6,901}$

5. $11)\overline{\$55.00}$ **6.** $29)\overline{\$31.03}$ **7.** $52)\overline{\$106.08}$ **8.** $26)\overline{13,078}$

9. $\frac{15,698}{31} =$ _____   **10.** $\frac{54,468}{65} =$ _____   **11.** $\frac{15,022}{37} =$ _____

Holt, Rinehart and Winston, Publishers • 5

Large portable radios use 30-volt batteries. Frederick's radio uses 10 of these batteries. How many volts does his radio use?

> **Remember**
>
> When multiplying by a multiple of 10, move the decimal point one place to the right for each zero that is in the multiple of 10.
>
> $$\begin{array}{r} 3.0 \\ \times\ 10 \\ \hline 30.0 \end{array}$$

Frederick's radio uses 30.0 volts.

Find $10)\overline{16.8}$.

> **Remember**
>
> To divide decimals by multiples of 10, move the decimal point one place to the left for each zero that is in the multiple of 10.
>
> $$16.8 \div 10 = 1.68$$
>
> Move the decimal point one place to the left.
> 16.8 divided by 10 is 1.68.

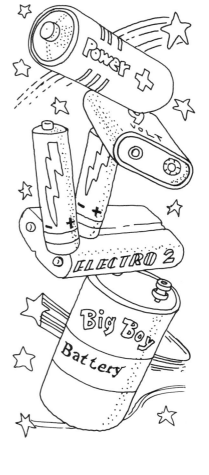

Multiply or divide.

1. $83 \times 10 =$ _____

2. $27.84 \div 10 =$ _____

3. $521.47 \times 100 =$ _____

4. $9{,}347 \div 100 =$ _____

5. $10 \times 624.5 =$ _____

6. $293 \times 100 =$ _____

7. $100 \times 0.87 =$ _____

8. $1{,}000 \times 9.167 =$ _____

9. $5{,}834 \div 1{,}000 =$ _____

10. $100)\overline{355.2}$

11. $10)\overline{160}$

12. $2.75 \times 100 =$ _____

13. $84.126 \times 10{,}000 =$ _____

14. $82{,}157 \div 10{,}000 =$ _____

Holt, Rinehart and Winston, Publishers • 5

When Stephanie was shopping, she noticed that a half
gallon of milk costs 2 times as much as a dozen small eggs.
Milk is selling for $1.24 per half gallon. What is the price of
the eggs?

Remember

Divide $1.24 by 2.

Divide the whole number.

```
   ⓪
2)1 . 2 4
  0
  1
```

Place the decimal point.
Divide the tenths.

```
  0 .⑥
2)1 . 2 4
  0 ↓
  1 2
 (1 2)
      0
```

Divide the hundredths.

```
  0 .⑥2
2)1 . 2 4
  0  |
  1 2|
  1 2↓
    0 4
     ④
      0
```

The price of the eggs is $0.62, or 62 cents.

Divide.

1. 5)8.35

2. 8)9.84

3. 7)17.92

4. 3)6.42

5. 4)3.28

6. 12)28.08

7. 13)81.12

8. 56)176.96

9. 29)38.28

10. 89)59.63

11. 7)60.2

12. 6)24.78

13. 26.32 ÷ 4 = _____

14. 91.325 ÷ 5 = _____

15. 57.5 ÷ 23 = _____

At Super Quick Supermarket, a 3-pound package of
hamburger is on sale for $3.18. What is the cost of 1 pound?

┌─ **Remember** ──┐

When you have to write a zero in the quotient, you must multiply by it as well.

Divide the whole number.   Divide the tenths.   Divide the hundredths.

Sometimes you may have to write zeros in the dividend.

Example:

$$
\begin{array}{r}
2.202 \\
15\overline{)33.030} \leftarrow \text{Write 0.} \\
\underline{30} \\
30 \\
\underline{30} \\
03 \\
\underline{0} \\
30 \\
\underline{30} \\
0
\end{array}
$$

└──┘

The cost of 1 pound of hamburger is $1.06.

Divide.

1. 3)6.12   **2.** 5)4.05   **3.** 4)8.12   **4.** 6)18.12

5. 2)4.16   **6.** 7)21.14   **7.** 8)24.32   **8.** 9)72.54

Holt, Rinehart and Winston, Publishers • 5

Throughout history, people made measurements with whatever tool was handy. Parts of the body have also been used for measurement. For instance, the distance from the elbow to the tips of the fingers was called a *cubit*. Lumberjacks used their ax handles for measuring. The most common system of measurement used today is the metric system. The numbers on the metric ruler below indicate lengths called *centimeters (cm)*.

Use a metric ruler to measure each object.

1.

The penny is _____ cm wide.

2.

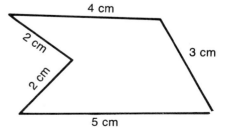

The calculator is _____ cm long.

Each centimeter can be divided into 10 units called millimeters (mm).

millimeters   centimeters

Measure each object to the nearest millimeter.

3.

The dime is _____ mm wide.

4.

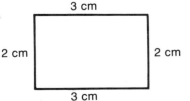

The paper clip is _____ mm long.

Find the distance around each shape.

5.

3 cm

2 cm   2 cm

3 cm

6.

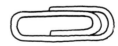

4 cm

2 cm

2 cm

3 cm

5 cm

At the Olympics, all measurements are made in metric units.
One lap around the track equals 400 meters (m). Ten laps
around the track equals 4,000 m, or 4 kilometers (km).

Remember these relationships:

1 centimeter (cm)   =   10 millimeters (mm)
1 meter (m)   =   100 centimeters (cm)
1 kilometer (km)   =   1,000 meters (m)

If Bob ran a 10,000-meter race, how many kilometers did he run?

Remember
Divide to rename smaller units with larger units. $10,000 \div 1,000 = 10$

Bob ran 10 kilometers.

Multiply to rename larger units with smaller units.

14 km = _____ m
 1 km = 1,000 m
14 km = 14,000 m

Which unit would you use to measure?
Write mm, cm, m, or km.

1. the length of your classroom _____

2. the length of your pencil _____

3. the height of a cat _____

4. the distance from your house to school _____

5. the length of a basketball court _____

6. the thickness of a quarter _____

Complete.

7. 3.5 mm = _____ cm

8. 3 km = _____ m

9. 5,000 m = _____ km

10. 150 cm = _____ m

11. 39 cm = _____ mm

12. 310 m = _____ km

13. 5 km = _____ m

14. 2.74 m = _____ cm

15. 905 m = _____ km

Solve.

16. Bob ran a 15-kilometer race. How many meters did he run?

_____

Holt, Rinehart and Winston, Publishers • 5

Peter kept a record of how much water his hamster drank each day for a year. He found that the hamster drank 1,460 milliliters of water during the year. How many liters of water did the hamster drink in one year?

1 liter (L)   =   1,000 milliliters (mL)

Remember

Divide to rename smaller units with larger units.

$1,460 \div 1,000 = 1.460$

The hamster drank 1.460 L of water in one year.

Which unit would you use to measure the liquid?
Write mL or L.

1. in a swimming pool _____   **2.** in a pail of water _____

3. in a bathtub _____   **4.** in a bottle of syrup _____

5. in a can of soup _____   **6.** in a bottle of vegetable oil _____

7. in a large water tank _____   **8.** in a test tube _____

Complete.

9. 5 L = _____ mL   **10.** 13 L = _____ mL   **11.** 0.9 L = _____ mL

12. 5.3 L = _____ mL   **13.** 0.3 L = _____ mL   **14.** 962 L = _____ mL

15. 182 mL = _____ L   **16.** 735 mL = _____ L   **17.** 38.027 L = _____ mL

18. 0.088 L = _____ mL **19.** 9,526 mL = _____ L   **20.** 92 mL = _____ L

Solve.

21. During the months of June, July, and August, Peter's hamster drank 0.357 L of water. During January, February, and March, the hamster drank 325 mL of water. Did the hamster drink more water in the winter or in the summer? How much more?

_____

In the metric system, a gram is the basic unit used to measure mass. A gram is made up of 1,000 units called milligrams. A kilogram is made up of 1,000 grams.

Remember these relationships:

1 gram (g)	=	1,000 milligrams (mg)
1 kilogram (kg)	=	1,000 grams (g)

John buys cat food for his cat, Alfie. He reads the label on the cat-food can. The label states that the can contains 1.81 kg of cat food. How many grams of cat food are there in the can?

Remember

Multiply to rename larger units with smaller units.

$$1.81 \times 1,000 = 1,810$$

There are 1,810 grams of cat food in the can.

Which unit would you use to measure the mass?
Write mg, g, or kg.

1. a matchbox car _____

2. a raindrop _____

3. a small dog _____

4. your mathematics book _____

5. a bicycle _____

6. a drop of water _____

7. a box of cereal _____

8. a fly _____

Complete.

9. 91 kg = _____ g

10. 2.1 kg = _____ g

11. 74 g = _____ kg

12. 52 kg = _____ g

13. 0.02 g = _____ mg

14. 948 mg = _____ g

15. 7,233 mg = _____ g

16. 4.32 g = _____ mg

17. 0.054 kg = _____ g

18. 756 g = _____ mg

19. 870 mg = _____ g

20. 98 kg = _____ g

Use with pages 212–213.

Mary has a baby-sitting job for 6 hours each day during the summer. Jill has a baby-sitting job for only 4 hours each day. What is the least number of days each girl will have to baby-sit to work for the same total hours? How many hours will that be?

Remember

To find the least number of days each must baby-sit to work for the same number of hours, find the least common multiple of 6 and 4.

The least common multiple of two numbers is the smallest number, other than zero, that is a common multiple of both numbers.

The first 6 multiples of 6 are

$0 \times 6 = ⓪$	$3 \times 6 = 18$
$1 \times 6 = 6$	$4 \times 6 = ㉔$
$\boxed{2} \times 6 = ⑫$	$5 \times 6 = 30$

The first 6 multiples of 4 are

$0 \times 4 = ⓪$	$\boxed{3} \times 4 = ⑫$
$1 \times 4 = 4$	$4 \times 4 = 16$
$2 \times 4 = 8$	$5 \times 4 = 20$

0, 12, and 24 are common multiples of 6 and 4. The least common multiple of 6 and 4 is 12.

So, Mary must baby-sit for 2 days and Jill must baby-sit for 3 days in order for each to work for 12 hours.

Find the least common multiple.

1. 2, 6 _____

2. 3, 4 _____

3. 4, 5 _____

4. 3, 5 _____

5. 2, 8 _____

6. 5, 9 _____

7. 6, 10 _____

8. 9, 12 _____

9. 12, 18 _____

10. 18, 24 _____

11. 3, 5, 6 _____

12. 2, 4, 6 _____

13. 3, 6, 9 _____

Holt, Rinehart and Winston, Publishers • 5

Jaime and Andy are making costumes for a school play. So far, Jaime has made 18 masks for the play, and Andy has made 24. What is the greatest common factor of 18 and 24?

Remember

To find the greatest common factor of two numbers, first find the common factors of the two numbers. To find the greatest common factor of 18 and 24, first find the common factors of 18 and 24.

The factors of 18 are all the numbers between 1 and 18 that divide 18 with a remainder of 0.

The factors of 18 are ①, ②, ③, ⑥, 9, and 18.

The factors of 24 are all the numbers between 1 and 24 that divide 24 with a remainder of zero.

The factors of 24 are ①, ②, ③, 4, ⑥, 8, 12, and 24.

The common factors of 18 and 24 are 1, 2, 3, and 6. They appear on both lists. The greatest common factor of 18 and 24 is 6.

List the common factors of these numbers.

1. 4, 6	**2.** 8, 10	**3.** 6, 9	**4.** 8, 12	**5.** 15, 20
_____	_____	_____	_____	_____
6. 12, 30	**7.** 18, 30	**8.** 30, 40	**9.** 3, 5	**10.** 15, 30
_____	_____	_____	_____	_____

Find the greatest common factor of these numbers.

11. 6, 8	**12.** 4, 10	**13.** 6, 9	**14.** 3, 12	**15.** 5, 15
_____	_____	_____	_____	_____
16. 12, 30	**17.** 18, 20	**18.** 12, 36	**19.** 3, 7	**20.** 2, 5
_____	_____	_____	_____	_____

Solve.

21. John and Kathy went fishing. John caught 18 fish, and Kathy caught 30 fish. What is the greatest number of fish each could catch per hour if they caught the same number of fish per hour?

Use with pages 228–229.

Is 81 a prime number or a composite number?

> **Remember**
>
> A **prime number** has only two factors: itself and 1. A **composite number** consists of more than two factors.
>
> List the factors of 81.
>
> The factors of 81 are 1, 3, 9, 27, and 81.

Since 81 has more than two factors, it is a composite number.

List all the factors of each number.

1. 7 _____   **2.** 18 _____   **3.** 27 _____

4. 35 _____   **5.** 52 _____   **6.** 69 _____

Write *prime* or *composite* to describe each number.

7. 8 _____   **8.** 19 _____   **9.** 37 _____   **10.** 77 _____

11. 91 _____   **12.** 84 _____   **13.** 54 _____   **14.** 87 _____

15. 63 _____   **16.** 79 _____   **17.** 83 _____   **18.** 57 _____

Draw a factor tree to write the prime factorization of each number.

19. 18   **20.** 48   **21.** 64

Holt, Rinehart and Winston, Publishers • 5

Kim cut a pizza into 8 pieces. She and her friends ate 6
pieces of the pie. What fraction of the pie is left?

Remember
The numerator shows the part of the pie that is left. The denominator shows the total number of pieces in the whole pie. numerator ——→ 2 parts ——————————— denominator ——→ 8 whole There were 8 pieces in the pie. There are 2 pieces left.

$\frac{2}{8}$ of the pie is left.

Write the fraction for the part that is shaded.

1.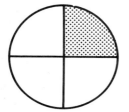

2.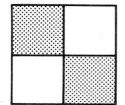

3.

4.

_____   _____   _____   _____

5.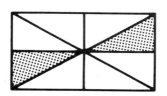

6.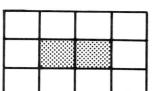

7.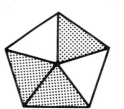

8.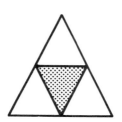

_____   _____   _____   _____

Solve.

9. Alan, a mechanic, is overhauling an 8-cylinder engine. He
has repaired 3 cylinders. What fraction of the cylinders
are repaired?

_____

Holt, Rinehart and Winston, Publishers • 5

In the early days of farming, most of the work was done by horses. Some farmers still use horses to help them with their work. Oscar has 8 horses on his farm.

Today, he used $\frac{1}{2}$ of his horses to plow the field. Write an equivalent fraction for $\frac{1}{2}$.

Remember

To find equivalent fractions, multiply the numerator and the denominator by the same number other than zero.

$$\frac{1}{2} = \frac{1 \times 2}{2 \times 2} = \frac{2}{4} \qquad \frac{1}{2} = \frac{1 \times 3}{2 \times 3} = \frac{3}{6} \qquad \frac{1}{2} = \frac{1 \times 4}{2 \times 4} = \frac{4}{8}$$

$\frac{1}{2}$ and $\frac{2}{4}$ are equivalent fractions.

Also: $\frac{1}{2} = \frac{2}{4} = \frac{3}{6} = \frac{4}{8}$

Write three fractions that are equivalent to each fraction.

1. $\frac{1}{2}$ _____

2. $\frac{2}{3}$ _____

3. $\frac{3}{4}$ _____

4. $\frac{4}{5}$ _____

5. $\frac{1}{3}$ _____

6. $\frac{2}{5}$ _____

7. $\frac{1}{6}$ _____

8. $\frac{2}{7}$ _____

9. $\frac{2}{9}$ _____

10. $\frac{3}{8}$ _____

11. $\frac{1}{10}$ _____

12. $\frac{7}{9}$ _____

Solve.

13. Oscar used 6 of his 8 horses to pull a plow. Write this as a fraction. Then write an equivalent fraction.

_____

Simplifying Fractions

Long ago, the McCade family had a farm and 18 horses. During harvesttime, they used 9 horses in the morning and the remaining 9 horses in the afternoon. In other words, they used $\frac{9}{18}$ of their horses in the morning and $\frac{9}{18}$ of their horses in the afternoon. How is $\frac{9}{18}$ written as a fraction in simplest form?

Remember

To write a fraction in simplest form, divide the numerator and the denominator by their greatest common factor. The greatest common factor of 9 and 18 is 9. Divide both the numerator and the denominator by 9.

$$\frac{9}{18} \div \frac{9}{9} = \frac{1}{2}$$

$\frac{9}{18}$ in simplest form is $\frac{1}{2}$.

Write these fractions in simplest form.

1. $\frac{9}{27}$ _____

2. $\frac{8}{10}$ _____

3. $\frac{7}{14}$ _____

4. $\frac{8}{12}$ _____

5. $\frac{6}{9}$ _____

6. $\frac{4}{6}$ _____

7. $\frac{10}{30}$ _____

8. $\frac{15}{20}$ _____

9. $\frac{12}{18}$ _____

10. $\frac{14}{24}$ _____

11. $\frac{12}{14}$ _____

12. $\frac{16}{18}$ _____

Solve.

13. If 4 of 36 horses were used to pull a plow, what fraction of the horses was used to pull the plow? Write this fraction in simplest form.

_____

Holt, Rinehart and Winston, Publishers • 5

Use with pages 238–239.

The world's largest known opal was found in southern Australia in 1956. It measured 10 inches by $5\frac{1}{2}$ inches by 5 inches.

Write $5\frac{1}{2}$ as a fraction.

Remember

To rename a mixed number as a fraction:

Multiply the whole number by the denominator.	Add the product and the numerator.	Write the sum over the denominator.
$5\frac{1}{2} \longrightarrow 2 \times 5 = 10$	$10 + 1 = 11$	$\frac{11}{2}$

$5\frac{1}{2} = \frac{11}{2}$

Write as a fraction.

1. $2\frac{1}{3}$ _____

2. $4\frac{3}{4}$ _____

3. $3\frac{2}{3}$ _____

4. $7\frac{5}{8}$ _____

5. $8\frac{6}{7}$ _____

6. $4\frac{1}{10}$ _____

7. $2\frac{2}{3}$ _____

8. $5\frac{1}{9}$ _____

9. $8\frac{3}{7}$ _____

10. $2\frac{1}{4}$ _____

11. $8\frac{5}{8}$ _____

12. $10\frac{3}{4}$ _____

Write as a whole number or as a mixed number.

13. $\frac{11}{3}$ _____

14. $\frac{16}{3}$ _____

15. $\frac{9}{4}$ _____

16. $\frac{13}{5}$ _____

17. $\frac{15}{6}$ _____

18. $\frac{9}{2}$ _____

19. $\frac{9}{3}$ _____

20. $\frac{8}{3}$ _____

21. $\frac{14}{7}$ _____

22. $\frac{16}{2}$ _____

23. $\frac{21}{5}$ _____

24. $\frac{39}{6}$ _____

Julie and Sandy each bought a pound of blueberries.
Julie used $\frac{2}{3}$ of her blueberries to make a blueberry pie.
Sandy used $\frac{5}{8}$ of her blueberries to make a fruit salad. Which
girl used more blueberries?

Remember

Before comparing $\frac{2}{3}$ and $\frac{5}{8}$, you need to write equivalent fractions for $\frac{2}{3}$ and $\frac{5}{8}$.

The least common multiple of the denominators 3 and 8 is 24.

$24 \div 3 = 8$; so multiply the numerator and the denominator by 8. Compare the numerators.

$$\frac{2}{3} = \frac{2 \times 8}{3 \times 8} = \frac{16}{24}$$

$24 \div 8 = 3$, so multiply the numerator and the denominator by 3.

$$\frac{\cancel{16}}{24} > \frac{\cancel{15}}{24}$$

$\frac{16}{24}$ is greater than $\frac{15}{24}$.

$$\frac{5}{8} = \frac{5 \times 3}{8 \times 3} = \frac{15}{24}$$

Julie used more blueberries.

Compare. Write $>$, $<$, or $=$ for $\bigcirc$.

1. $\frac{2}{5} \bigcirc \frac{3}{5}$ **2.** $\frac{3}{7} \bigcirc \frac{4}{7}$ **3.** $\frac{3}{10} \bigcirc \frac{5}{10}$ **4.** $\frac{5}{8} \bigcirc \frac{3}{8}$

5. $\frac{2}{7} \bigcirc \frac{3}{4}$ **6.** $\frac{2}{3} \bigcirc \frac{4}{6}$ **7.** $\frac{3}{6} \bigcirc \frac{1}{2}$ **8.** $\frac{2}{3} \bigcirc \frac{7}{8}$

9. $3\frac{1}{2} \bigcirc 2\frac{1}{3}$ **10.** $3\frac{5}{8} \bigcirc 2\frac{7}{8}$ **11.** $3\frac{3}{4} \bigcirc 5\frac{1}{4}$

12. $2\frac{1}{2} \bigcirc 2\frac{3}{8}$ **13.** $\frac{4}{5} \bigcirc \frac{5}{7}$ **14.** $3\frac{1}{3} \bigcirc 4\frac{1}{4}$

Solve.

15. Kay and Alan had a race. They agreed that the winner would be the person who did more mathematics homework in an hour. After one hour, Kay had done $\frac{3}{4}$ of her homework, and Alan had done $\frac{6}{7}$ of his homework. Which one did more homework in one hour? _____

Holt, Rinehart and Winston, Publishers • 5

Use with pages 242–243.

Susan cut the grass today. She used $\frac{5}{9}$ of a gallon of gas to cut the front lawn and $\frac{2}{9}$ of a gallon to cut the back lawn. How much gas did Susan use to cut both sections of the lawn?

Remember

To add fractions that have like denominators, add the numerators only. Write the sum over the denominator.

$$\frac{5}{9} \quad + \quad \frac{2}{9} \quad = \quad \frac{5+2}{9} \quad = \quad \frac{7}{9}$$

Add. Write the answer in simplest form.

1. $\frac{2}{8} + \frac{3}{8} =$ _____

2. $\frac{3}{5} + \frac{1}{5} =$ _____

3. $\frac{3}{7} + \frac{2}{7} =$ _____

4. $\frac{3}{10} + \frac{4}{10} =$ _____

5. $\frac{1}{9} + \frac{4}{9} =$ _____

6. $\frac{1}{3} + \frac{1}{3} =$ _____

7. $\frac{1}{5} + \frac{2}{5} =$ _____

8. $\frac{2}{9} + \frac{4}{9} =$ _____

9. $\frac{7}{15} + \frac{4}{15} =$ _____

10. $\frac{3}{10} + \frac{2}{10} =$ _____

11. $\frac{1}{4} + \frac{3}{4} =$ _____

12. $\frac{1}{2} + \frac{3}{2} =$ _____

13. $\frac{4}{6} + \frac{5}{6} =$ _____

14. $\frac{5}{12} + \frac{9}{12} =$ _____

15. $\frac{3}{8} + \frac{7}{8} =$ _____

16. $\frac{5}{11} + \frac{6}{11} =$ _____

17. $\frac{9}{22} + \frac{7}{22} =$ _____

18. $\frac{7}{15} + \frac{4}{15} =$ _____

Estimate $\frac{11}{20} + \frac{1}{6} + \frac{7}{8}$.

Remember

In order to estimate the sum of fractions, you need to estimate the value of each fraction by comparing the numerator and the denominator.
- When the numerator is much smaller than the denominator, round the fraction to 0.
- When the denominator is about twice as large as the numerator, round the fraction to $\frac{1}{2}$.
- When the numerator is nearly the same as the denominator, round the fraction to 1.

Estimate $\frac{11}{20} + \frac{1}{6} + \frac{7}{8}$.

Round each fraction to 0, $\frac{1}{2}$, or 1.

about $\frac{1}{2}$	about 0	about 1
$\frac{11}{20}$	$\frac{1}{6}$	$\frac{7}{8}$

$$\frac{1}{2} + 0 + 1 = 1\frac{1}{2}$$

The sum $\frac{11}{20} + \frac{1}{6} + \frac{7}{8}$ is about $1\frac{1}{2}$.

Write 0, $\frac{1}{2}$, or 1 to complete.

1. $\frac{5}{9}$ is close to _____

2. $\frac{13}{14}$ is close to _____

3. $\frac{3}{17}$ is close to _____

Estimate.

4. $\frac{1}{9} + \frac{15}{19}$ _____

5. $\frac{24}{75} + \frac{19}{20}$ _____

6. $\frac{11}{12} + \frac{17}{18}$ _____

Solve.

7. Paul used $\frac{3}{8}$ of a can of paint to paint his living room, $\frac{6}{7}$ of a can of paint to paint his dining room, and $\frac{1}{6}$ of a can of paint to paint his bathroom. Estimate how many cans of paint Paul needed to paint these three rooms.

8. Alice used $\frac{14}{15}$ of a can of paint to paint her bedroom, $\frac{5}{9}$ of a can of paint to paint her kitchen, and $\frac{7}{30}$ of a can of paint to paint her den. Estimate how many cans of paint Alice needed to paint these three rooms.

_____

_____

Holt, Rinehart and Winston, Publishers • 5

It's sheep-shearing time on Tom and Jenny's ranch. Today, they sheared $\frac{1}{4}$ of their herd. Tomorrow they will shear $\frac{1}{5}$ of the remaining sheep. By the end of the workday tomorrow, what portion of the sheep will have been sheared?

Remember

To add fractions that have unlike denominators, you need to write equivalent fractions that have common denominators.

$$\frac{1}{4} \quad + \quad \frac{1}{5} \quad = \quad \frac{1 \times 5}{4 \times 5} \quad + \quad \frac{1 \times 4}{5 \times 4}$$

$$= \quad \frac{5}{20} + \frac{4}{20} = \quad \frac{5+4}{20} = \quad \frac{9}{20}$$

$\frac{9}{20}$ of the sheep will have been sheared.

Add. Write the answer in simplest form.

1. $\frac{1}{2} + \frac{1}{4} =$ _____

2. $\frac{2}{9} + \frac{1}{3} =$ _____

3. $\frac{1}{5} + \frac{2}{10} =$ _____

4. $\frac{3}{4} + \frac{5}{8} =$ _____

5. $\frac{1}{7} + \frac{3}{14} =$ _____

6. $\frac{2}{7} + \frac{1}{3} =$ _____

7. $\frac{4}{5} + \frac{2}{3} =$ _____

8. $\frac{5}{10} + \frac{3}{8} =$ _____

9. $\frac{4}{5} + \frac{5}{9} =$ _____

10. $\frac{5}{6} + \frac{3}{8} =$ _____

11. $\frac{7}{11} + \frac{5}{6} =$ _____

12. $\frac{3}{7} + \frac{3}{4} =$ _____

13. $\frac{4}{5} + \frac{5}{6} =$ _____

14. $\frac{4}{9} + \frac{3}{4} =$ _____

Holt, Rinehart and Winston, Publishers • 5

Use with pages 250–251.

Lisa's school is holding a dance. All the tickets have been sold. The cheerleaders sold $\frac{2}{5}$ of all of the tickets. The basketball team sold $\frac{1}{10}$ of all the tickets. How many more tickets did the cheerleaders sell than the basketball team?

Remember

In order to subtract unlike fractions, write them as equivalent fractions that have a common denominator.

$$\begin{array}{l} \frac{2}{5} = \frac{4}{10} \\ -\frac{1}{10} = \frac{1}{10} \\ \hline \frac{3}{10} \end{array} \qquad \boxed{\frac{2}{5} = \frac{2 \times 2}{5 \times 2} = \frac{4}{10}}$$

The cheerleaders sold $\frac{3}{10}$ more tickets.

Subtract. Write the answer in simplest form

1. $\frac{5}{7} - \frac{2}{7} =$ _____

2. $\frac{5}{9} - \frac{4}{9} =$ _____

3. $\frac{5}{6} - \frac{2}{6} =$ _____

4. $\frac{3}{4} - \frac{1}{4} =$ _____

5. $\frac{7}{10} - \frac{3}{10} =$ _____

6. $\frac{5}{6} - \frac{3}{12} =$ _____

7. $\frac{2}{3} - \frac{2}{6} =$ _____

8. $\frac{9}{12} - \frac{2}{8} =$ _____

9. $\frac{4}{9} - \frac{3}{27} =$ _____

10. $\frac{4}{4} - \frac{5}{8} =$ _____

11. $\frac{7}{12} - \frac{4}{8} =$ _____

12. $\frac{3}{5} - \frac{3}{7} =$ _____

13. $\frac{2}{3} - \frac{1}{4} =$ _____

14. $\frac{1}{5} - \frac{2}{15} =$ _____

Holt, Rinehart and Winston, Publishers • 5

Adding Mixed Numbers

Mark and Sara are baking muffins for their club's bake sale. They baked $5\frac{1}{2}$ dozen blueberry muffins and $4\frac{2}{3}$ dozen cranberry muffins. How many dozens of muffins did they bake altogether?

Remember

Find equivalent fractions that have common denominators before adding. Add the whole numbers and the numerators only.

Find equivalent fractions that have common denominators.	Add the fractions.	Add the whole numbers.
$5\frac{1}{2} \longrightarrow 5\frac{3}{6}$ $+4\frac{1}{3} \longrightarrow +4\frac{2}{6}$	$5\frac{3}{6}$ $+4\frac{2}{6}$ $\frac{5}{6}$	$5\frac{3}{6}$ $+4\frac{2}{6}$ $9\frac{5}{6}$

They baked $9\frac{5}{6}$ dozen muffins.

Add. Write the answer in simplest form.

1. $6\frac{3}{7}$
$+4$

2. 7
$+9\frac{5}{8}$

3. 12
$+3\frac{1}{4}$

4. $3\frac{2}{7}$
$+4\frac{3}{7}$

5. $6\frac{1}{5}$
$+3\frac{2}{5}$

6. $2\frac{1}{3}$
$+4\frac{1}{3}$

7. $6\frac{2}{5}$
$+3\frac{4}{10}$

8. $9\frac{1}{8}$
$+7\frac{3}{16}$

9. $5\frac{1}{6}$
$+4\frac{3}{18}$

10. $7\frac{1}{3}$
$+1\frac{1}{2}$

Solve.

11. Gerald works for a small bakery. One week, he worked $4\frac{1}{2}$ hours overtime. The next week, he worked $6\frac{1}{3}$ hours overtime. For how many hours did he work overtime in 2 weeks?

Holt, Rinehart and Winston, Publishers • 5

Jules and Jim are picking berries. Jules picks $11\frac{3}{4}$ pounds and Jim picks $8\frac{5}{8}$. How many pounds of berries do they pick altogether?

You can add to answer this question.

Add $11\frac{3}{4} + 8\frac{5}{8}$.

Remember			
Find fractions with a common denominator.	Add the fractions.	Add the whole numbers.	Write the sum in simplest form.
$11\frac{3}{4} = 11\frac{7}{8}$ $+\ 8\frac{5}{8} =\ 8\frac{5}{8}$	$11\frac{3}{4} = 11\frac{7}{8}$ $+\ 8\frac{5}{8} =\ 8\frac{5}{8}$ $\frac{12}{8}$	$11\frac{3}{4} = 11\frac{7}{8}$ $+\ 8\frac{5}{8} =\ 8\frac{5}{8}$ $19\frac{12}{8}$	$19\frac{12}{8} = 19 + 1\frac{4}{8}$ $20\frac{4}{8} = 20\frac{1}{2}$

Jules and Jim picked $20\frac{1}{2}$ pounds of berries.

Add. Write the answer in simplest form.

1. $\quad 3\frac{5}{8}$
$\quad +4\frac{1}{2}$

2. $\quad 3\frac{1}{5}$
$\quad +3\frac{7}{8}$

3. $\quad 4\frac{2}{3}$
$\quad +5\frac{3}{5}$

4. $\quad 5\frac{8}{9}$
$\quad +4\frac{1}{6}$

5. $\quad 6\frac{7}{9}$
$\quad +4\frac{1}{2}$

6. $\quad 9\frac{5}{6}$
$\quad +5\frac{2}{3}$

7. $\quad 12\frac{13}{14}$
$\quad +\ 4\frac{4}{7}$

8. $\quad 7\frac{2}{3}$
$\quad +7\frac{14}{15}$

9. $7\frac{7}{8} + 8\frac{7}{16}$

10. $5\frac{2}{3} + 6\frac{6}{7}$

11. $6\frac{3}{4} + 7\frac{13}{16}$

12. $6\frac{9}{10} + 7\frac{1}{3}$

13. $5\frac{2}{9} + 3\frac{17}{18}$

14. $6\frac{2}{5} + 4\frac{14}{15}$

15. $6\frac{7}{8} + 9\frac{3}{10}$

16. $4\frac{5}{12} + 8\frac{5}{6}$

Holt, Rinehart and Winston, Publishers • 5

Don's fruit farm has $6\frac{3}{4}$ acres of strawberries
and raspberries. He has $2\frac{1}{4}$ acres of raspberries.
How many acres of strawberries does Don have?

Find $6\frac{3}{4} - 2\frac{1}{4}$.

Remember

Subtract the whole numbers and the numerators, not the denominators.

Subtract the fractions.

$$6\frac{3}{4}$$
$$-2\frac{1}{4}$$
$$\overline{\quad\frac{2}{4}}$$

Subtract the whole numbers.

$$6\frac{3}{4}$$
$$-2\frac{1}{4}$$
$$\overline{4\frac{2}{4} = 4\frac{1}{2}}$$

Don has $4\frac{1}{2}$ acres of strawberries.

Subtract. Write the answer in simplest form.

1. $4\frac{3}{8} - 1\frac{1}{8} =$ _____

2. $3\frac{3}{4} - 3\frac{1}{4} =$ _____

3. $4\frac{5}{8} - 2\frac{1}{2} =$ _____

4. $9\frac{4}{7} - 6\frac{1}{7} =$ _____

5. $5\frac{1}{2} - 3\frac{1}{4} =$ _____

6. $9\frac{2}{5} - 3\frac{1}{6} =$ _____

7. $7\frac{5}{8} - 5\frac{1}{2} =$ _____

8. $9\frac{6}{7} - 4\frac{1}{3} =$ _____

Solve.

9. Don had $10\frac{3}{4}$ pints of strawberries. He sold $6\frac{1}{2}$ pints of strawberries. How many pints of strawberries does Don have left?

_____

Holt, Rinehart and Winston, Publishers • 5

Dan and Beth had an 8-hour baby-sitting job. Dan baby-sat first for $5\frac{1}{4}$ hours, and Beth sat next for the remaining hours. For how many hours did Beth baby-sit?

Remember

Sometimes, you must rename a fraction or a whole number in order to subtract.

Rename.   Subtract.

$$
\begin{array}{r}
8 \\
-5\frac{1}{4} \\
\hline
\end{array}
\longrightarrow
\quad
\begin{array}{r}
7\frac{4}{4} \\
-5\frac{1}{4} \\
\hline
2\frac{3}{4}
\end{array}
$$

$$8 = 7 + \frac{4}{4} = 7\frac{4}{4}$$

Beth baby-sat for $2\frac{3}{4}$ hours.

Subtract. Write the answer in simplest form.

1. $5\frac{1}{4} - 2\frac{3}{4} =$ _____

2. $4\frac{3}{10} - 1\frac{5}{10} =$ _____

3. $8\frac{1}{7} - 2\frac{1}{7} =$ _____

4. $3\frac{5}{16} - 1\frac{7}{16} =$ _____

5. $7\frac{1}{5} - 6\frac{1}{20} =$ _____

6. $12\frac{1}{3} - 3\frac{5}{6} =$ _____

7. $5\frac{2}{3} - 2\frac{7}{10} =$ _____

8. $9 - 2\frac{5}{7} =$ _____

Solve.

9. Mark mowed 8 lawns each week. By noontime on Wednesday, he had mowed $5\frac{1}{4}$ lawns. How many lawns did Mark have left to mow?

_____

10. Allison is a prospector for gold. She finds a large ingot that weighs $14\frac{1}{8}$ grams. After she scrapes away $3\frac{5}{24}$ grams of dirt from the ingot, she is left with pure gold. What is the weight of the pure gold ingot?

_____

Holt, Rinehart and Winston, Publishers • 5

A hailstorm destroyed $\frac{1}{4}$ of a farmer's sunflower crop. He had $\frac{3}{4}$ of his crop left. Sunflower beetles destroyed $\frac{1}{2}$ of the remaining crop. What part of the sunflower crop remained?

Remember

You need to find $\frac{1}{2}$ of $\frac{3}{4}$ of his crop. You can draw a picture to show $\frac{1}{2}$ of $\frac{3}{4}$.

$\frac{3}{4}$ of the crop

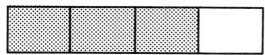

You can multiply fractions to find $\frac{1}{2}$ of $\frac{3}{4}$.

$\frac{1}{2}$ of $\frac{3}{4}$ of the crop

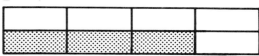

$\frac{3}{8}$

$\frac{1}{2}$ of $\frac{3}{4}$ $\longrightarrow$ $\frac{1}{2} \times \frac{3}{4} = \frac{1 \times 3}{2 \times 4} = \frac{3}{8}$ (Multiply the numerators.)
(Multiply the denominators.)

So, $\frac{3}{8}$ of the sunflower crop remains.

Multiply. Write the answer in simplest form.

1. $\frac{1}{5} \times \frac{1}{6} =$ _____

2. $\frac{1}{3} \times \frac{1}{4} =$ _____

3. $\frac{1}{2} \times \frac{1}{2} =$ _____

4. $\frac{1}{4} \times \frac{3}{5} =$ _____

5. $\frac{1}{3} \times \frac{5}{6} =$ _____

6. $\frac{3}{4} \times \frac{1}{3} =$ _____

7. $\frac{5}{8} \times \frac{2}{3} =$ _____

8. $\frac{3}{4} \times \frac{2}{3} =$ _____

9. $\frac{5}{8} \times \frac{2}{5} =$ _____

Solve.

10. Duane harvested $\frac{1}{3}$ of his wheat crop during the last week of July. He harvested $\frac{3}{4}$ of the remaining crop during the first week of August. How much of the crop did he harvest during the first week of August?

_____

Holt, Rinehart and Winston, Publishers • 5

There are 15 students who work for the Parks Department during the summer. Of these, $\frac{2}{3}$ are members of various sports teams. How many students play on sports teams?

Remember

To multiply a fraction and a whole number, you must write the whole number as a fraction.

$$\frac{2}{3} \text{ of } 15 \longrightarrow \frac{2}{3} \times 15$$

Write 15 as $\frac{15}{1}$. Multiply the fractions.   Simplify.

$$\frac{2}{3} \times \frac{15}{1} \qquad\qquad \frac{2}{3} \times \frac{15}{1} = \frac{30}{3} \qquad\qquad \frac{30}{3} = 10$$

10 students play on sports teams.

Multiply. Write the answer in simplest form.

1. $\frac{1}{3} \times 6 = $ _____

2. $\frac{1}{2} \times 8 = $ _____

3. $\frac{2}{5} \times 15 = $ _____

4. $8 \times \frac{1}{4} = $ _____

5. $6 \times \frac{1}{3} = $ _____

6. $3 \times \frac{2}{3} = $ _____

7. $4 \times \frac{5}{9} = $ _____

8. $5 \times \frac{4}{20} = $ _____

9. $\frac{1}{6} \times 18 = $ _____

Solve.

10. There are 24 students who work on park and recreation programs during the summer. Of these, $\frac{3}{4}$ work on recreation programs. How many students work on recreation programs?

_____

11. At the Xeno Zoo, $\frac{2}{3}$ of the monkeys are from Africa. If the zoo has a population of 39 monkeys, how many of them are from Africa?

_____

Holt, Rinehart and Winston, Publishers • 5

Multiplying Fractions and Mixed Numbers

David had a berry-picking agreement with his father. David kept $\frac{1}{4}$ of the berries he picked. His father kept the remaining berries. If David picked $11\frac{1}{2}$ pints, how many pints of berries did he keep?

Remember

To multiply a mixed number by a fraction, first rename the mixed number as a fraction.

Rename the mixed number.	Multiply the fractions.	Simplify.
$11\frac{1}{2} = \frac{23}{2}$ $\begin{array}{l}11 \times 2 = 22 \\ 22 + 1 = 23\end{array}$	$\frac{23}{2} \times \frac{1}{4} = \frac{23}{8}$	$\frac{23}{8} = 2\frac{7}{8}$

David kept $2\frac{7}{8}$ pints of berries.

Multiply. Write the product in simplest form.

1. $\frac{1}{2} \times 3\frac{1}{4} = $ _____

2. $\frac{1}{3} \times 2\frac{5}{8} = $ _____

3. $\frac{3}{4} \times 1\frac{2}{3} = $ _____

4. $9\frac{1}{2} \times \frac{1}{3} = $ _____

5. $3\frac{1}{2} \times \frac{1}{4} = $ _____

6. $7\frac{3}{4} \times 3 = $ _____

7. $5\frac{2}{5} \times 2 = $ _____

8. $4\frac{1}{8} \times 3 = $ _____

9. $6 \times 3\frac{1}{2} = $ _____

10. $9 \times 9\frac{1}{2} = $ _____

11. $3 \times 1\frac{5}{6} = $ _____

12. $2 \times 2\frac{1}{9} = $ _____

Solve.

13. David picks $10\frac{3}{4}$ pints of berries. His dad decides to let him keep $\frac{1}{3}$ of the berries. How many pints does David keep?

_____

14. David picks $14\frac{2}{5}$ barrels of apples. He discovers that $\frac{1}{4}$ of them have been spoiled. How many barrels of apples were spoiled?

_____

Giorgio will serve 6 melons to his friends for dessert. Each friend will receive $\frac{1}{2}$ a melon. How many friends does Giorgio have?

Remember

You need to find how many halves there are in 6.

There are 12 halves in 6.   Check by multiplying.

$$6 \div \frac{1}{2} = 12$$

$$12 \times \frac{1}{2} = 6$$

Giorgio has 12 friends.

Divide.

1. $4 \div \frac{1}{3} =$ _____

2. $3 \div \frac{1}{2} =$ _____

3. $5 \div \frac{1}{4} =$ _____

4. $1 \div \frac{1}{5} =$ _____

5. $2 \div \frac{1}{4} =$ _____

6. $8 \div \frac{1}{4} =$ _____

7. $6 \div \frac{1}{3} =$ _____

8. $9 \div \frac{1}{2} =$ _____

9. $10 \div \frac{1}{5} =$ _____

10. $7 \div \frac{1}{6} =$ _____

11. $3 \div \frac{1}{6} =$ _____

12. $4 \div \frac{1}{2} =$ _____

13. $9 \div \frac{1}{3} =$ _____

14. $7 \div \frac{1}{5} =$ _____

15. $5 \div \frac{1}{3} =$ _____

Solve.

16. It takes $\frac{1}{4}$ foot of pine board to make a floor for a birdhouse. How many birdhouse floors can be made from a pine board 16 feet long?

_____

Holt, Rinehart and Winston, Publishers • 5

A dairy farmer begins to milk his cows at 5:20 each morning. He finishes milking the cows at 7:30. How much time does it take to milk the cows?

Remember

To find elapsed time, count the minutes and then the hours.

5:20   5:30   5:30   7:30

5:20 to 5:30 equals 10 minutes.   5:30 to 7:30 equals 2 hours.

It took the farmer 2 hours 10 minutes to milk his cows.

A.M. is the time between 12:00 midnight and 12:00 noon. P.M. is the time between 12:00 noon and 12:00 midnight. How much time has passed from

1. 8:00 A.M. to 11:15 A.M.?

_____

2. 7:15 P.M. to 9:20 A.M.?

_____

3. 9:30 A.M. to 12:00 noon?

_____

4. 9:15 A.M. to 1:15 P.M.?

_____

5. 10:00 A.M. to 4:00 P.M.?

_____

6. 9:30 A.M. to 4:45 P.M.?

_____

7. 7:30 A.M. to 8:30 P.M.?

_____

8. 11:00 A.M. to 10:45 P.M.?

_____

Solve.

9. Toji went to bed at 8:30 P.M. and set her alarm clock to ring at 7:15 A.M.. If Toji wakes up when the alarm rings, for how long will she have slept?

_____

Holt, Rinehart and Winston, Publishers • 5

Adding and Subtracting Time

Karen spent 1 hour 20 minutes mowing part of the lawn.
Kathy spent 1 hour 45 minutes mowing the rest of the lawn.
How much time did it take Karen and Kathy to mow the
lawn?

Remember

Add 1 hour 20 minutes and 1 hour 45 minutes, and regroup if necessary.

Add the minutes.	Add the hours. Regroup if necessary.	Regroup. Think:
1 h 20 min + 1 h 45 min 65 min	1 h 20 min + 1 h 45 min 2 h 65 min	2 h 65 min = 2 h + 1 h + 5 min = 3 h 5 min

It took 3 hours 5 minutes for Karen and Kathy to mow the
lawn.

Add.

1. 4 h 17 min
    + 3 h 36 min

2. 3 h 38 min
    + 2 h 21 min

3. 4 h 29 min
    + 7 h 14 min

4. 3 h 45 min
    + 1 h 20 min

5. 1 h 58 min
    + 4 h 11 min

6. 2 h 53 min
    + 7 h 42 min

Subtract.

7. 8 h 42 min
    − 4 h 17 min

8. 7 h 46 min
    − 4 h 22 min

9. 9 h 38 min
    − 6 h 16 min

10. 9 h 28 min
    − 7 h 41 min

11. 3 min 12 s
    − 1 min 15 s

12. 9 min 36 s
    − 3 min 45 s

Solve.

13. Lisa left home at 6:15 P.M.. She arrived at the ball game
    at 7:25 P.M. How much time did it take Lisa to arrive at
    the ball game?

Holt, Rinehart and Winston, Publishers • 5

                                                                 Use with pages 286–287.

Janet plays oboe in an orchestra. Like many oboe players, she makes her own wood reeds. A **reed** is the part of the mouthpiece of an oboe that, when blown upon, vibrates to produce sound. Janet prefers her reeds to be at most $1\frac{5}{16}$ inches long. Is this reed too long?

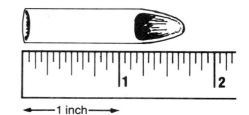

←—1 inch—→

┌─ **Remember** ─────────────────────────────┐

These are the units on a ruler.

The reed measures
2 in. to the nearest inch.

$1\frac{1}{2}$ in. to the nearest $\frac{1}{2}$ in.

$1\frac{3}{4}$ in. to the nearest $\frac{1}{4}$ in.

$1\frac{6}{8}$ in. to the nearest $\frac{1}{8}$ in.

$1\frac{11}{16}$ in. to the nearest $\frac{1}{16}$ in.

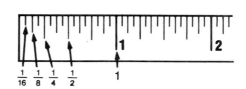

$\frac{1}{16}$ $\frac{1}{8}$ $\frac{1}{4}$ $\frac{1}{2}$ 1

The reed measures $1\frac{11}{16}$ inches long. It is too long.

Find the distance around.

1.

9 in.

3 in.

9 in.

_____

2.

6 in.   8 in.

10 in.

_____

3.

10 in.

3 in.

_____

Solve.

4. In Problem 1, how much longer is the rectangle than it is wide?

_____

5. In the triangle in Problem 2, how much shorter than the longest side is the shortest side?

_____

6. Measure the length of this page. How long is it? _____

7. Measure the width of this page. How wide is it? _____

12 inches (in.) = 1 foot (ft)
        3 ft = 1 yard (yd)
   1,760 yd = 1 mile (mi)

A parking lot is 72 ft long and 63 ft wide. How many yards long is it?

Remember

You must divide to rename a unit of measure with larger units.

72 feet = ☐ yards

72 ÷ 3 = 24 | 3 feet = 1 yard |

72 feet = 24 yards

The parking lot is 24 yd long.

Complete.

1. 4 ft = _____ in.

2. 3 yd = _____ ft

3. 4 yd = _____ ft

4. 6 ft = _____ yd

5. 72 in. = _____ ft

6. 2 mi = _____ yd

7. 10 ft = _____ in.

8. 108 in. = _____ ft

9. 6 ft = _____ in.

Solve.

10. The rows of vegetables in Alice's garden are 15 ft long. How many yards long are they?

_____

Remember these units:

2 cup (c) = 1 pint (pt)
    2 pt = 1 quart (qt)
    4 qt = 1 gallon (gal)

Maria has to fill a 5-gallon tub in order to wash her puppy in her backyard. How many times will she have to fill a quart container with water in order to fill the tub?

Remember
You must multiply to rename a unit of measure with smaller units.

5 gal = ☐ quarts   4 qt = 1 gal
5 x 4 = 20
5 gal = 20 qt

She will have to fill the container 20 times.

Complete.

1. 3 gal = _____ qt   **2.** 5 pt = _____ qt   **3.** 7 qt = _____ gal

4. 9 c = _____ pt   **5.** 3 qt = _____ pt   **6.** 9 pt = _____ c

7. $3\frac{1}{2}$ gal = _____ qt   **8.** $2\frac{1}{2}$ pt = _____ c   **9.** $10\frac{1}{2}$ gal = _____ qt

Solve.

10. Janet and her scout troop are camping. Janet made 6 quarts of vegetable stew for dinner. If each scout is served 1 cup of stew, how many scouts will her stew serve?

_____

11. Janet's troop leader, Maggie, brought 3 gallons of milk to drink with dinner. If each scout is served 1 cup of milk, how many scouts will receive milk?

_____

12. Maggie decides Jill will make juice for breakfast. Maggie wants Jill to make 4 gallons of juice. How many quarts must Jill make?

_____

The highest temperature recorded in North Dakota was 49°C at Steele on July 6, 1936. The lowest temperature recorded in North Dakota was ⁻50°C at Parshall on February 15, 1936. By how many degrees did the temperature vary in North Dakota in 1936?

Remember

From 49 to 0 is 49. From 0 to ⁻51 is 51.

49 + 51 = 100

The temperature in North Dakota varied 100°C in 1936.

How many degrees are there between

1. 30°C and 15°C? _____

2. 27°C and 5°C? _____

3. 18°C and 2°C? _____

4. 33°C and ⁻12°C? _____

5. 40°C and ⁻40°C? _____

6. ⁻10°C and ⁻33°C? _____

Solve.

7. The highest temperature recorded in Winnipeg, Manitoba, Canada, was 34°C. The lowest temperature recorded in Winnipeg was about ⁻38°C. How many degrees are there between these two temperatures?

_____

8. When Harold boarded an airplane in San Francisco, California, the temperature was a comfortable 24°C. When Harold got off the plane at Juneau, Alaska, the temperature was a frigid ⁻21°C. How many degrees are there between these two temperatures?

_____

9. Water begins to boil at 100°C and freezes to ice at 0°C. How many degrees are there between these two temperatures?

_____

10. Jenny took a glass of water with a temperature of 34°C and heated the water to 97°C. How many degrees are there between these two temperatures?

_____

Holt, Rinehart and Winston, Publishers • 5

In 1981, Mayville, North Dakota, celebrated its one hundredth birthday. At that time, Mr. Forseth had taught mathematics at Mayville State College for 34 years. Write a ratio to compare his years of teaching to the age of the city.

> **Remember**
>
> When you compare numbers in a ratio, be careful to write the numbers in the correct order.
>
> Compare years of teaching to the age of the city.
> 34 to 100
>
> You can write this ratio in three ways.
> 34 to 100, or 34:100, or $\frac{34}{100}$

Write each ratio as a fraction.

1. 3 to 4 _____   **2.** 5 to 7 _____   **3.** 19 to 35 _____   **4.** 12:18 _____

5. 9:4 _____   **6.** 15:100 _____   **7.** 347:1,000 _____   **8.** 10 to 1 _____

9. 50 to 1 _____   **10.** 1 to 100 _____

Solve.

11. During a certain year, the number of daily newspapers published in the United States for each 1,000 people was 287. Write this fact as a ratio.

_____

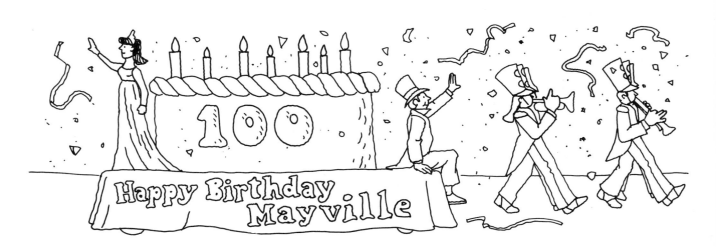

Use with pages 308–309.

Rafe's class is going on a field trip to the Natural History Museum to study prehistoric life. On all field trips, there must be 1 chaperon for every 6 children. How many chaperons are needed for his class of 24 children?

Remember

Two ratios are equal if they can be written as equivalent fractions. You can use equal ratios to find how many chaperons are needed.
Draw a ratio table.

Chaperons	1	2	3	4	5	6
Children	6	12	18	24	30	36

Rafe's class will need 4 chaperons for 24 children.

You can tell if two ratios are equal by checking to see whether they are equivalent fractions.

Are the ratios $\frac{1}{6}$ and $\frac{4}{20}$ equal?

Think: $\frac{1}{6} = \frac{1 \times 4}{6 \times 4} = \frac{4}{24}$, not $\frac{4}{20}$.

$\frac{4}{24} \neq \frac{4}{20}$

Write a number to make the ratios equal.

1. $\frac{1}{2} = \frac{}{6}$

2. $\frac{3}{4} = \frac{6}{}$

3. $\frac{2}{5} = \frac{4}{}$

4. $\frac{3}{8} = \frac{}{16}$

5. $\frac{}{3} = \frac{4}{6}$

6. $\frac{4}{} = \frac{8}{6}$

7. $\frac{3}{} = \frac{12}{20}$

8. $\frac{1}{} = \frac{7}{49}$

Holt, Rinehart and Winston, Publishers • 5

What length should be used to represent dimension *A* of the V block shown in the scale drawing at the right?
The scale is 1 in. = 6 in.

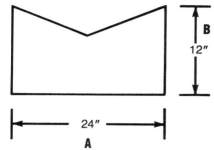

Remember

The scale of 1 in. : 6 in. means that 1 inch in the drawing is equivalent to 6 inches of the actual length. You can use equal ratios to find the actual length.

$$\frac{1}{6} = \frac{\text{length in drawing}}{\text{actual length}}$$

or $\frac{1}{6} = \frac{\square}{24}$.

So, $\frac{1 \times 4}{6 \times 4} = \frac{4}{24}$

The length of *A* in the drawing should be 4 inches.

Use the scale drawing at the right to answer each question.

1. How long is the kitchen? _____

2. How wide is the kitchen? _____

3. How wide is the bathroom? _____

4. How long is the laundry room? _____

5. How wide is the living room? _____

6. How long is the bedroom? _____

7. How wide is the house? _____

8. How long is the house? _____

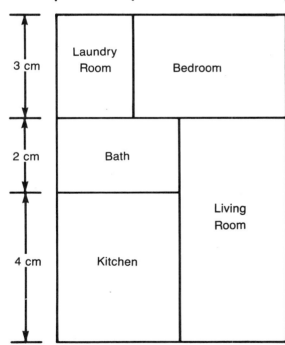

Solve.

9. The scale drawing of a room is 3 inches wide and 4 inches long. The scale is 1 in. = 5 ft. Find the length and the width of the actual room.

_____

SCALE: 1 cm = 3 m

Use with pages 314–315.

85

Ann's class surveyed students at their school to see how they spend their Saturday afternoons. The survey showed that 10 of 100 students watch television on Saturday afternoons. Write this ratio as a percent.

> **Remember**
>
> You can think of a percent (%) as the ratio of a number to 100. You can rename a ratio with a percent by using the numerator and the percent (%) symbol.
>
> 10 of 100 can be written as $\frac{10}{100} = 10\%$

10% of the students surveyed watch television on Saturday afternoons.

Write each ratio as a percent.

1. $\frac{25}{100}$ _____   **2.** $\frac{37}{100}$ _____   **3.** $\frac{86}{100}$ _____   **4.** $\frac{5}{100}$ _____

5. $\frac{19}{100}$ _____   **6.** $\frac{75}{100}$ _____   **7.** $\frac{88}{100}$ _____   **8.** $\frac{73}{100}$ _____

9. $\frac{2}{100}$ _____   **10.** $\frac{42}{100}$ _____   **11.** $\frac{50}{100}$ _____   **12.** $\frac{25}{100}$ _____

Solve. Write each ratio as a percent.

13. sugar $\frac{2}{100}$ _____   minerals $\frac{2}{100}$ _____

　　 fiber $\frac{2}{100}$ _____   fat $\frac{4}{100}$ _____

　　 starch $\frac{45}{100}$ _____   water $\frac{37}{100}$ _____

　　 protein $\frac{8}{100}$ _____

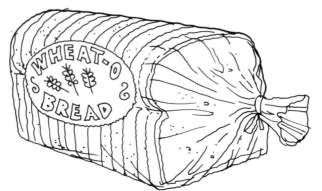

Holt, Rinehart and Winston, Publishers • 5

Use with pages 318–319.

The girls' basketball team at Sandro's school has won every home game. Approximately 70% of the students in the school show up for each home game. That is 5% more than came last year. Write 70% as a decimal. Write 5% as a decimal.

Remember

Think of 70% as 70 of 100. Think of 5% as 5 of 100.

$70\% = \frac{70}{100}$ Write: 0.70 or 0.7. $5\% = \frac{5}{100}$ Write: 0.05.

Written as decimals, 70% is 0.70 and 5% is 0.05.

Write as a decimal.

1. 34%   2. 89%   3. 15%   4. 6%   5. 27%   6. 75%

_____   _____   _____   _____   _____   _____

7. 99%   8. 3%   9. 45%   10. 49%   11. 25%   12. 35%

_____   _____   _____   _____   _____   _____

Write as a percent.

13. 0.23   14. 0.51   15. 0.48   16. 0.36   17. 0.5

_____   _____   _____   _____   _____

18. 0.02   19. 0.9   20. 0.6   21. 0.01   22. 0.75

_____   _____   _____   _____   _____

Copy and complete the chart. Write each percent as a decimal.

23. The percents of student attendance at other events are listed below.

Boys' basketball games	75%	
Cheerleading competitions	55%	
Football games	85%	
School dances	50%	

Holt, Rinehart and Winston, Publishers • 5

At the cast party for the production of *A Midsummer Night's Dream,* 30% of the fifth-grade students attending are members of the cast. What fraction of the fifth-grade students at the cast party are cast members?

Remember

To express a percent as a fraction, write the percent as a fraction that has a denominater of 100. Then write the fraction in simplest form.

Percent	Fraction	Write in simplest form.
30% $\longrightarrow$	$\frac{30}{100}$ $\longrightarrow$	$\frac{3}{10}$

Of the fifth-grade students attending the cast party, $\frac{3}{10}$ of them are cast members.

Write each percent as a fraction in simplest form.

1. 9% _____   **2.** 12% _____   **3.** 40% _____   **4.** 45% _____   **5.** 57% _____

6. 84% _____   **7.** 97% _____   **8.** 25% _____   **9.** 52% _____   **10.** 17% _____

Write each fraction as a percent.

11. $\frac{4}{50}$ _____   **12.** $\frac{9}{10}$ _____   **13.** $\frac{3}{4}$ _____   **14.** $\frac{3}{5}$ _____   **15.** $\frac{7}{50}$ _____

16. $\frac{9}{20}$ _____   **17.** $\frac{27}{50}$ _____   **18.** $\frac{13}{20}$ _____   **19.** $\frac{1}{5}$ _____   **20.** $\frac{4}{25}$ _____

Solve.

21. At the end of the cast party, $\frac{7}{25}$ of the food is uneaten. What percent of the food is uneaten?

_____

Holt, Rinehart and Winston, Publishers • 5

The fifth-grade class had a lasagna party and ate 15 pounds of lasagna. If lasagna is 13% protein, how many pounds of protein did the fifth-grade class eat?

Remember

To calculate with a percent, first change the percent to a decimal.

$$13\% \longrightarrow \frac{13}{100} \longrightarrow 0.13$$

Multiply.

$$\begin{array}{r} 15 \\ \times\, 0.13 \\ \hline 45 \\ 150 \\ \hline 1.95 \end{array}$$

The fifth-grade class ate 1.95 pounds of protein.

Find the percent of each number.

1. 25% of 300 _____

2. 75% of 150 _____

3. 50% of 275 _____

4. 10% of 22 _____

5. 8% of 95 _____

6. 2% of 500 _____

7. 15% of 36 _____

8. 3% of 20 _____

9. 5% of 950 _____

10. 63% of 720 _____

11. 25% of 243 _____

12. 88% of 1,200 _____

Solve.

13. The fifth-grade class invited the sixth-grade class to join them for a lasagna party. The classes ate 25 lb of lasagna. If the sixth-grade class ate 55% of the lasagna, how much lasagna did the sixth-grade class eat?

_____

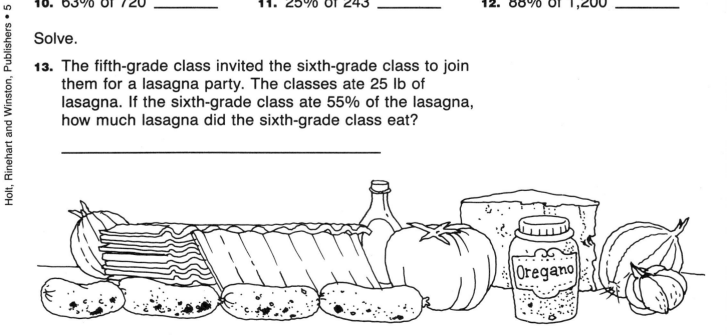

Holt, Rinehart and Winston, Publishers • 5

More Cases of Percents

Of the fifteen players on the MayPort Middle School girls'
basketball team, 3 of the girls are fifth graders. What percent
of the players are fifth-grade girls?

Remember

Compare the part to the whole and write a fraction. Then find an equivalent fraction
that has a denominator of 100. Write the equivalent fraction as a percent.

Write a fraction.	Find an equivalent fraction that has a denominator of 100.	Write the fraction as a percent.
part $\longrightarrow$ whole $\longrightarrow$ $\dfrac{3}{15} = \dfrac{1}{5}$	$\dfrac{1 \times 20}{5 \times 20} = \dfrac{20}{100}$	20%

Of the fifteen players, 20% are fifth-grade girls.

Find the percent that each part is of the whole.

1. 7 white mice
20 mice

_____

2. 3 black dogs
5 dogs

_____

3. 12 girls
20 team members

_____

4. 6 red cars
10 cars

_____

5. 8 white horses
25 horses

_____

6. 2 boys
5 ball players

_____

Solve.

7. What percent of 20 is 5?

_____

8. 15 is what percent of 50?

_____

9. What percent of 35 is 7?

_____

10. 16 is what percent of 40?

_____

11. What percent of 180 is 54?

_____

12. 6 is what percent of 20?

_____

Solve.

13. The middle-school soccer team has 16 team members.
Of these, 10 are fifth graders. What percent of the team
are fifth graders?

_____

Holt, Rinehart and Winston, Publishers • 5

Use with pages 326–327.

A **ray** has one endpoint and goes on forever in one direction. A ray is named by an endpoint and any other point on it.

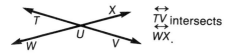

ray *JK*, or $\overrightarrow{JK}$.

A **line segment** is a part of a straight line. A line segment is named by its two endpoints.

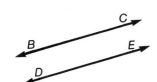

line segment *YZ*, or $\overline{YZ}$

Intersecting lines meet or cross each other. *U* is the point of **intersection.**

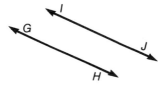

$\overleftrightarrow{TV}$ intersects $\overleftrightarrow{WX}$.

Parallel lines never intersect.

Identify and name each figure.

1.

G ———————— *H*

2.

B

O

3.

I
G
J
H

_____

4.

A   *C*
Z
D   *B*

5.

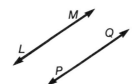

M
L   *Q*
P

6.

H
J

_____

Name each figure.

7. $\overrightarrow{CA}$ _____

8. $\overline{BE}$ _____

9. $\overleftrightarrow{GH}$ and $\overleftrightarrow{AE}$ _____

10. $\overline{CF}$ _____

11. $\overrightarrow{DF}$ _____

12. $\overleftrightarrow{GD}$ and $\overleftrightarrow{AE}$ _____

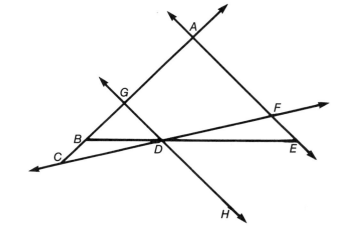

Holt, Rinehart and Winston, Publishers • 5

An **angle** ∠*BAT* is formed by rays *BA* and *AT*. $\overrightarrow{AB}$ and $\overrightarrow{AT}$ are the sides of the angle. *A* is the vertex of the angle.

A **right angle** forms a square corner. It measures 90°.

An **acute angle** is smaller than a right angle.

An **obtuse angle** is larger than a right angle. An obtuse angle measures more than 90°.

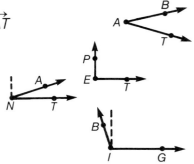

Name the angle and the vertex.

1.

2.

3.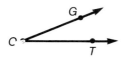

_____   _____   _____

4.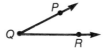

5.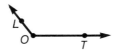

6.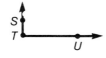

_____   _____   _____

Identify the angle as *right, acute,* or *obtuse.*

7.

8.

9.

_____   _____   _____

10.

11.

12.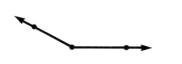

_____   _____   _____

13.

14.

15.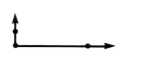

_____   _____   _____

16.

17.

18.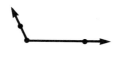

_____   _____   _____

Holt, Rinehart and Winston, Publishers • 5

Use with pages 342–343.

Measure the angle. Use a protractor.

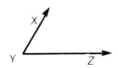

Remember

Since ∠XYZ is less than 90°, choose the number on the protractor that is less than 90°.

The numbers that $\overrightarrow{YX}$ passes through are 60° and 120°.

∠XYZ measures 60°

Use a protractor to measure the angle.

1.

_____

2.

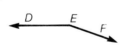

_____

3.

_____

4.

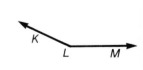

_____

5.

_____

6.

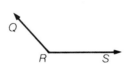

_____

7.

_____

8.

_____

On another sheet of paper draw each angle.

9. 180°   **10.** 50°   **11.** 145°   **12.** 120°

13. 70°   **14.** 90°   **15.** 40°   **16.** 15°

17. 150°   **18.** 5°   **19.** 60°   **20.** 175°

21. 87°   **22.** 96°   **23.** 130°   **24.** 156°

A **triangle** is any figure that has three sides and three angles. Some triangles have special names.

     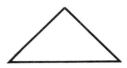   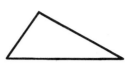

equilateral
All three sides
are of equal length.

isosceles
At least two sides
are of equal length.

scalene
Each side is a
different length.

     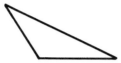

right
has one right angle

acute
has three acute
angles

obtuse
has one
obtuse angle

Remember

A right angle forms a square corner.
An acute angle is smaller than a right angle.
An obtuse angle is larger than a right angle.

Write whether each triangle is *equilateral, isosceles,* or *scalene.*

1.   **2.**   **3.**

_____   _____   _____

Write whether each triangle is *right, acute,* or *obtuse.*

4.   **5.**   **6.**

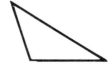

_____   _____   _____

Holt, Rinehart and Winston, Publishers • 5

Polygons are closed figures that consist of three or more line segments. There are many different kinds of polygons.

A **quadrilateral** is a polygon that has four sides.

A parallelogram whose sides are all the same length is a **rhombus.**

A parallelogram that has four right angles is a **rectangle.**

A rectangle whose sides are all the same length is a **square.**

Here are some other polygons.

pentagon
five sides

hexagon
six sides

octagon
eight sides

decagon
ten sides

Name each polygon.

1.

_____

2.

_____

3.

_____

4.

_____

5.

_____

6.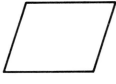

_____

7.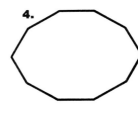

_____

8.

_____

Every point on a circle is the same distance from a point called the **center** of the circle.

A **chord** is a line segment that has its endpoints on the circle. $\overline{IT}$ and $\overline{IS}$ are chords.

A **diameter** is a chord that passes through the center of the circle. $\overline{IS}$ is a diameter.

A **radius** is a line segment. It has one endpoint on the circle and one endpoint on the center. $\overline{AZ}$ is a radius. A radius is one half the length of the diameter.

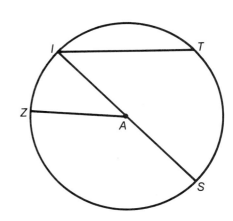

Write *chord, radius,* or *diameter* for the given segment.

1.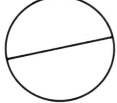

_____

2.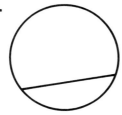

_____

3.

_____

4.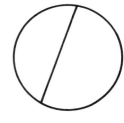

_____

Complete.

5. Write the diameter. _____

6. Write the four radii. _____

7. Write the two chords. _____

8. Write a chord that is also a diameter. _____

9. If the diameter is 8 cm, how long is the radius? _____

10. Write a 60° angle whose vertex is point *A*. _____

11. Write a right angle whose vertex is point *A*. _____

12. If the radius is 6 cm long, how long is the diameter? _____

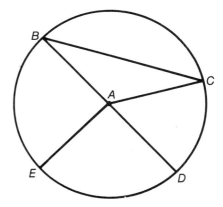

Holt, Rinehart and Winston, Publishers • 5

Use with pages 352–353.

Line segments that have the same length are **congruent segments.**

Angles that have the same measure are **congruent angles.**

Polygons that have the same size and shape are **congruent polygons.**

Remember

If two polygons are congruent, the matching or corresponding parts are congruent.

Is the line segment congruent to $\overline{AB}$? Write *yes* or *no.* Use a ruler to measure. Trace to check.   A •————————• B

1.

2.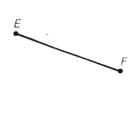

3.

4.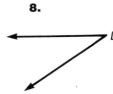

_____   _____   _____   _____

Is the angle congruent to ∠H? Write *yes* or *no.* Use a protractor to measure. Trace to check.

5.

6.

7.

8.

_____   _____   _____   _____

Is the figure congruent to △ABC? Write *yes* or *no.* Use a protractor and ruler to measure the angles and sides. Trace to check.

9.

10.

11.

12.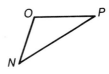

_____   _____   _____   _____

Holt, Rinehart and Winston, Publishers • 5

Symmetric shapes can be folded so that both halves match perfectly. A kite is a symmetric shape. A line down its middle is its **line of symmetry.**

Some shapes have more than one line of symmetry.

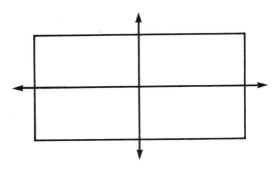 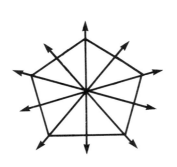 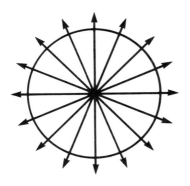

Some shapes have no lines of symmetry.

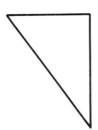  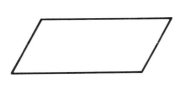

Trace each figure. Draw the line or lines of symmetry for each and count them.

1.   **2.** H   **3.** S   **4.** B

Is the line a line of symmetry? Write *yes* or *no*.

5.   **6.**   **7.**   **8.**

_____   _____   _____   _____

Solve.

9. Write two capital letters that have lines of symmetry.

_____

Holt, Rinehart and Winston, Publishers • 5

Figures that have the same shape but not the same size are **similar figures.** All of the octagons in the picture are similar. They are the same shape because they are all regular octagons. They are not the same size.

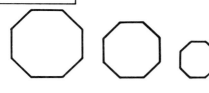

These two triangles are similar.

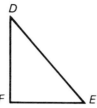

Write: △ABC ~ △DEF.
Read: Triangle ABC is similar to triangle DEF.

In similar figures, corresponding angles are congruent.

We write: If △ABC ~ △DEF, then ∠A ≅ ∠D
∠B ≅ ∠E
∠C ≅ ∠F

Is the figure similar to Figure ABC? Write *yes* or *no*.

1.   **2.**   **3.**

   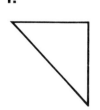   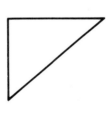

_____   _____   _____

Figure ABCD is similar to figure EFGH. Write *true* or *false*.

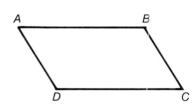   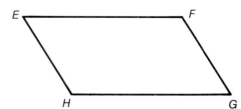

4. ∠A ≅ ∠E _____   **5.** ∠F ≅ ∠B _____   **6.** ∠G ≅ ∠D _____

7. ∠B ≅ ∠C _____   **8.** ∠H ≅ ∠D _____   **9.** ∠E ≅ ∠F _____

Holt, Rinehart and Winston, Publishers • 5

The famous pirate Blackbeard buried treasure on an island. He made a map and a set of directions. The map at the right is a **coordinate grid.**

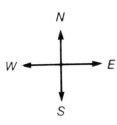

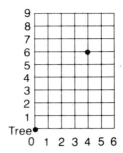

At the corner of the grid is a large palm tree. The top of the map is north. The treasure was buried 4 paces east and 6 paces north of the palm tree.

Give an ordered pair of numbers that identifies the treasure.

> **Remember**
>
> The first number of the ordered pair indicates movement to the east, that is, 4 paces east. The second number of the ordered pair indicates movement north, that is, 6 paces north.

The treasure is located at ordered pair (4,6).

Name the ordered pair for **each** point.

1. A   **2.** B   3 C

4. D   **5.** E   **6.** F

7. G   **8.** H   **9.** I

Graph each set of points on a grid. Connect the points to form a geometric figure. Is the figure symmetrical? Write *yes* or *no.*

10. (9,3), (7,1), (4,1), (2,3), (2,6), (7,8), (9,6), (9,3) _____

11. (5,3), (5,6), (7,7), (7,2), (5,3) _____

12. (1,7), (1,5), (3,3), (6,3), (6,9), (3,9), (1,7) _____

13. (6,1), (1,3), (1,7), (6,9), (10,5), (6,1) _____

14. (2,1), (2,5), (9,3), (2,1) _____

15. (1,1), (1,6), (3,6), (3,1), (1,1) _____

Holt, Rinehart and Winston, Publishers • 5

Juan likes to walk through the nature park near his home. This is the route he takes.

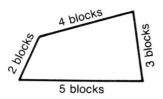

The **perimeter** of a figure is the distance around it. To find the perimeter, add the measures of its sides. What is the perimeter of the figure?

Remember

Perimeter means "distance around something" So, we are asking: How far does Juan walk to get around the park?

He walks 5 blocks + 3 blocks + 4 blocks + 2 blocks, or he walks 5 + 3 + 4 + 2

Juan walks 14 blocks.

The perimeter of the figure is 14 blocks.

Find the perimeter of each figure.

1.

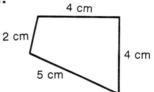

_____

2.

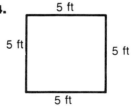

_____

3.

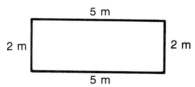

_____

4.

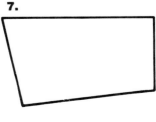

_____

5.

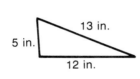

_____

6.

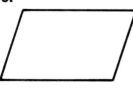

_____

Use a centimeter ruler to find the perimeter of each figure.

7.

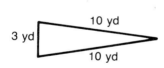

_____

8.

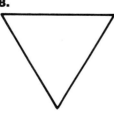

_____

9.

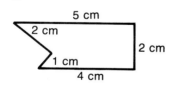

_____

Holt, Rinehart and Winston, Publishers • 5

The soccer field is 120 yards long and 75 yards wide. What is the area of the soccer field?

> **Remember**
>
> The **area of a rectangle** is its length times its width. A soccer field has the shape of a rectangle.
>
> $$A = l \times w$$
> $$A = 120 \times 75$$
> $$A = 9{,}000$$

The soccer field has an area of 9,000 square yards.

Count to find the area.

1.

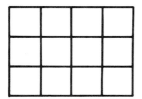

_____

2.

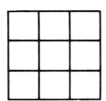

_____

3.

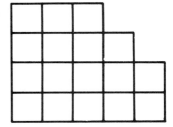

_____

Multiply to find the area.

4.

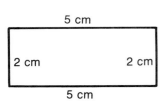

5 cm

2 cm   2 cm

5 cm

_____

5.

3 yd

3 yd   3 yd

3 yd

_____

6.

3 ft

6 ft   6 ft

3 ft

_____

Multiply to find the area of the quadrilateral.

7. $l = 12$ cm, $w = 5$ cm _____

8. $l = 15$ ft, $w = 3$ ft _____

9. $l = 7.5$ in., $w = 3.5$ in. _____

10. $l = 8$ cm, $w = 8$ cm _____

11. $l = 49$ yd, $w = 15$ yd _____

12. $l = 1.5$ mi, $w = 2.25$ mi _____

Holt, Rinehart and Winston, Publishers • 5

Use with pages 366–367.

The sail on Mr. Weiler's sailboat has the shape of a right triangle. The sail is 15 feet high and has a 6-foot base. How many square feet of sail cloth are there in this sail?

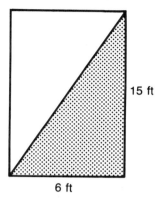

Remember

The **area of a right triangle** is $\frac{1}{2}$ the area of a rectangle. The height of this triangle is 15 feet. The base of this triangle is 6 feet.

Area of rectangle = length x width

$A = l \times w$
$A = 15 \times 6$
$A = 90$

Area of triangle = $\frac{1}{2}$ (base × height)

$A = \frac{1}{2}(b \times h)$
$A = \frac{1}{2}(6 \times 15)$
$A = \frac{1}{2} \times 90$
$A = 45$

The area of the sail is 45 ft².

Multiply to find the area.

1.

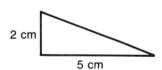

2 cm
5 cm

_____

2.

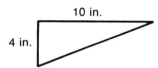

10 in.
4 in.

_____

3.

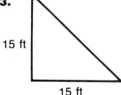

15 ft
15 ft

_____

Find the area of these triangles.

4. $b = 6$ cm, $h = 3$ cm _____

5. $b = 5$ yd, $h = 8$ yd _____

6. $b = 1.5$ ft, $h = 3.6$ ft _____

7. $b = 9$ m, $h = 9$ m _____

Solve.

11. Mr. Buendia must replace the sail on his sailboat. The sail is 7 yards high. The base of the sail is 4 yards. How many square yards of sailcloth does Mr. Buendia need to replace the sail?

_____

Here are some solid figures

rectangular
pyramid

rectangular
prism

cylinder

sphere

Name the basic shape of the building in the drawing.

Remember

A circle is the name of a plane figure. The building is a solid figure.

The building is a cylinder.

Copy and complete the table.

	Solid figure	Name of solid figure	Number of faces	Number of edges	Number of vertices
1.		Rectangular prism	_____	12	_____
2.		Rectangular pyramid	_____	_____	_____
3.		_____	5	_____	_____
4.		Cube	_____	_____	8

Write an example of these solid figures.

5. sphere _____

6. cylinder _____

Holt, Rinehart and Winston, Publishers • 5

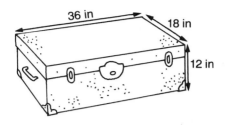

36 in
18 in
12 in

Steve is a Boy Scout. He has many pieces of scouting equipment and many uniforms. Uncle Henry gave Steve a footlocker so that he would have some place to keep all of his scouting gear. The footlocker is 36 inches long, 18 inches wide and 12 inches high. What is the volume of the footlocker?

Remember

Multiply to find the volume of a rectangular prism.
Volume = length × width × height

$$V = l \times w \times h$$
$$V = 36 \times 18 \times 12$$
$$V = 7{,}776 \text{ } cubic \text{ inches}$$

The footlocker contains 7,776 cubic inches.

Find the volume of each.

1.

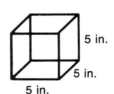

5 in.
5 in.
5 in.

_____

2.

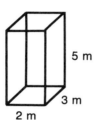

5 m
3 m
2 m

_____

3.

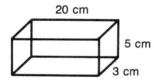

20 cm
5 cm
3 cm

_____

Use the formula $V = l \times w \times h$ to complete.

4. $l = 10$ m, $w = 7$ m, $h = 5$ m _____

5. $l = 12$ mi, $w = 8$ mi, $h = 3$ mi _____

6. $l = 7.5$ in., $w = 5.5$ in., $h = 2.5$ in. _____

Solve.

7. On a scouting trip, the scouts were told to dig a pit for a fire. The pit had to be 8 inches deep, 16 inches wide, and 24 inches long. How many cubic inches of dirt do they remove?

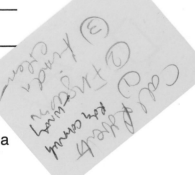

_____

The table shows the maximum wind speed in miles per hour recorded by certain weather stations in 1980.

MAXIMUM WIND SPEED IN MILES PER HOUR

Station	Wind Speed
Atlanta, Ga.	70
Bismarck, N. Dak.	72
Cape Hatteras, N.C.	110
Denver, Colo.	56
Fort Smith, Ark.	58
Galveston, Tex.	100

WIND SPEEDS RECORDED AT SELECTED WEATHER STATIONS

Make a bar graph from these data.

1. Draw a vertical axis and a horizontal axis. Write a title above the graph.
2. Label the vertical axis and the horizontal axis with appropriate titles.
3. Choose an appropriate scale. Mark intervals on both axes.
4. Draw the bars.

Solve.

The average rise and fall of tides for selected cities is given in the table below. Graph these data. Make an appropriate bar graph.

AVERAGE RISE AND FALL OF TIDES

Places	Ft	In.
Baltimore, Md.	1	1
Charleston, S.C.	5	2
Eastport, Me.	18	2
Galveston, Tex.	1	5
Halifax, N.S.	4	5
Portland, Me.	9	0

Holt, Rinehart and Winston, Publishers • 5

Use with pages 384–385.

The average salaries of major-league baseball players have increased steadily during the past few years. The table shows the average salaries from 1980 to 1985.

Year	Average salary in dollars
1980	150,000
1981	200,000
1982	250,000
1983	300,000
1984	330,000
1985	360,000

Use the data from this table to draw a pictograph.

Steps for drawing a pictograph

1. List the years along one axis. Use the horizontal axis.

2. Choose appropriate dollar units on the vertical axis. Use units of $50,000.

3. Choose a symbol to represent each unit. Let one baseball represent $50,000. Let a triangle represent $10,000.

4. Replace the numbers on the table with an appropriate number of baseballs and triangles on the graph.

5. Write the title, the symbols chosen, and the value of the symbols.

AVERAGE MAJOR LEAGUE BASEBALL SALARIES: 1980–1985

= $50,000
△ = $10,000

Solve.

The number of cattle, sheep, and hogs kept on farms in the United States in 1980 is listed in the table. Draw a pictograph of these data.

Animal	Number of animals
Cattle	111,192,000
Sheep	12,687,000
Hogs	67,353,000

Holt, Rinehart and Winston, Publishers • 5

The average price for a gallon of gasoline in the United States for each of the first six months of 1985 is listed in the table.

Month	Price per gallon
January	$1.15
February	1.14
March	1.16
April	1.21
May	1.23
June	1.24

Draw a broken-line graph. Use these steps.

1. Draw a vertical axis and a horizontal axis. Write zero at the base of the vertical axis.
2. Write the title, and label the axes.
3. Mark appropriate scales on each axis.
4. Use the table to help you to place the points on the graph.
5. Connect the points with line segments.

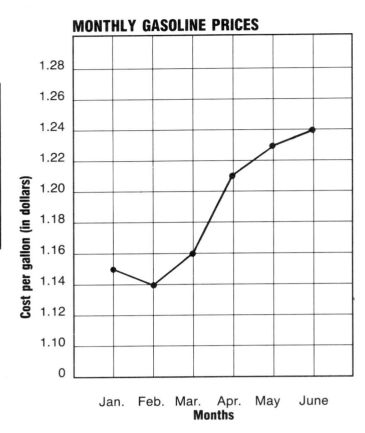

MONTHLY GASOLINE PRICES

Solve.

Use the data in the table below to draw a broken-line graph.

UNITED STATES DEFICITS

Year	Deficit in billions
1976	66.4
1977	44.8
1978	48.8
1979	27.7
1980	59.6
1981	110.6
1982	195.4
1983	175.3

Holt, Rinehart and Winston, Publishers • 5

During the first nine weeks of school, Kay scored 95, 90, 97, 93, 95, 85, and 82 on mathematics tests. Find the mean, the median, the mode, and the range of these scores.

To find the mean, you add the scores; then divide by the number of addends.

$95 + 90 + 97 + 93 + 95 + 85 + 82 = 637$

7 addends

sum → 637

number of addends $\left.\begin{matrix} \\ \\ \end{matrix}\right\}$ $\dfrac{637}{7} = 91$ ← mean

The mean is 91.

To find the median, arrange the scores from the least to the greatest. Find the middle score.
$82 + 85 + 90 + 93 + 95 + 95 + 97$
93 is the middle score. So, 93 is the median.

The mode is the score that appears most often.
$82 + 85 + 90 + 93 + 95 + 95 + 97$
The mode is 95.

The range is the difference between the greatest score and the least score.
$82 + 85 + 90 + 93 + 95 + 95 + 97$
The range is 15.

greatest score = 97
least score = $-$ 82
_____
15

Solve.

The Peewee Baseball Team played 7 games. After each game, the team stopped at a hot-dog stand. The batboy recorded the number of hot dogs eaten after each game. Find the mean, the median, the mode, and the range of the numbers of hot dogs eaten.

The batboy's record book looked like this.

Game	Hot Dogs
1	17
2	19
3	14
4	20
5	17
6	18
7	21

Mean _____

Median _____

Mode _____

Range _____

Use with pages 392–393.

Three fruit-juice varieties, A, B, and C, are being tasted by a person who is blindfolded.

What is the probability that the person will rank C first?

Remember
Probability can be shown as a fraction.
$\dfrac{\text{favorable outcomes}}{\text{possible outcomes}} \qquad \dfrac{1}{3}$

The probability of picking C first is $\frac{1}{3}$.

Solve.

A number cube, which has 6 sides, is tossed. Find the probability of each of the following events.

1. The number showing is a 3. _____

2. The number showing is odd. _____

3. The number showing is less than 5. _____

4. The number showing is less than 7. _____

5. The number showing is prime. _____

Suppose the cards are turned face down and arranged randomly. You pick one card. Then you return it.

Find the probability of each event. Write a fraction for each probability. What is the probability of picking

6. the star? _____

7. the circle? _____

8. the flower or the line? _____

9. a rounded shape? _____

Use with pages 396–397.

What is the probability that the spinner will
stop on an even number?

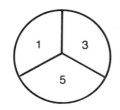

> **Remember**
>
> When the number of favorable outcomes divided by the
> number of possible outcomes equals 0, the event is
> impossible. When the number of favorable outcomes
> divided by the number of possible outcomes equals 1,
> the event is certain.
>
> $\dfrac{\text{Favorable outcomes (even number)}}{\text{Possible outcomes (1, 3, and 5)}} = \dfrac{0}{3} \text{ or } 0$

The probability is 0. It is *impossible* that the spinner will land
on an even number.

Susan has a bag with 10 apples in it. There are 4 green
apples and 6 red apples. Suppose, with her eyes closed,
Susan picks an apple from the bag.

Predict the probability of each event. Write *certain or
impossible* for each event.

What is the probability of Susan picking

1. a yellow apple? _____

2. a red or a green apple? _____

3. an orange apple? _____

4. a green or a red apple? _____

5. a yellow or a white apple? _____

6. a purple apple? _____

Suppose you spin the spinner a total of 60 times.
Predict the number of times the spinner will stop on each
color. Copy and complete the chart.

Outcome	Prediction
7. White	
8. Green	
9. Brown	
10. Red	

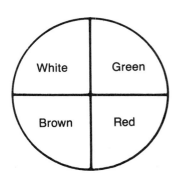